SOME NERVE

SOME NERVE

*Lessons Learned
While Becoming Brave*

PATTY CHANG ANKER

RIVERHEAD BOOKS

a member of Penguin Group (USA)

2013

RIVERHEAD BOOKS
Published by the Penguin Group
Penguin Group (USA) LLC
375 Hudson Street
New York, New York 10014

USA · Canada · UK · Ireland · Australia
New Zealand · India · South Africa · China

penguin.com
A Penguin Random House Company

Library of Congress Cataloging-in-Publication Data

Anker, Patty Chang.
Some nerve : lessons learned while becoming brave / Patty Chang Anker.
p.   cm.
Includes index.
ISBN 978-1-59448-605-0
1. Fear.   2. Change (Psychology).   3. Self-realization.
4. Anker, Patty Chang.   I. Title.
BF575.F2A55   2013   2013015484
152.4'6—dc23

Printed in the United States of America
1   3   5   7   9   10   8   6   4   2

Book design by Gretchen Achilles

For G. and R.

It is not because things are difficult that we do not dare,
it is because we do not dare that they are difficult.

—LUCIUS ANNAEUS SENECA

CONTENTS

SOME NERVE

Fear Itself

'm in a bathing suit, and people are laughing. Oh, this can't be good.

The sun was a spotlight on the diving board. *It must be twenty degrees hotter up here,* I thought. My forehead was sweaty, and, come to think of it, so was everything else. I bent over. The image of Tiffany Chin skating her 1987 U.S. Nationals long program with a wedgie in her blue Lycra costume flitted through my head. I dug my toes into the nubby wet board and tried to get a grip on my own situation.

Do I have a wedgie? I don't think so.

With my arms stretched overhead, I tucked my chin and swallowed at the same time, which made me want to cough. *Don't cough! Don't fall in!* The board was wobbling. Ergo, my thighs were wobbling. *Great.*

A line of teens jostled one another behind me. Were they watching me? I wasn't sure. The water below looked cold and deep. I closed my eyes.

I'm almost forty years old. Lord, help me. I don't know what I'm doing.

≈

IN THE STORY of my life there are many times when I did not, literally or metaphorically, dive in. I was raised by Chinese immigrant parents who wanted my sister and me to excel in school, succeed in our careers. In my mind, that meant focusing on things I was good at (reading and writing, pioneer crafting) and avoiding areas where I might fall short (most everything else). I was not only afraid of failing, but I was afraid of the fear I would feel while trying not to fail. Afraid of feeling fear itself.

Diving into a swimming pool, with its associated risks of belly flops, drowning, and public humiliation, was something I had successfully avoided all my life. Until now.

My husband and I have two daughters, Gigi and Ruby. Gigi was eight years old and scared to jump off the diving board at camp. "Go ahead, try it, don't worry what everyone else thinks, you'll be fine!" I said, praying for her not to ask the obvious: "Mommy, do you dive?" Ruby, then three years old, was already asking why everyone in the family had a bike helmet but Mom. I wanted them to worry less and enjoy life more, to take risks and try new things. But I rarely sought to go out of my comfort zone myself.

In fact, given my nervous nature, my bookish upbringing, my midlife responsibilities, and my boundless propensity for tripping and falling and hurting myself, my comfort zone was less a zone and more a skittish zigzag from car to coffee shop to supermarket to office to sofa to fridge to bed, where I lay awake, worrying. The day I realized I wanted something more for my girls was the day I realized I had to do something more myself. And the day all our lives changed for the good.

I scheduled two diving lessons with my daughter's swim coach, Jenny Javer. Zoe, an old college friend, had always wanted to learn how to dive and asked to join in. Jenny is exactly who you'd want by your side if your ship was on fire and you had to jump off the deck to save yourself. "A belly flop is like stubbing your toe—it hurts, but you get over it, right?" she said, instantly dispelling a lifelong fear for both Zoe and me. We were diving (that is, falling with style) from the side of the pool within a half hour; and by the end of the first lesson, she'd deemed us ready to try the diving board the next time.

Yet at the beginning of the second lesson, Zoe and I had lingered in the shade, meticulously applying sunscreen, as if a layer of SPF would protect us from all pain. We watched the teens lined up for the diving board push and shove and dare each other into ever more dangerous stunts. *Do we have to do this?* our expressions must have said loud and clear, because Jenny broke in: "Don't think."

The two of us, Chinese-American straight-A students for life, stood blinking at her, uncomprehending.

"You know what to do," Jenny said, appealing to our knowledge base. "It's the same as what you've done before, just a little higher. Come on now."

It sounded so sensible on the ground. I tucked my hair into a ponytail, put one last smear of sunscreen on the back of my neck, and took my place in line. A few minutes later, and ten steps down the plank, I was suspended over the county pool, sweating through my Speedo. *I'm on the diving board. This feels a lot higher up than it looks.*

I took a deep breath, and dove in. With a big fat splash.

It was one of the proudest moments of my life.

Not only did Zoe and I survive, we became divers that day. Not only did we become divers that day, we got a new lease on life. *If I can do this, something I never thought I could do . . . well, then anything is possible.* I was captivated by how fears held for decades could be dispelled in a matter of minutes. How many of us are held back by fears that make our lives smaller than they need to be, fears that, before we know it, define who we are?

I started a blog about facing fears and trying new things in midlife, called *Facing Forty Upside Down.* I figured if I committed myself in writing, at least Gigi could follow along and hold me to my promises. I wasn't sure if anyone else would read it. Everywhere I looked I saw confident, successful people. I wasn't sure anyone else could relate.

It turned out I was far from alone. Friends from all phases of my life and around the world responded from cyberspace. New acquaintances and neighbors from around the corner pulled me aside at the coffee shop or the playground to tell me how afraid they were. Afraid to swim, to drive at night, to ride a chairlift. Afraid of getting hurt, of looking dumb, of growing old. Some were tentative by nature and nurture. Others remembered living exuberantly until a bad experience scarred them. Still others, spread thin by life's responsibilities, no longer had the energy to shake things up. It struck me how universal the emotions were beneath the specific fears. It all boiled down to fear of pain, fear of rejection, fear of death, a sense of powerlessness. And the stranglehold these feelings had on us made us less than who we wanted to be.

Not that there was any lack of advice out there. The self-help section of any bookstore had lots of suggestions for how to face fear. Unfortunately, they all seemed to conflict. *It doesn't matter why you're afraid, just do what you fear* was one school of thought, while another cautioned, *Stop, think, why are you afraid?* It's because of your brain, your genes, your upbringing, your chakras, your past lives, your diet, your pets or lack thereof. If you could focus on your future, if you could reframe your past, if you could just be in the present, all might be well.

There were books that profiled extraordinary heroes—jet pilots, prisoners of war, Olympic athletes, world leaders—stepping up to extreme challenges. There were books about putting life on hold for a spiritual quest, or doing *Fear Factor*–type challenges like skydiving or shark cage diving. I loved those stories. But how did they relate to my life? I was tempted to chuck it all and buy *The New Encyclopedia of Flower Remedies*.

And then it came to me.

I want to write a book about how ordinary people face everyday fears. About what motivates us, what keeps us going, what helps us most of all. About how our lives change when we become our best, bravest selves.

Of course, fear is a valuable self-protecting mechanism, so I left some life-preserving intuitive fears (snakes, lightning, blood, clowns, for example) well enough alone. But other common surmountable fears were fair game and I had a theory that different methods would be effective in different situations, so I cast a wide net. I joined Toastmasters and did ropes courses and self-defense classes and put myself in more ridiculous predicaments than I'd ever imagined. I wore helmets and harnesses, high heels and swimsuits (not at the same time), and over and over again, I looked at myself, thinking, *I'm about to do something completely different now.* And I loved every nerve-racking minute.

Along the way, I met so many inspiring people: a priest, a rabbi, and a swami; therapists; multiple swim coaches; and two car crash survivors. I heard about near-death experiences by plane and boat and hanging off a cable way above the ground. I saw shaking people step up to a mic and grown men pedal undersized bikes. I watched adults working with kids and discovered that who learned more from whom was entirely up for grabs. I encountered breakthroughs and setbacks and surprises I certainly didn't see coming.

Every single person in this book opened my eyes in a different way, and collectively they showed me how much we are the same. For it's not just fear we have in common but our endless capacity for joy.

What began as a challenge that I took on for the sake of my kids became a series of lessons in how to open my heart to the elements. The payoff—exhilaration, irrepressible laughter, gratitude, and lo! courage, too—is what I want to share with you.

You can face your fears. You can learn and grow. And you can have the time of your life doing it, too. You can go from being an armchair adventurer to the heroine of your own story, and you don't need a personality transplant or a sudden windfall to do it. You don't even need to do anything crazy (unless you discover, as I did, that you really kind of want to).

All you need is some nerve.

CHAPTER 1

THE UNEXPECTED
Boogie Boarding

Splash! The foam football, heavy with seawater, bonked my head on its way into the ocean, landing with a wet thud that kicked salt water into my eyes.

"Sorry, lady!" the tattooed man to my right called out. I was floating on my brand-new boogie board, just behind where the waves were breaking, and had been watching him and his friend play catch in the waist-high water for a while. They gradually drifted closer to me, until the ball was sailing over my head. Or into my head. It was the second time I'd been hit with it.

In the past, I might have assumed they, like the rest of the world, were out to get me. But not today. I was in a great mood today. I picked up the ball, wrung it out, and tossed it toward a blurry tattooed form, yelling cheerfully, "Your friend has lousy aim!" Blurry tattooed man number two, behind me, waved sheepishly.

"Do you think those guys are flirting with me?" I asked Barb, floating on her board a few feet away. "Or was I just the monkey in the middle?"

"They were definitely flirting with you," Barb said. "No question." She leaned her head back into the water.

"I love you, Barb." I laughed. "You always know what to say."

I sighed happily, touching the ocean floor with my feet, just to make sure it was there, before I let them float back up. This was no tropical vacation—we were at Jones Beach, that is to say, the Atlantic Ocean with a few million New Yorkers mixed in. The water was cold and brown, with objects I didn't want to look too closely at drifting by. But still, it was bliss. I was here with my friend, stealing a few hours while the kids were in camp. I had just turned forty-one, and after more winters of discontent than I cared to think about, it was glorious summer and things were looking up.

Hazy sunshine soaked through the topmost layer of water. I hugged the warm board, feeling almost comfy enough to be lulled to sleep. I marveled for a moment at how relaxed I was. Me. Having fun. In moving water!

I have never enjoyed the sensation of being off my feet, and since an ill-fated tubing incident on the Esopus Creek—gosh, was it nearly twenty-five years ago?—being off my feet in fast-moving water that could drown me had long been off my list of how to have a good time.

The list wasn't very long to begin with. Growing up, when my friends were out climbing trees and skinning knees, I was in the library reading about Laura Ingalls climbing trees and skinning knees. I guess you could say I was more of an armchair kid.

As I grew up, the list shrank. First there was the career to think of, and then the children. The real, and what felt like real, battles between life and death, success and failure, took every ounce of my energy. To my sleep-deprived brain it was all about conserving strength: If it didn't have to be done; if I didn't know how; if it was too scary, too complicated, too inconvenient, too expensive, too time-consuming, too embarrassing, too cold, too hot, too wet, too icky; if I could get bit or dizzy or fall over; if it could hurt my bad back, bad neck, bad ankle; if it made me or my mother (or the mini-version of her I carry in my head) cluck and say, *Why would you want to do that?* it went by the wayside.

"Mommy doesn't do that," my kids would say—she doesn't ski or sail or ride a bike. Mommy doesn't play catch or do roller coasters or program the TV. She's busy! She's tired! She has Important Things to Do! If I had died in 2009, my headstone would probably have read: *Mom: She Worried a Lot.*

But then, *I changed.* So much that my husband is still searching the back of my neck for signs of alien abduction. Who can explain it?

Maybe it was turning forty and realizing that it wasn't just days but decades slipping by in the same worn paths that somehow grew narrower with each foray. Maybe it was the sense among friends that as we got older we were becoming more like ourselves, but not in a good way. *I love you, but didn't we have the same conversation last week?* Maybe it was the hypocrisy of stuffing my children into snowsuits and shin guards and helmets and sending them out into the fray while I cheered from a bench. Maybe it was a combination of all that and a last-gasp, premenopausal burst of hormones.

Whatever it was, after a lifetime of living nowhere near the edge, I had had enough. I started diving in.

The sounds of teenagers teasing and splashing each other and children screaming happily filled the air around me and Barb. *This is what it feels like to be part of the fun,* I thought, my own pleasure suddenly tinged with guilt. Gigi, my older daughter, loves the water, but I had avoided taking her to the beach for years, because I was so afraid. The last time I'd waded into waves with her, I squeezed her slippery little wrist so hard my own hand hurt. Ruby, my younger daughter, hated putting her face in the water at the pool; who even knew how she would take to the ocean? My own limitations had limited us all for so long.

It's not too late. I'll bring them to the beach before the summer is out.

My toes broke through the surface of the water and I wiggled them proudly. "My feet look like the feet of a *CSI: Miami* victim," I said to Barb, pointing to the chipped polish.

"That means you're having a good summer," Barb said. I *was* having a good summer, a great one, in fact. I'd been to the pool countless times to prepare for this outing. I still had a panicky response underwater, where my go-to relaxation technique, deep breathing, remained singularly ineffective. Navigating moving water was a work in progress.

Barb rested her chin on her board, long brown hair fanning out around her. "Can you believe how far you've come? Do you remember the first time we did this?"

I certainly did.

☰

IT'S PAINFUL EVEN TO think of now, how sad and lost I was when I first got to know Barb, just two years earlier. I'd stumbled into Antoinette's Patisserie with Ruby on my hip, as I did each morning. Ruby, at age three, was too old to be carried, but she had eczema all over, down to the soles of her feet. She scratched constantly, cried often, and slept rarely. Some days all we did was cling to each other. In the warmth of the coffee shop we self-soothed with milk and butter cookies for her, coffee and a chocolate chip muffin for me.

At the time, I had few friends in the village. I had left my full-time career in publishing ten years before, when we adopted Gigi and then Ruby, and it seemed as if I'd left my confidence behind along with my commuter rail pass. My girls were the center of my world, but with special needs in the mix, that world revolved around doctors and therapists, not Girl Scouts or T-ball. Often I felt like a foreigner in my own town.

But here was Barb, spilling over the bistro table in front of her, with cups and plates, books, a journal, a laptop, and people, so many people, all within arm's reach. I'd met her once before without our kids but felt too shy to break in here to say hello. It was overcast, and although I was sitting by the window, the light over their cluster glowed brighter by far. They were laughing, and when Barb laughed, her thick wavy hair shook in a way that looked so soft and warm, I wanted to rest my head on her ample bosom and go to sleep.

"Hi, there!" Barb said, catching me looking at her longingly. She said it in a friendly way, but I blushed deep red as her companions looked at me curiously. "Who's this?" she asked, smiling at Ruby. I introduced ourselves to the group and then as soon as I could, I high-tailed it out of there.

Our next interaction was better. She had asked, "What's your favorite misheard lyric?" and I chimed in, "I always thought 'Secret Agent Man' was 'Secret Asian Man.'" Barb thought that was hilarious, and we sang the lyric together for the entire coffee shop to hear.

"Don't laugh," I said, laughing. "I loved Secret Asian Man. He was so intriguing. I still feel robbed."

She invited me to sit with her at the popular table, where I was out of my element entirely. Here was a Little League dad, a Boy Scouts leader, a La Leche mother, a community organizer, or two or three. I couldn't keep track. Barb, a local music festival producer and the mother of two active boys, was connected to everyone in town. I did nothing but smile and nod at the whirl around her, while bouncing Ruby gently on my knee.

After a while my head started to hurt. It was warm already; the day was going to be oppressive. I needed to get out of there.

"It's so busy here today!" Barb declared, dabbing her brow. Then she sighed dreamily and said, "I can't wait for tomorrow. I'm going to the beach."

"Family vacation?" I asked absentmindedly. I was already mentally in the rest of my day, ticking off errands to do.

"No, just by myself. For the morning."

I stopped and stared. "You're going to the beach by yourself?"

"Yeah," she said, smiling. "It's heaven. Just sit with a book, watch the waves, listen to music." She stopped and looked at me. "Wanna come?"

"Hell, yeah!" I spluttered. But what was I saying?

I can't just go to the beach tomorrow! I have things to do.

Ah, there it was, the imaginary Greek Chorus of Perpetual Doubt. It was a little slow on the uptake today—usually it would not have allowed me to say yes in the first place. I tried talking back to it, in my head. *Well, actually, Ruby's nursery school has a camp; I could put her in for a day . . .*

Oh! The Greek Chorus did not like that one bit. *What kind of mother pays for child care so she can go to the beach? What if something happens to the kids and you're far away? What if you drown? Who would raise the children? You don't even like the beach! And, hello: What if Barb was just being polite? She doesn't really want to go to the beach with you. Don't go.*

"Are you serious?" I asked her.

"Uh, sure!" Barb said, nodding. She looked like she was thinking it through at lightning speed. She had asked and I had answered without thinking it through at all. Didn't Malcolm Gladwell have a theory about this? That big decisions often happen in the blink of an eye?

I looked into her big green eyes. She seemed sincere. It felt so good to be invited. I wanted to go. I never did anything spontaneous anymore. I wanted something different in my life, to be different from how I was. Patty Chang Anker would never do this. I blinked.

"Then I'm in," I said. The Greek Chorus opened its mouth, staggered backward a step, and passed out cold.

I told no one I was going. My husband, Kent, worked long hours at a law firm in the city and hadn't breathed fresh air in a decade. I crumpled with guilt at the thought. My Chinese immigrant parents would not approve. Had they sacrificed everything for their eldest child to squander her "Ivy League" education (honestly, was Penn even in the Ivy League?) and leave her job at *The New York Times* (*The New York Times*! At last, a place people had heard of!), to stay home with children, and then have her put those children in camp, and leave laundry in the hamper, so she could go *sit in the sun*? I felt downright naughty.

The next day, when I opened the back of Barb's SUV to put my tote bag inside, an avalanche of gear—towels, beach umbrella, helmets, mitts—started sliding out. I put my hands out to stop a beach chair from unfolding on top of me. Barb laughed, leaning into the trunk.

"Can you tell I'm a mom?" she asked. "I'm ready for anything."

My trunk had exactly zero gear in it for having fun. My insides shifted at the thought.

"Take the cooler out, would you?" she asked. "Ooh, and the *Cosmo*, too. Let's put those up front."

I pulled the glossy magazine out of the trunk and shoved my little bag in, feeling giddy. Was I really going to get in this car with a woman I barely knew?

Once we were on our way, Barb flipped me her iPod. "Feel free to pick some music," she said. I was at a loss. I didn't know how to work an iPod. I didn't even know what kind of music I liked. My husband usually picked the music. Five minutes into the drive and I was already inadequate—what were we going to talk about for the next six hours? This was a mistake.

As we started to chat, it became clear that I would not be able to sustain a facade of fun-loving gal, ready for any adventure. The truth was going to come out. Around minute seven, it did.

"I don't know how to ride a bike." So it began.

"Really?"

"Not one with hand brakes. Or gears. I've never gone camping. I'm scared of the ocean. And rivers. And most things in nature, to be honest. I don't even know how to dive into a swimming pool. Or do a handstand. I think it's because I hate being upside down." I was starting to gather steam. This was too much information, and I knew it, but I was like a woman on a blind date who cannot stop talking even though she knows she's taking the evening down in flames.

"I'm married to my high school boyfriend."

"Really?"

"Look out, Barb!" She pulled the car back into its lane.

"You've been with the same man since you were a teenager?" she asked.

I nodded, then wailed, "I was afraid of dating!"

We both burst out laughing. "I mean, he's also a really nice guy," I said, as we laughed some more. I realized I was being myself and it was going well—we were having fun. It was a relief actually, coming clean.

We were driving through the Bronx, near where I grew up, on our way out to the shore. I looked out at all the aging concrete. It was like looking at myself from a distance.

"My problem is, I'm so afraid of getting hurt or looking stupid that I don't try things," I said. I looked around for Gigi and Ruby, as if they would be in car seats behind me. My heart skipped a beat, then I remembered where I was. Suddenly, I had the kind of out-of-the-box insight one can only get when plucked out of one's box.

I don't want my girls to grow up scared.

Right then and there, I decided. I was going to turn over a new leaf. *I'm going to start saying yes to things that scare me.*

At the beach, Barb dived into the trunk and came up with two boogie boards. "Want one?" she asked.

"Uh, *yes!*" I said brightly. She handed me a purple foam board and then turned to look for towels. There was something that looked like a leash attached to the board. I furrowed my brow. *How do you use this thing?* Barb handed me my bag, a towel, and some magazines as I clumsily tried to tuck the board under my arm. She expertly carried all her stuff plus a beach umbrella as we scouted for a place in the sand. Gulls swooped all around. A lone city pigeon pecked on by, looking lost. "You and me both," I whispered, quickening my pace to keep up with Barb.

The next hour went by in a dreamy haze of sunbathing, chatting, snacking, and listening to music. So far, doing things outside my comfort zone was extremely pleasant. When Barb asked, "So what about going upside down scares you?" I answered, "It's like my brain freezes and I don't know what to do." But as I lay in the warm sand, the fear seemed quite remote. "Maybe I should learn how to do a handstand," I murmured lazily. This out-of-the-box thinking was getting out of hand.

Then Barb said, "Wanna go in the water?"

I stiffened. "Uh, *okay!*" I said, my body all at once cold and twice as sweaty.

Barb put her boogie board's leash around her wrist—that answered that question—and led us out past where the waves were breaking so we could float while hanging on our boards. I watched the kids bodysurfing and felt a tumult of terror inside. A wave washed over my head and I came up coughing.

"I don't see how you can stand facing away from the waves," Barb said. "I like to see what's coming." I turned around reluctantly. I'd always hated advice like "Don't turn your back to the ocean" or "Keep your eye on the ball." Seeing the thing about to hit me in the face only made me want to squeeze my eyes shut and cry.

We watched a wave come toward us. "What do we do?" I squeaked.

"Jump up!" Barb called out, and it went past us. "You know that part when the wave is coming and you're not sure whether to jump or dive under or ride it in? That's my favorite part."

Is she kidding? I thought, scanning the horizon worriedly. *The not knowing part? That's the part I hate.*

A big wave was building. "Oooh, good, ride this one in!" Barb said.

"What, how?" My brain froze. *What do I do?*

"Belly on the board, hold on, now go!"

I went. Every which way. The light foam board, perhaps half the length of my body, was no match for the elements at play. I felt like a Barbie doll put through the wash, arms and legs splayed, head and torso churning in opposite directions, the hair will never be the same. In the roiling surf I tumbled like a gymnast, a really bad gymnast, in to shore. I lurched upright just in time to hear Barb screaming excitedly, "Patty, you did it!!"

Did what?

"You were totally *upside down!*"

On the way home, Barb marveled at the moment she saw me go under the water and then both my feet popped up. "Your legs were sticking straight up in the air—you did a handstand without even trying!"

I laughed and my body ached from the underwater pummeling, the sun, and exposure to the elements. The experience felt completely new. "Maybe I should write about this," I mused out loud. "I could start a blog about trying new things. I could call it *Facing Forty Upside Down.*"

I stayed up late that night after everyone else was in bed, looking at what I'd drafted for my inaugural post. I declared I would learn how to dive into a swimming pool, ride a bike (without crashing into a tree), and do a handstand, all before I turned forty.

The Greek Chorus had a conniption. *What will the neighbors think? I'll tell you what the neighbors will think. They'll think: Who does she think she is, learning how to dive? Doesn't she have kids to raise? Money to earn? If she's got spare time, shouldn't she be donating it to charity? She's got some nerve.*

"Who cares what other people think?" a voice interjected, almost startling me from my seat. It was my voice, the clear, confident one I use with my kids all the time. It had never spoken to me like this before. I hit Publish. *Nothing ventured, nothing gained,* I thought. I shut down the computer and sat for a moment in the dark. *I wonder what's going to happen now.*

What happened was this: I wasn't alone. Friends from every phase of my life came out of the woodwork, saying they, too, were tired of feeling tired. Of living a more limited life in the little slices of time they had between work and family. Some, like me, had never been very adventurous, but with time ticking by they were thinking, *If not now, when?* Others, who'd been very outgoing as kids and young adults, looked up in middle age to discover that their fears and fatigue had nibbled away at their enjoyment of life to the point that they couldn't remember the last time they'd done something they never thought they could do. They forwarded my posts to their friends. "Take me with you!" was the common refrain.

And so I learned how to dive with my old college friend Zoe and took a bike lesson at dawn arranged by my friend Kim. It took a year of practice before I could do a solid handstand. Five days before my fortieth birthday, when I was about ready to quit trying, Victoria Ramos, my tough-love yoga teacher, said, "Have you ever seen toddlers learn how to walk? How they fall and fall and never give up?" I kept going, until at last I felt the sensation of walking on air. My brain did not freeze. Quite the opposite: My upside-down grin said it all.

Everything changed. In facing my fears and encouraging others to face theirs, I found my calling. In writing our stories, I found my voice. After a career spent promoting other people's writing, I decided to write my own book about how ordinary people face everyday fears. After a string of mostly pleasant surprises and successful outcomes (Diving, check! Handstand, check! Bicycling, at least I didn't crash!), I was starting to look forward to new experiences with excitement rather than dread. In fact, I was looking forward to attending my first writers' conference, Bread Loaf, in Vermont in a couple of weeks.

But first I wanted this day at the beach with Barb.

This time, two summers after our first date, I'd plugged my own iPod into Barb's car stereo and put on Sheryl Crow's "Soak Up the Sun." At the beach shack, I picked out a peppy blue Hawaiian print boogie board; I was ready for one of my own. "This is a sign of my new life," I'd said, plopping down the cash to pay for it. And now I was hanging out in the ocean, as if I was the kind of person who could just do these things. All this was what Barb was talking about when she said, "Can you believe how far you've come?" Neither of us could believe it. Of course not. It was too good to be true.

≫

BARB'S SHOULDERS WERE turning pink. "We should go soon," I said.

"One last run?" Barb asked, and before I could answer, a big wave rose out of nowhere, filling my vision, top to bottom, side to side, taking all my words away. In that moment of not knowing what to do that Barb loves and I hate, the wave decided for me. It pushed me in to shore, in a massive whoosh of water and noise.

I clutched my board, my brand-new board, to my chest. *Check me out!* I whooped to myself, feeling the rush under my belly. *This is scaring the crap out of me! And I'm doing it anyway!* The wave kept going— when would it stop? My eyes were shut, there was no way to know. *Oh crap!* The board ran aground and then the wave receded, sucking backward with such force that I thought it might rip the skin off my body. I staggered to my feet.

I'm alive! I hoisted my board up over my head like the Stanley Cup. *I am the champion! I am a cool mom! Prepared for anything! Put this baby in my trunk! I AM FACING . . .*

The wrong way.

Boom! The next wave didn't so much crash as *detonate*. I both heard and felt it strike me down from behind, like lightning and thunder combined. It hit the back of my head and shoulders, popping the board out of my hands and knocking me off my feet. I gasped, sucking water up my nose and spitting it out of my mouth as I got dragged under.

The water IN MY MOUTH was FROM MY NOSE! THAT IS SO GROSS! I gagged. *Air! I need air!* Held by the leash, I was tossed against the board like a rubber ball against a wooden paddle. I had no idea which way was up, until *bam!* the wave threw me against the sandy bottom. My left foot made a sickening yet oddly clarifying *crunch*. *Ouch. Okay. That way is down.*

I pushed myself onto all fours, then lurched upright. But my foot didn't want to take my weight, and I crumpled down again. *This is ridiculous*, I thought. I'd always been afraid of getting sucked out to sea, never of being thrown *toward land*.

What came next was a series of poor decisions. I probably shouldn't have crawled back out into the ocean to rest my foot. Yes, it felt good to dangle it weightless in the water while I coughed seaweed out my ears. But the cold probably also numbed it, so I didn't believe it could be broken.

"I'm fine," I told Barb, as we packed up our things. Although when I tried to lift my bag onto my shoulder, my foot sank into the sand and I felt something inside it go *crack*. It was the strangest thing. My foot was attached to me, just like always. It was clearly my foot. But it didn't feel like my foot anymore.

"I'm fine," I told the couple who had seen the whole thing and now offered me some ice from their cooler. "You sure?" the man said doubtfully. "You've got some big scratches on your leg. And your arm."

I probably shouldn't have walked the two hundred steps to the lifeguard shack, picking my way around each picnic blanket en route, leaning on the boogie board for support.

"You know we could have come to get you, right?" the lifeguard said when I hobbled past the Lifeguards Only sign to collapse onto a bench. "I didn't want to bother anyone," I said. "I just need an ice pack for the ride home."

I should not have listened to the EMT who treated me, a young man in shades who rode in on a Kubota jeep, ready to save the day. After asking about vital things like chest pain and dizziness, he looked at my foot. It had not yet begun to swell. "You probably just bruised it," he said. "Rest, ice, elevate. If it doesn't get better, go to your doctor. You definitely didn't break it." *Whew.*

The lifeguards lounging around the shack seemed calm. Maybe my fear of oceans was overblown. "What kinds of injuries do you usually see here?" That, I should not have asked.

"Cuts, sprained ankles, that kind of thing. Occasionally we have someone helicoptered out of here for something more serious," the EMT said importantly.

I gulped. Thousands of people were spread out across the beach, children everywhere. Any one of them could end up on a stretcher. *This is a death trap!* I wanted to shout it into a megaphone. *Clear the beach!*

But I didn't. Instead, Barb brought the car around, and I went home with a fourth metatarsal bone in my left foot that, as the doctor later said, was "most definitely broken." And a fierce desire never to go to the beach again.

〰

I PUT AN *It-could-have-been-worse-at-least-I-have-a-good-story-to-tell* gloss on the situation, but back at home I felt like the worst mother in the world. I couldn't cook or clean. I couldn't bathe Ruby or hold the girls' hands crossing the street. I'd be counting on the whole family to fill in for me in the weeks ahead at a time when Kent was crazy busy at work. I was useless.

My fears of moving water had been justified all along, obviously, and with that realization all my newly minted courage drained away. A week later, crutching my way slowly across the rural campus of the Bread Loaf Writers' Conference in the pouring rain, it all caught up with me.

My whole body hurt—my foot from swelling, my armpits and hands from crutching, and my heart worst of all. I worried about falling with every step on the slippery gravel paths. Each time I planted the crutches, *crunch*, and swung my foot, *swing*, I heard my mother's gentle voice, my constant companion, saying, "*Xiao xin. Xiao xin,*" "be careful, small heart." My heart contracted, a little bit smaller, with every step.

Crunch, swing,

Xiao xin,

Xiao xin,

Xiao xin.

I stopped and looked around me. I was across from the nurse's cabin, set prettily in a field of wet wildflowers. I made my way across the threshold and collapsed in a parlor chair, pouring puddles of rainwater onto every surface I touched.

The nurse came to greet me, and I asked whether I could get a brace that would give me a break from the crutches. She set to work looking up medical supply stores in the area, then asked, "So what are you writing about?"

It was an innocent question.

"I'm supposed to be writing about how people face fears," I said. And then I burst into noisy tears.

The nurse, looking slightly alarmed, gave me some tissues, as I tried to speak between sobs. "I wanted my book to inspire people, but how can I help anyone if I can't be brave myself? I can't go back in the ocean—just look at me! I'm a mess! I can't hold an umbrella, my clothes are muddy. *I can't even do my laundry.*"

I bawled.

The nurse patted my hand. She offered me an apple, the first of many gifts. "Oh, honey, I can help you with the laundry," she said, and she ran through the rain, took my dirty clothes from my dorm to the laundry shed, and popped them in the machine, lickety-split, filling me with longing for the ability to do anything with ease. She also arranged for me to get a walking boot, so I could have breaks from the crutches. I finally let myself start taking the Vicodin my doctor had prescribed. I hadn't wanted to be woozy, but wooziness was called for, I decided.

Things were looking up.

That night, sick of hiding in my room, I put on a dress and started crutching my way toward the Barn. There was a dance party going on, and I wanted to be near the music, instead of wishing it away. I figured I could sit on the sidelines and put the crutches down, and stop talking about what happened to me. I could fade into the background and try to forget.

It was dark, and the gravel path was uneven. Partway there, I stalled, unsure whether to keep going or give up and go back to the dorm. It wasn't worth twisting my good ankle.

"Hey, do you want a flashlight?" a man's voice called over. It was Jamie, a fiction writer from New York.

"I can't hold a flashlight and crutch at the same time," I said.

"It's a headlamp," he replied. He caught up to me and put it on my head, but it was too big, and it slid down around my neck. So there I was, a headless crippled woman haunting the grounds, seen only by the pool of light illuminating her conspicuously modest cleavage. So much for my plan to fade into the night.

Once in the Barn, I "danced." With the boot, I could stand without crutches for a few songs at a time, flinging my arms about freely. It felt great to stand upright, until people high-fived or hip-bumped me too vigorously and almost toppled me over. When I got tired, I crutched my way outside for some air and found Jamie standing against the porch rail.

He was next to another man, whom he introduced as I made my way over. "Patrick writes about surfing." Between the Vicodin, the thud of music, and the chatter around us, I wasn't sure I'd heard correctly. "What?" I said, listing a little. But Jamie was already turning to chat with someone else, and Patrick nodded at my crutches and asked the inevitable. "How did you hurt your foot?"

"I was boogie boarding," I began.

"Really?" Patrick looked surprised. "I'm a surfer. I teach surf culture."

"Really?" I replied. I had heard correctly, but it still sounded implausible. Could you really get paid to write and teach surf culture? Wasn't surfing essentially high-risk fooling around on a beach? And wasn't he a little old for that? Patrick's hair was more white than not, the lines around his eyes crinkled like he was thinking something funny.

"Do you surf?" he asked, seeming excited to have a love of water sports in common. I hurried to correct the misperception.

"Oh, no way," I said. "I'm actually afraid of the ocean, period. I'm writing a book about facing fears, and let's just say my field research didn't go so well. This may be a very short book." I made myself sound lighthearted but I ached inside. How could I write about finding courage when I no longer knew where I'd put mine?

"Well, you need to learn how to surf, then!" Patrick declared. "To face your fears." I groaned. I should have seen where this was going. I recognized the look on his face. I got that look myself, every time I saw an opportunity to encourage someone else to try something new.

I tried deflecting. "Are you kidding? The wave that broke my foot knocked me down when I was standing in ankle-deep water. I'm wondering if I'll be brave enough to go back in the ocean at all, let alone try something as crazy as surfing."

"You can do anything you set your mind to," Patrick said. He said it effortlessly, like it was some simple truth.

For a moment I felt torn. I wanted to say "Hell, yeah!" I wanted him to think well of me. When I was a girl growing up in the Bronx I may have been afraid of most things outside my door, but I had a good imagination. Hiding in my bottom bunk with my books, I was Laura Ingalls on the prairie, Jane Eyre on a windswept moor. I tried for a split second to imagine myself surfing. It could not be done.

"You don't know me," I said. "My daughter calls me a 'magnet for disaster.' With my luck, if I tried to surf, I'd get sucked out in a riptide, attacked by a shark, and then thrown back on land, whereupon a wave would break my *other* foot."

Patrick looked at me quizzically. There were plenty of young, hale, and hearty people around he could talk to about surfing. Why was he wasting energy on this middle-aged housewife, crippled by fear? He'd probably leave me alone now.

"Well, I believe you can do it," he said quietly. He wasn't being a bully, I realized, and my defenses softened, a little. "And then, when you stand up on a wave," he added, his face brightening, "you'll know what it's like to smile *the biggest smile of your life.*"

It could have been the porch light reflecting off his hair and his Hawaiian shirt, or maybe it was the Vicodin, but Patrick was glowing. *He looks like he's absorbed a lot more sunshine and fresh air in his life than I have in mine*, I thought. I looked down at my black hair, black dress, black boot. We were dressed for entirely different parties.

When I'd first started facing my fears, I felt like I'd been living my life in a narrow hallway, where I'd shut all the doors to anything that seemed too much for me to handle. "Don't make fear the end point," my therapist had said. "Don't let it stop you from doing what you want and need to do." When I started opening doors, I realized that fear is not the end point but the entry—to new experiences I could not have imagined while I was stuck in the hallway.

As long as the risks ended in triumph, it was great. But getting hurt . . . *hurt*. Patrick smiled at me encouragingly and I looked back at him, wanting to believe and wanting to be left alone in equal measure, as the Greek Chorus wailed, *Pay no attention to the surfer! You have responsibilities! You're facing fears for your kids, this is not about you. The biggest smile of your life is beside the point.*

The evening mist around us was turning to rain.

I was suddenly almost painfully thirsty.

"Do you dance?" I asked Patrick, resorting to what I usually do when feeling out of my element by changing the subject and running— well, hobbling—away. "Waving my arms to Salt-N-Pepa on a nice solid wood floor is more my speed than surfing." As we returned to the warmth of the Barn, I shook raindrops out of my hair, feeling like I'd gotten away with something. I'd chatted with a surfer and escaped without committing to doing anything crazy. Door closed. I'd have to figure out some way to face my fears, it was true. But one step at a time. For now, I was glad to be safe and dry.

I put my crutches aside and considered plopping into a chair, but the sight of so many normally self-conscious writers cutting loose on the dance floor drew me in again. I joined the crowd and waved my arms to the music, feeling energized for the first time since the accident. I smiled a little smile, not realizing this was just the beginning, having no idea of the joyride to come.

CHAPTER 2

LETTING GO

Clutter

The desk I was sitting under had been mine since I was fourteen years old. I'd outgrown it in every way. Its little drawers, perfect for a young girl's diary with lock and key, had been crammed to capacity long ago. The computer now sat atop it like Jabba the Hutt, belching piles of paper overboard with each move of the mouse. "Stop stepping on my work!" I'd yell at the kids. "Then why is it on the floor?" they'd yell back.

It was all over the floor—work, bills, medical forms, school notices, kids' art, toys, photos, cables, Christmas cards, clothes—and that was just the layer I could see. I'd returned from Bread Loaf with a box of new books and nowhere to put them, a file of story ideas I already couldn't find. Poking apprehensively at a stack with a crutch, I wondered if I needed to rethink my approach.

Back at *The New York Times* and the publishing houses where I worked as a publicist, everyone knew better than to step into my office. My piles were a sign of my productivity. *I'm too busy to file! Look at* ALL THIS WORK! *Someone make me some copies! I* knew where everything was. My piles spoke to me in the voices of the writers, the editors, the executives wanting to know where things stood. "I'll get to you and you and you," I would tell the stacks, as nine p.m. approached and the cleaning lady passed by my office again. No way you're getting to vacuum this floor today, lady, I've got work to do. I was in charge.

But here in the home office I share with Kent, the cacophony had grown unbearable. Now the voices from the piles were those of my two daughters, their teachers and doctors, my husband, my students and clients. The thank-you notes, the half-knit sweater (and vest and scarf) clamored, too: *What about me? Did you forget me? When will you get to me? Take care of me!* And from the corners came the whispers: *It's too late for me.*

Surveying the mess, I felt frantic: *Yes, I promise I will. I'll get to you tomorrow. I can't believe I haven't taken care of this yet. I hate myself. Why am I like this? God help me.*

Which is why I was under my desk. I had to register Ruby for kindergarten, and I had three problems. I couldn't find the forms, her immunization records, or a pen. Declaring war on clutter, I'd started toppling piles. Eventually, the only clear place to sit was under the desk.

Most of my friends felt good when they cleared space around them; they were afraid of clutter and of being hemmed in. For me, the opposite was true. The very idea of coming home to empty surfaces filled me with anxiety. "I've lived in the Bronx," I'd deadpan to friends. "My first instinct would be—*WHO STOLE MY STUFF?!*"

The truth is, I would have wondered, *Who lives here? Why is she important? What does she do? What does she have to live for?*

≋

MY MOTHER GREW UP in wartime China, and in 1949, when she was seven years old, her family fled to Taiwan. "I could take one toy car with me," she'd once told me with sadness. "Because it was small enough to hold in one hand." Everything else stayed behind. She wrapped her favorite doll in the blanket she'd knit for her, laid her in the toy crib in the closet, and closed the door.

I, on the other hand, as a child had scores of hand-me-down Barbies and Fisher-Price people and all the accessories. My mother saved scraps of cloth to make us doll dresses and puppets; she fashioned animals out of homemade play dough, made glue out of rice and water. We collected things—stamps, rocks, leaves, and seeds. Other kids loved playing at our house. It was full of love.

Maybe that's why once I became a mother myself I flipped past the "Declutter your life!" articles in women's magazines, the same way I ignored my husband's pleas to at least clear the doorway of the day's detritus so he could enter the house. I turned away, so I felt more than saw the raised eyebrows of friends watching our kids spread finger paint off the paper and onto the floor. "I wish I could be so . . . relaxed," they'd say before rushing their children home for a bath. Even when more than one friend asked if I'd ever watched the show *Hoarders*, I clung to the notion that there was something heroic about putting parenting before organizing.

Until the kids themselves started speaking up.

"Mom, you are so disordered," said ten-year-old Gigi, the backseat clinician, the morning I left the car a third time to retrieve a forgotten item from the house. Gigi has ADHD, and because it takes one to know one, suspected I had issues, too. "You need fish oil," she prescribed kindly, the time I couldn't find the house phone I needed to call the cell phone I had lost.

"You need sleep," my doctor said at my checkup. I had asked him if I had ADD or early-onset senility. "You have so much going on—your brain is like a computer with too many applications open at once. It glitches. It happens." He had never seen our house.

But Karen Clay, a licensed social worker, had. Ruby's allergies and skin issues made her extra sensitive to her surroundings, and Karen came weekly for a time to help us work with her sensory needs. Karen's soft Southern drawl made everything she said sound chatty and benign, and I found I could accept parenting advice from her far more easily than from friends or relatives.

At our next meeting I cleared a corner of the dining room table so we could sit. "I love everything the girls make," I said, pointing at five unfinished craft projects on the table. "I love that we're spontaneous and creative. But the mess is getting a little out of hand. I can't bring myself to throw an old button away, let alone anything they've worked on. Is this a problem? I've never really thought of myself as a hoarder, but . . ."

"You are a clutterer, not a hoarder," Karen said. "Your house is clean, you're not putting anyone in physical danger—believe me, I would tell you if you were. But . . ." She said the next part slowly, watching me closely for my reaction: "Kids have a harder time regulating and organizing themselves internally if they are surrounded by disorganization externally."

I looked into Karen's quiet brown eyes. Closing mine, I saw Gigi and Ruby, whirling dervishes, me, the supposed adult, whirling alongside them, none of us able to stop.

It was time to make a change.

After Karen left, I did some research online. Clearly I wasn't alone. There are seventy-seven chapters of Clutterers Anonymous in the United States, a 12-step program modeled on Alcoholics Anonymous, with weekly in-person meetings. But adding another meeting to my schedule meant having to find my calendar, and that was not happening anytime soon.

I also discovered the Institute for Challenging Disorganization's clutter–hoarding scale that professional organizers use to assess how serious the problem is in a given household. To my relief, it supported Karen's conclusion, placing us decidedly on the clutter end of the scale.

Finally, my research led me to the National Association of Professional Organizers, which has about 4,200 members. I was skeptical, though. I'd had two well-meaning organizers work with me before, and all that remained of their work was some neat labels on files and shelves that bore no relation to their current contents. We come across them occasionally, like hieroglyphs from a civilization that died off long ago.

This time, though, I was serious. A friend recommended the author of three books on getting organized, Mary Carlomagno of Order-period.com. I made an appointment a week and a half away and then told everyone I knew to hold me accountable. *I'm not going to fail in front of the world,* I thought. *This is for the kids. I'm not going to fail, period.*

≈

MARY'S BOOK *Secrets of Simplicity* opens with a quote from the Chinese philosopher Lao Tzu: "A journey of a thousand miles begins with a single step." What I dubbed Operation: Find My Floor began with baby steps. With nine days before Mary's first visit, I eased myself in by thinking about it, reading about it, talking about it, taking "before" pictures, and buying clothes to clean in. Oh, that last bit is bad, I know.

"I'm breaking the golden rule of decluttering," I muttered, raiding the clearance rack at Target. "I should be giving away my T-shirts, not buying a new one. But how cute would I look cleaning in this?"

I wasn't all talk. On Day 1, I dumped twelve nearly empty bottles of toiletries, freeing up a section of bathroom counter, and on Day 7, I found twenty-five pens scattered around the office where on Day 6 I'd sworn I had none. On Day 8, I discovered a still-full hot water bottle under a stack of work, my embarrassment at not remembering how it got there balanced by my elation that moving it reduced the stack by two inches in one go.

On Day 9, however, panic hit. *The organizer is coming! This house looks like a crazy woman was locked in here with wild animals for the winter! I can't show her this! Who can live like this?*

Even the porch was a disaster. I moved aside a pop-up tent, two cardboard boxes, a bucket of chalk, three spray cans of sunscreen, two pairs of Crocs, three newspapers, and a bag of last winter's ice melt so she had a chance of entering. And escaping.

And then I saw her walking up the path. Short, in her early forties, with a friendly smile and a head of brown curls, Mary was wearing a long-sleeved black T-shirt and comfortable jeans, looking ready to work.

"Be careful around the broken bricks," I cautioned, leading us up the front steps. "We have to get those fixed." Already, seeing my life through a stranger's eyes was giving my to-do list new urgency. Our front door opens into our foyer/parlor. Once upon a time, this room had housed an adult sitting area with antique Chinese furniture and comfortable cushions for sitting on the left and a small, clear space for yoga to the right.

I started doing yoga around the time I stopped working full-time, and in typical type A fashion, decided to justify my time spent lying down doing nothing by getting a credential while I was at it. I became a certified yoga teacher, and for the first time in my life, learned, at least while I was on the mat, to quiet the Greek Chorus.

Then one Christmas Santa filled it with a mini-trampoline and a profusion of stocking stuffers, and it was all downhill from there. As fast as I could move things out, more came in—laundry to be sorted, swimming bags to be emptied, a printer, a *drum set*, for crying out loud.

"I'll never get my meditation space back," I'd moaned to my yoga teacher. "And even if I do, the stuff will just pile up again."

"You don't need much," he'd said, "just room to sit." And then I could see it. A cocoon. Clearing an entire room was too much to take on. But Dumpster-diving through mountains of clutter, I unearthed my altar, a candle, and a cushion, and set a Japanese screen around it in the corner of the foyer. Two square feet of peace. Now my Secret

Hiding Place was the only space in the house clear of clutter. I showed it off to Mary.

"Yeah, that may have to move," she said. "It's prime real estate for organizing the whole foyer."

Move my *altar*? My sacred space? The one place I felt good about, the one place I felt was mine? This was no "make it pretty" organizer. This was a clutter slayer.

I was horrified, yet fascinated. I needed someone to help me get to the source of my attachments and learn to release them. I couldn't do it alone. So I resisted the urge to kick her out then and there.

"Let's go see your office," she said.

Going upstairs, Mary praised our arrangement of family photos on the wall. "I like that you have all black frames—even if the pictures are different sizes and colors, it's less busy and easier on the eye." I puffed up with pride before my fall. We opened my office door.

The walls inside were a deep, jazzy blue, chosen by my husband in a romantic mood, the first and last thoughtful gesture we put into the room. In went two desks, two bookcases, a kid's art table, and every stray object we didn't know what to do with. The overall effect was part storage unit, part preschool frat house.

"This is a good-sized office," Mary said, squeezing past a waist-high stack of books and a fan. "What's in this box?" In a room teeming with piles of crap, she'd alighted on my one nice file box, sitting quietly in front of the closet, guarding the mayhem spilling from the shelves above. It was one box we didn't have to worry about. I'd packed it ten years ago.

"It's my files from *The New York Times* and Norton," I replied.

"Oh, good," she said, cracking open the lid. "Let's start here."

"What? Why?" I was confused. "This stuff is organized. I know what's in it—call lists, press kits, my phone logs."

"Yes, and it's taking up prime real estate in this office. Let's say bye-bye." She looked as happy as my kids with a bowl of potato chips, ready to attack until there was nothing left but fingerprints.

"Wait, I might need that stuff someday," I protested. But then I stopped. Even I didn't believe that. Every freelance job I'd done required building updated lists. I changed tack. "It's a record. Look, every call I've ever made is in these steno pads."

Mary is a petite but commanding presence. Inside her Jersey-girl-next-door exterior beats the heart of an Italian mama. She used to run celebrity events for Barnes & Noble before she started her own business. Her books have punchy titles in the imperative form: *Give It Up!* and *Live More, Want Less*. She speaks frankly, and I guessed by the look she gave me that she'd heard this one before.

"Patty, if the IRS comes knocking on your door saying, 'We need to see where the money went,' you show them the files with your tax returns." Pause. "I guarantee you: *No one* you worked with ten years ago is going to come knocking on your door asking if you pitched *Good Morning America*."

The absurdity of that cracked us up as I rifled through a pad, pretending to look up what *GMA* said. "It's here! See? I made the call. I did my best." I wiped tears of laughter away as I caught my breath. "This represents so much talking, so much work. All the energy I put into each writer, each project, is here."

"Oh, I see—this is about how good you were at your job," Mary responded. She took my hand and looked me right in the eye. "Okay, let me say this for you: You were *SO GOOD* at your job. You worked *SO HARD*. And we all appreciate it." Is this what I needed? To hear that I was good at something? To hold in my hand proof that people respected me once, even if today's reality was me screaming, "Pants! On! Now!" to little backsides skipping away in glee?

Mary opened a trash bag. "Now say bye-bye. You cannot make room for your future if this office is about the past."

She was right. I could easily locate the fax numbers of editors from 2001, but I couldn't find the book I was writing about for a deadline a week away. In one go, I dumped about ten steno pads. Bye, voice mails. Publicists don't even use voice mail anymore. Bye, lists. Bye, Conan O'Brien contact from the show before *The Tonight Show*.

This was the moment home decorating shows turned on. The catharsis! Let the healing begin. Mary was proud, I, *verklempt*. But purging the rest of the room was easier. After I'd released something of such symbolic value, what was the point of holding on to the rest of this junk? Five garbage bags filled themselves.

We sifted real gold from fool's gold, like the photograph of my husband as a child taken by his dear grandfather (real) crushed in the closet by the broken lamp I was intending to fix one day (fool's). "It's not only about what you let go but treasuring what you keep," Mary said. All things are not of equal value, but when underfoot or shoved in a corner, they're all treated equally badly.

Lastly, Mary took my active box, which could not hold one more thing, and removed everything having to do with the kids and the house. "This box should be about work," she said. "We'll put the rest in a file drawer."

"But my kids are my work," I said. I was used to squeezing my professional work around their needs. Without their stuff, the box looked terrifyingly empty. "We are going to put beautiful, new files in here," Mary promised, getting ready to go. "You're going to be excited to fill them. Your creativity is going to flow!"

Later that night, exhausted in bed, I considered going under the porch and retrieving my ten-year-old files. I could do it—the garbage wouldn't be picked up for two days. That box represented solid triumph. Without it, all that was left was the mess that life had become since—X-rays and doctors' reports, schools and therapies tried, so many hopes, so many false starts. Gigi's and Ruby's medical needs filled the days with appointments, the nights with worry, and the office with paperwork. I filed their records, five years' worth spread all over the house, into four two-inch binders, as if by wrangling them into one place I could control the outcome for both. Now they stood in a row on the shelf, declaring, "This is what I've been doing with my life. This is how hard I have worked. I am good at my job." Even if it often felt like I was failing.

What if my writing career didn't take off? What if, like many times before, the family's needs put my work on the back burner? So much easier to rest on the laurels of achievements already achieved. So much easier to say I was too busy to try.

As a supposed advocate for facing fears, it had never occurred to me that holding my belongings close was tantamount to fear. I would readily admit to being too busy, too lazy to be bothered with housework, but would I ever say too afraid?

The way we commonly distinguish fear from anxiety and stress is this: *Fear* is a physical response to an immediate threat, *anxiety* is our mind's way of worrying about what might happen in the future, and *stress* is the overall feeling of being overwhelmed by what we have to deal with.

Up until this moment, I'd thought that my wanting to save things for a rainy day, or as proof of my worth, was a sign of some anxiety (okay, a lot of anxiety), and being surrounded by chaos was a breeding ground for stress, but I never would have said letting go of clutter was a real fear I needed to add to my list of things to face. Lord, help me, not another thing to face.

But lying in my bed staring through the French door to the empty spaces I could imagine in my office beyond, I felt as if I was being robbed. There was nothing abstract or equivocal about this sensation, and it was happening *right now*: I was scared out of my mind.

I curled up and hugged myself, covered in nightclothes and blankets but feeling naked to the core. My children couldn't sleep without their loveys. I wanted my files back. They made me feel safe.

≋

WHILE I WAS LYING AWAKE, thinking about my past, Mary had been up with her sleepless baby, thinking about my future. Her morning e-mail linked to sky-blue file folders to buy and reminded me to do my homework, one task being to move five bulging boxes of pictures out of the office closet. I was at my computer, thinking up delay tactics, when I heard a low moan from above. "Did you hear that?" I asked Kent, who was working at his desk across the room. Either the top shelf housing the pictures was peeling off the closet wall, or God was speaking to me. Or both.

Kent leaped up and caught the shelf just as screws started popping off. My husband was about to be crushed by the weight of our memories. Okay, okay. Time to move the pictures.

Mary's edict "Purge as you go!" only made me dump the worst offenders, the snapshots that made me thankful I hadn't come of age in a world with cyberhazing. All the rest, I couldn't bear to part with— there we were, high school sweethearts, college, wedding, vacation, vacation, more vacation, in our lives before kids. When did these pictures start looking so historic?

When I finished filling the large archival box Mary had had me buy and closed its long, rectangular lid, it lay there on my side of the bed, looking exactly like . . . a coffin. And then it got stuck. It was supposed to slide under the bed, but because I'd overstuffed it, half of it stuck out. I heaved, I shoved, and finally it went in with a thud.

"Well, we're never going to see that again," my husband observed.

As in his high school pictures, he was still tall and fair, with brown wavy hair and glasses; with a little gray coming in and a stronger jaw-line, he was actually getting better looking with age.

"You're right. But after I die, my children will know what my life was like," I said.

The clutter issue was probably our longest-running dispute. Kent's family is German and Estonian. They like order. And efficiency.

"It seems to me," he said, after another weekend of patiently moving furniture, boxes, and bags around at my behest, "that you're moving everything out of the office and into other rooms."

The next day, I floated the idea to five-year-old Ruby that the little art table and chair by my desk could one day go to her room. "No rush, honey, I love having you nearby when I work. But my office tends to get collaged and Play-Dohed and I need more space for my files."

Ruby, a lion prowling my newly cleared floor, stopped midroar. "Can we do it now?"

Ruby is like her dad. Practical. Efficient. Both of them are lean in build and impatient by nature. When I sorted a stack of cards with handwritten notes for Kent to file, he took one look, said, "I've seen these already," and tossed them out. No reminiscing, no saving them for future gift tags. Bye-bye.

"Well, Ruby, we could move the table to your room, but then we'd have to move the rocking chair in there out."

"Let's do it right now!" she shouted, bounding away on all fours.

This was going a lot faster than I was ready for. I hadn't even thought about saying good-bye to the rocking chair. And it was covered with stuffed animals. Where would they go?

"I'm done with this one," Ruby announced from her room, flinging Elmo out the door. "And this one, and this one—you can give these away."

I made her sit with me in the rocker for a couple of pictures. Her thin face, framed by short tomboy hair, burst into a broad smile for the camera. She was already a year old when we'd adopted her from China; in my hungry heart we've never had enough time for cuddling here. But she'd moved on, clapping her hands, excited to have a place to sit and "work" in her room.

I moved the rocker to the foyer for now, and put the two worn Elmos and Gymbo the Clown into a trash bag without looking in their eyes. And then Gigi came home.

Gigi is like me. Sentimental. Emotional. Her long hair is thick and black; her round, soft face reminds me of my mother and me, all of us holding on to so much at all times. One look at the rocker by the door, and: "What's going on here? Are you getting rid of the rocker? This is the rocker from when I was a baby! This rocker is like part of the family!"

Then she spied the bag. "Not *Gymbo*! Ruby loves Gymbo—how could she give him up?" I knew what she meant. We'd sung "Gymbo the Clown goes up and down" every week for a year at Gymboree, how could she let that go? Gigi shook her head sadly. "These Elmos still laugh. I remember she bought this one with her own money." It was a wake. I silently apologized to Tickle Me Elmo for shaking him violently the time I couldn't make the laughing stop and for sticking him in the fridge so he wouldn't wake the baby. "Maybe Ruby will change her mind," I said.

"Yeah," Gigi replied. "Let's hold on to them a while longer just in case."

The next day, I found dozens of black construction paper dots all over the family room. I didn't know where they came from, but I gathered them up, thinking, *These could go on a Dalmatian costume, or we could draw faces on them with white chalk, or we could make big dominoes.* Then I reconsidered. *They could be all those things, but what they are right now is a mess.* I put them in the throwaway box. Which Gigi stumbled upon like long-lost friends: "My black dots! I found these at school. These could be tokens. Or checkers. Or . . ."

≋

IN 2002, AFTER MANY YEARS of wanting a child, Kent and I had brought one-year-old Gigi home from an orphanage in central China. Our entire extended family poured love and affection, and, yes, toys, all over her. It was never enough. Still she couldn't sleep, still she could never get enough to eat, still she needed more toys. We knew from adoption preparation classes to look for signs of hoarding behavior, but it wasn't that. She didn't stash food, she didn't steal from other people. But she was never satisfied.

When Gigi was four years old, we went to see the Christmas tree at Rockefeller Center. It was overwhelming—the crowds, the noise, the street vendors hawking their wares. Every two feet, Gigi stopped and pointed to another tchotchke, saying, "I need this!" I dragged her along until she dug in her heels in front of a man peddling Spider-Man toys: "I need more Spider-Man!"

"You do not need more Spider-Man," I said. "You have plenty of Spider-Man stuff. You have a Spider-Man bed, for crying out loud." There was a moment of silence, before Gigi opened her mouth wide and wailed: "IT'S NOT ENOOOOOOUGH!" All foot traffic on Fifth Avenue stopped.

We wondered if we were spoiling her. We lectured her about being happy with what you have, about how nice it is to share.

Watching her struggle through playdates, it was clear that sharing did not make her feel happy or nice. She looked upset, unsettled, and scared. One night, after a kindergarten classmate had left with hard feelings, I sat on the edge of Gigi's bed to tuck her in and thought about what to say. A large stuffed lion guarded her pillow. They both looked up at me expectantly.

"Imagine you have a cookie jar inside your heart," I began. She perked up. She liked cookies. "Inside the jar are cookies that are made out of love. You act like you only have one or two cookies, and you're afraid that if you give any away, you won't have enough for yourself. But—"

I was about to go on, about how love doesn't run out, how we can always make more, but before I could, Gigi took in a sharp breath and cried. A deep, deep cry. "My cookie jar is broken," she sobbed. "There's only crumbs."

I held her and rocked her for a long, long time.

RIDING THE TRAIN HOME from a rare day in the city and a welcome break from decluttering, I ran into a friend of my sister's, Wendy Tomkiel, a psychotherapist who practices Emotionally Focused Therapy. Wendy, perfectly suited to her profession, is easy to talk to; and although I tried to rein it in (people probably tap her for free advice all too often), going through all my belongings was dredging up every old memory and raising all my deepest fears for the future. Before I knew it I was spilling my guts.

"I'm afraid for my kids; I'm afraid of failure; I'm afraid of life taking that sudden, irrevocable turn for the worse," I said. "I know my fears are holding me back. I'm trying to speak to myself in a positive way, loudly, to drown out the negative voices."

"The thing is, fear serves a function," Wendy said. "You can't just say, 'Fear, go away!' and expect it to. You need to ask, 'Fear, why are you here? What are you trying to protect me from? Is it something I need protection for? Or is it a response to a situation that resolved years ago or that maybe even happened to somebody else?' If so, you can recognize the fear for what it is and say this isn't necessary anymore."

Wendy's words resonated deep in my brain. Yogis have long used breathing and meditation to quiet the mind. Allowing thoughts and feelings to come and go without getting caught up in them is the key to equanimity. Recent research shows that we use the prefrontal cortex of the brain, which is responsible for abstract thinking and decision making, when we're anxious or stressed, worrying and then worrying about worrying—"Calm down!" we might shout at ourselves as we get ever more wound up. Meanwhile, the deep limbic system is the part of the brain that governs our feelings, and we can't order it around with the prefrontal cortex. We need to sit with the feelings, breathe into them, let them come and go.

What was this fear of letting go protecting me from? Could my holding on and saving everything for posterity, for a rainy day, be a response to my daughter's losses and my mother's losses and completely unnecessary for my own life right now? Could I simply thank it for trying to protect me and then say, "I'm really okay, you can go now"?

The train rattled on. Something shifted. Something small, but strong.

»

MARY'S SECOND VISIT BEGAN with the sound of me complaining: "I'm tired. Everything is out in the open and bringing back memories. I can't shut them off. The house is a mess, my kids are unsettled, I'm fighting with my husband over what to purge."

"Chaos precedes order," Mary said sympathetically. "But remember, stuff is just stuff. Organize the piles, not the emotions. You need real file drawers. Are you going to order a bigger desk?"

A new desk. She had no idea what a family drama that had caused.

When I'd broached the subject of getting rid of my old desk with my mother, we'd said, "It's teak!" in unison—she aloud, I in my head. I knew that was coming. Teak was expensive back in the day, and they'd saved up to buy that desk. For a Chinese daughter, whose job it was to study, this desk was home and workplace. My parents had inherited hardly a thing from their parents. How could I throw away their gift to me? "Give it to Gigi," my mother directed.

At first, Gigi agreed. But when it came time to move it into her room, she balked. "I never wanted it," she admitted. "I just felt sad for you saying good-bye to your old desk." So much like me. Except that, at age ten, she'd learned to say no.

My mother was a freecyclist before it was trendy. Coworkers, neighbors, relatives gave her things, knowing she wouldn't say no. You never knew what would be sitting in her foyer, waiting for a new home. More often than not, I said yes to the finds she wanted to pass along to me. Yes to the stray cat I was allergic to. Yes to the ironing board, even though I already had one I never used because I couldn't find the iron. But I had drawn a line at the sewing machine.

"Take it," she'd told me. In her short barbershop haircut and at-home clothes, every ounce of her thrifty under-five-foot frame humbled me.

"But I don't know how to use a sewing machine."

"Take it. You might learn."

"Ma, I do not have time to learn how to use a sewing machine. Try Sandra. She machine sews." My sister, Sandra, and I used to help our mother hand sew old sheets into duvet covers. Sandra has evolved the process with technology; we now go to her for perfectly hemmed pants.

"She already has one," my mother said, disappointed. I was usually a reliable dumping ground. "It's a good machine—what a waste."

"Why don't you learn to use it?"

"No, it's too late for me. I'm not young, like you. Plus, I don't have a house. You could store it in the basement until you're ready to learn."

I thought about the sewing, beading, and crocheting books I'd been saving for the same reason. I am my mother's daughter, and it was all I could do not to break down and take it. But with Kent shaking his head behind my mother and mouthing *"no,"* I stood firm.

"Love things that love you back," Mary says in *Live More, Want Less.* There's a difference between a sewing machine and a stray cat. Between an old desk and my daughter's life. *This desk does not have feelings. It's just stuff. I am not going to burden Gigi with it. Thank you, fear, for asking me to hold on to the desk in case we need it one day, or in case we need to remember our parents' love for us. But this desk is falling apart and I know how much my parents care. You can go now.*

Mary was excited to hear my change of heart. We measured the space for a new desk.

"Can we start decorating yet, please?" I was looking for some pay-off for all this work.

"Not yet," she said. "We need to clear these doorways."

≈

IT SOUNDED A BIT LIKE FENG SHUI, clearing doorways. Because I am Chinese-American, people expect me to know something about feng shui, the ancient Chinese system of determining auspicious placements of homes, properties, and tombs, based on the heavens (astronomy) and the earth (geography). It has become an approach to interior design that connects how you organize your space with how energy and good fortune flow in and out of your life.

My family, however, considered feng shui a little superstitious and a lot indulgent. Basic tenets, like "Don't store things under your bed" and "Keep your prosperity corner clear" made no sense in crowded apartments. You were lucky to have a place to live—who could afford to be picky about which direction the building faced?

Still, in purging my office I'd found *Clear Your Clutter with Feng Shui*, one of several organizing books it turned out I owned, each with its spine uncracked. Paging through it for wisdom, I noted a section titled "Why You Need to Clear Your Colon." Now I remembered why I'd given up learning about feng shui in the first place. That, and the chapter "Clutter and the Feng Shui Bagua."

The bagua is a grid with nine sections that assign areas of the home to corresponding life issues. Depending on the layout of your home, your living room might correspond to Health, the dining room to Family, etc. Where there's clutter, there's more likely to be difficulty in the corresponding aspect of life. Judging by my home, we were up the creek in Prosperity, Reputation, Love, Family, Health, Offspring, Wisdom, Career, and, oh yes, Compassion. Was that nine? Yep. All nine.

It didn't help that the bagua covers your entire property, so there's no use stashing stuff in a basement or a garden shed. No matter where you put it, it will sink some critical life issue. The only way to thrive is to not have clutter anywhere.

The overall point, though, is that energy needs space to travel, and where there is clutter, energy gets stagnant. Mary didn't frame it as feng shui, but spelled it out just as clearly: "Your office is kind of like a pinball machine." *Boing, boing, boing!* She bumped from doorway to bookshelf to desk and back again. Every piece of furniture jutted out awkwardly; none of the doors opened all the way because of wedding presents stashed behind them.

"We're going to move that file cabinet into the closet, and then you'll be able to go through the doorway and into your bedroom."

"But we're used to it sticking out like that. It's not a big deal to walk around," I said.

Mary stuck to her guns, and after a huge amount of work unloading the closet and loading the file drawers in, the doorway was clear. It was so clear I could see through to the bedroom. It looked the way it had the first time I'd seen it, five years ago. The skylight over the bed, dappled light creating a tree house effect. Light, air, and hope.

"You can't have marital problems if you sleep in this bedroom," I'd whispered to the realtor. This is what you buy when you buy a house. Not the roof, the floor, or the furnace but the fantasy. We bought it, hook, line, and sinker.

Once our stuff moved in, so did we, with all our old anxiety dreams and more. But now, with the entrance clear, a fresh start seems possible. I stepped from the office into the bedroom and back. And then I did it again, with more confidence—there was nothing to stub my toe, bang my knee or elbow on. *I could swing my arms. I could sashay my hips. I could do a little dance . . .*

"HOW'S THE DECLUTTERING GOING?" my friend Melanie asked. Melanie likes things in their place and is blessed with children who feel the same way. She has a peaceful, orderly house and I always wondered what she thought of the mess in mine.

"It's going," I replied. Before I broke my foot we'd talked about going for power walks to exercise, but now we were consuming calories at the coffee shop instead. "But it's so much work. I wonder if I'll be able to keep it up." Honestly, I was starting to regret having told everyone I knew that I was facing my fear of housework.

"It *is* a lot of work to maintain," Melanie said, eating her salad. Suddenly, she confided that she had thought twice about meeting me that morning. "I felt like I had too much to do. But when I thought about it, do you know what I would have done if I hadn't met with you? I would have polished the dining room table. Isn't that ridiculous? I wonder, sometimes, if my wanting things to be clean and in order keeps me from doing other things that would be more valuable."

I did some more research and discovered that what's true for clutterers is true for neatniks—when the desire for order, cleanliness, and space goes from a personality preference to a problem is when it interferes with your ability to do what you need to do, when it affects your relationships or the quality of your life or the lives of those close to you. So a woman who likes to put her shoes in pairs so she can find them prefers that. A woman who cannot sleep unless all her shoes are lined up in pairs exactly where they belong may have obsessive-compulsive disorder.

According to clinical psychologist Jonathan Abramowitz, "The main difference between 'neat freaks' and people with OCD is that 'neat freaks' like being neat. They want to be that way because they feel like it helps them and keeps them productive. People with OCD wish they weren't that way, but feel they have to do their rituals in order to prevent some dreaded catastrophe that is unlikely in the first place."

But what of those who are functioning well but wondering if their desire for neatness is getting in the way of their relationships and their enjoyment of life? Kids and pets can throw the best-laid systems for a loop, and order-seeking parents can reach a level of stress they've never felt before, thinking things like: "I hate coming home after a long day at work to chaos. It makes me dread coming home." And wondering, "Is this my problem for being too uptight, or theirs for being slobs?"

Talking to a qualified mental health care professional who can help assess your situation objectively is a good place to start. People sometimes use cleaning to avoid doing things they fear, like socializing or finding a new career. Or an obsessive need to organize one's exterior world may be a way of expressing anxiety and an unsettled internal landscape. Therapy focused on managing anxieties and relating to others with less tension can also help ease the pressure of daily life.

Those on the milder end of the spectrum can try to challenge their beliefs, the way Melanie had the morning she decided that catching up with a friend was a better use of her time than polishing a table. In our forty-five-minute lunch we'd socialized but also brainstormed how to handle sticky situations in her work and in our families, and swapped ideas for her husband's book proposal. "I'm trying to not just do things out of habit or routine, but think about what I really want to accomplish," she said.

≋

MARY THE CLUTTER SLAYER saved the hardest part for her third and last visit: "I think you should move a bookcase from upstairs into your secret hiding place," she said. "If you want to hold on to your books, you need to use your shelves."

For someone who writes books herself, Mary is surprisingly unattached to them. "When you're done with your copy of *Secrets of Simplicity*, pass it on to a friend," she said. I was planning to have her autograph all three of her books so I could hold on to them forever.

Our family loves books. Mary's suggestion "Get rid of anything you're not going to read" doesn't apply in our house, because Kent reads everything again and again (including his twenty-one-volume set of Patrick O'Brian's Napoleonic-era seafaring novels, in hardcover and paperback, and his hundred-volume-and-counting Library of America collection, all the mysteries in the Bill James series, and so on). We purged five boxes' worth and still had piles of books and hurt feelings spilling forth everywhere we looked.

"You care about the books more than you care about us," I huffed at him, feeling cranky and provocative. It was an old argument, my resenting his reluctance to make space for our growing children, his recounting of how adult space in his house growing up was off-limits to kids, my superiority complex over how we had so little space growing up that my sister and I and all our stuff were welcome everywhere, and isn't that what a home should be?

"I have so little in this house that's mine," he said, the overworked lawyer who got home with only enough energy to read before bed. "And now you want me to get rid of my books, too?" *You have a whole office in the city that's yours,* I thought to myself. *All I have is a cushion behind a screen.*

And now Mary wanted to give it away.

"Make him a happy man," she said, revising her plan after hearing my account of events. "These books are important to him, they're part of what makes his house a home. Put them in a nice bookcase in the first room he walks into after a long day away. He'll feel a part of things. Let's find somewhere else you can altar it up."

I was not ready. Not yet.

≋

"CLUTTER IS LIKE THE TIDES," Mary said. "It flows in and out." That was a rude awakening. I had kind of hoped for a home makeover show, a "reveal" that would have me breaking down in gratitude, shrieking in joy that I'd seen the light and would never clutter again. Doesn't that usually happen within twenty-two minutes on the show? In my case, it was taking longer.

"*What the hell is this?*" Mary exclaimed when she opened the office closet. Uh-oh. Now that we'd organized the shelves, all their contents were visible at a glance. "Is that a *Rolodex?* I thought you got rid of those." Yes, I had proudly shown her two Rolodexes in the trash. I just hadn't told her about the third. "Are you *hiding* things from your organizer?" Yes, yes, I was.

"Those are people I want to remember to look up online," I said.

"Okay, just make sure you do it. Clutter is delayed decisions. Got it?" Got it.

"You're making great progress, Patty," she said, gathering the twenty pounds of spare change we'd found around the house to bring to the bank. As I walked Mary out the door she said, "I love your front steps!" Our newly rebuilt, safe, sturdy steps. Progress, indeed. "Everyone wants a quick fix," she said in parting, "but real change takes time."

I AM PUTTING IN THE TIME. I've lost count of the days I've spent sorting out, an hour here and a half hour there, with three bags before me—one for trash, one for items to donate, one for things to put away. The admonishing voices—"Be thrifty, be creative, be green. Remember this? Remember this!"—have gotten easier to bear.

The donation bags are good karma. The first time I gave Karen, the social worker, an armload of dresses our tomboys never wore for the foster kids she serves, her eyes filled with tears of happiness. "I know just the little girl who will love these," she said. I vowed never again to let clothing hang unused in a closet for years.

The trash bags remind me to not accumulate so much in the first place. My mother has every gift we've ever given her displayed or carefully stored away in their apartment. She has towels, bedding, clothing from twenty years ago. But her apartment still has space because she doesn't buy new things. She's not out shopping clearance sales for T-shirts to clean in.

In *Secrets of Simplicity,* Mary says many of us fantasize that we'll be rescued from our troubles by a grand stroke of luck, like winning the lottery, and then not have to deal with the messes around us. I have definitely prayed for miracles. In the hardest times, when I was most overwhelmed, I have closed my eyes as the piles grew and waited for someone to rescue us all. The process of organizing myself has been like opening my eyes and seeing our lives laid bare, and owning it.

"Inhale what you need, exhale what you don't," I teach my yoga students all the time. The lesson is both literal and figurative. We take in life-giving air and let go of toxic waste every moment we're alive. I'm finally applying this in daily decisions, keeping what nourishes and releasing the rest. Taking responsibility for what I can. Surrendering the things I can't. Living with palms open.

I had been so afraid of letting go. But in the clear spaces on my floor, on my desk, on the walls, I do not see someone who has no reason to live but one who has every reason to live, because there's so much yet to come.

Slowly, it's getting easier to see, to walk, to *breathe* in different areas of the house. Gigi loves her homework basket with all her supplies in one place. Ruby can actually help herself to toys because she knows what's in each bin. "Our house seems bigger," Kent says, for the first time ever. My sister has started purging her house, friends are sending before and after pictures of theirs. "You're inspiring me!" they say, and I laugh that it's the blind leading the blind.

But honestly, I feel more capable every day. I don't need my old files to tell me so. I love opening the clean white drawers of my big new desk and seeing sky-blue files, so full of potential. I love working in my office, writing, planning, dreaming into the night.

In my past attempts to get organized, backsliding started as soon as the organizer left the scene. Now I realize why. It wasn't enough to force myself to behave differently. Eventually, the feelings of fear and insecurity would resurface and I'd start behaving the way I always had. It wasn't until I released the fear, telling it I could take care of things from here, that I gained a true sense of power.

I want Gigi and Ruby to be in charge of their things, and not the other way around. Clearing clutter, once just a burdensome chore, is becoming a practice with a purpose.

One day, Gigi said, "I want to organize my room. I've got a lot of stuff I don't need." I couldn't believe my eyes as she scaled a mountain range of toys, sorting the truly cherished from the rest. "I remember when I made this stuffed animal. I was very proud, I'll keep it. I never liked this game, but I feel bad giving it away. What if my friend who gave it to me finds out? This toy is basically new but I don't play with it. Should we let someone else have a chance?" All the guilt, the sentimental journeys, the letting go.

The letting go is what brought tears to my eyes. It's been five years since Gigi told me her cookie jar was broken. In that time we have worked on fixing her jar in many different ways. We talked about being hurt, about not having enough, about being afraid. About new beginnings, healing, and trust. We poured love and reassurance into the jar. Sometimes it would hold ("Mom, I have so many cookies to share today!") and sometimes it wouldn't.

On this day, though, it's solid.

"I don't need this Spider-Man anymore," Gigi said, adding it to a pile for Ruby. "I have plenty."

I smiled.

The cookie jar is full.

☇

DURING MY TRAINING to become a yoga teacher, a swami in saffron robes preached the principle of *vairagya*, nonattachment, as the path to peace. If we are not attached, we do not become consumed by desire, hope, fear, or disappointment. By letting go, we become free. "But what," I asked, "if we are attached to yoga?" "I guess it's better to be attached to yoga," the wizened woman replied with a twinkle, "than attached to a joint."

I am attached to my meditation space. I love the bronze tree branches of my favorite sculpture hanging on the wall above, the flickering candle on the altar below. The blossoms on the branches catch the light and remind me of my Chinese name, Mei, for "plum blossom," which blooms in late winter and symbolizes strength. As the old Chinese song goes, "Of ice, snow, wind, and rain, it is not afraid, it is my nation's flower." Here I sit, breathing in, breathing out. Of children, health, finances, and career, I am not afraid. I am mother of this house, ruler of this nation.

Now that my office is clear, down to the pretty Oriental rug I'd forgotten was so pretty, I've been feeling less desperate to defend my territory. Maybe I could find a new location for my altar. But where? Our house is small; there are other places to hang my beloved branches but no space to sit beneath them. There's a window I could move the altar under, but I'd lose the sculpture as the object of my meditation. Dragging my altar under the window, I thought, *I'll try this, but I won't like it*, and sat down with my eyes closed.

Natural light played on my face, an unfamiliar sensation. I opened my eyes and there, framed by the window, were the branches of a mulberry tree, in the exact shape of the sculpture. As if the sculpture, which I bought at a flea market in Texas, was made by an artist looking at this tree outside my house in New York.

This living sculpture will change with the seasons, with the light of day. It will bear up in wind and under snow, and I'll sit in its shade as I meditate. I can see it now, how the room will look, lined with books. Cozy. A family room. Not me, hiding from the kids. Not my husband forging a narrow, solitary path to get to the stairs. A room for all of us.

Like all good teachers, Mary taught me all she knew, and then gave me space to absorb the lessons into my life. Three afternoons with her and months of homework later, I hear her words in my own clear voice: *Love things that love you back.*

Love the people who love you back. Love the things that help you grow. Love the open windows and all the surprises yet to come. Let everything else go.

I sneak another peek at my new view, laughing out loud at how beautiful it is. I blow out the candle. *I'm home.*

CHAPTER 3

IN TOO DEEP

Water

Ruby stood like a stick bug in the sand, her knobby brown knees and elbows akimbo. *What if the sand is hot? What if a crab bites me? What if a jellyfish stings me? What if the water is cold? I can't swim. You know I can't swim!* My five-year-old daughter, putting words to all the free-flowing anxiety I felt, had fretted all the way to the beach. Now, she was motionless and mesmerized by the water, until a gentle wave came in her direction. She shrieked and ran back toward us.

Kent and I were sitting on beach chairs with a direct view of Ruby playing on land and ten-year-old Gigi wading in the water. It was late afternoon, late in the season on Long Island Sound. I had promised to bring the girls to the beach before the summer was out, but after breaking my foot I stretched the definition of summer all the way to Columbus Day. It was a beautiful fall day, warm enough for the girls to beachcomb, for Gigi to go in for a quick dip, if we made it really quick. "Let's do it," I said, packing the sand toys in the trunk. I wanted to be brave. I wanted this to be fun. Wasn't that the whole point of facing my fears—so my daughters could grow up with confidence?

But now, watching Gigi venturing waist-deep while rummaging

around with her feet for pretty rocks on the bottom, my stomach tightened.

It's okay, I told myself. *It's low tide. Look how calm that water is.*

The Greek Chorus of Perpetual Doubt in my head begged to differ. *People drown in bathtubs,* it stage-whispered. I tried waving it away with the sand flies.

It's okay. Kent's here. My husband used to be a lifeguard.

Yeah, twenty years ago—before his bad back . . .

Stop it! Nothing bad will happen. But my foot, broken by an ocean wave at Jones Beach less than two months ago, was still in its brace, and my heart was still in my mouth. The Greek Chorus rested its case.

"I'm glad Ruby has some sense of fear," I said out loud, looking on the bright side. I watched her tiptoe around some shells, her baseball cap, rash guard, and swim trunks bone-dry. If Ruby wouldn't get wet, she couldn't drown.

Ruby was fearless in many things. She could outclimb a howler monkey any day, scaling the playground equipment while cackling at my pleas for her to come down. She could keep up with Gigi, five years older, on any amusement park ride. But water was not her element.

Both our girls are Pisces—fish. After years of swim lessons, however, Ruby still would not put her face in the pool. Gigi, on the other hand, was born to swim. When she was still too little to stand in the shallow end of the town pool, she would spy something—a leaf, a penny—at the bottom, and before I could check her goggles or remind her to hold her breath, down she'd go. I'd scramble to put on my own goggles and go under to make sure she was okay. "Swim up! Swim up before you run out of air!" I'd instruct, frantically pointing toward the surface. In the water it sounded like *"Mmphblub! Mmphblubeyuruhanwha!"*

Above water, there was so much for Gigi to be anxious about— what the other kids were up to, whether to say hello or try to join a game. Below the surface, everything was simple. Her expression under water was beatific.

Once, I came upon her lying still in the bathtub, fully submerged, face up, eyes open. "GIGI!" I screamed, lunging toward her. She sat up, crying, *"What?! Mommy, what's wrong!"* She'd just been relaxing, and I'd scared us both half to death.

But I couldn't stop worrying about her in the water, especially at the beach. *She wouldn't realize she was out of her depth until it was too late,* I thought. When she became too quick for me to keep up with, I stopped taking her. Until today.

Now a wave knocked Gigi off her footing and she fell neck deep, then staggered back up with a frown.

"Oh no," Kent said, under his breath. "No, no, no. Do not come stomping out of there saying you want to go home."

Stomp, stomp, stomp. "I want to go home!" Gigi declared, stopping at my feet and dripping water and indignation all over my leg. "Did you see that? I fell down and *scraped my butt.* I am done."

"No," Kent said emphatically. "No, we can't leave on that note. Go back out there and have fun."

When Gigi was younger, she'd been impervious to pain. No one threw herself into life with more abandon. But ever since she'd broken her arm falling off the monkey bars in first grade, she had become more careful, which was a good thing, and more easily intimidated, which was not. I was starting to see more of me in her by the day.

Gigi stomped away, fuming. "My butt hurts. I don't want to go out there and have fun. It's not fun—I'm going to fall again . . ." Her voice faded but the sentiment hung in the air.

Let's just go to the movies! I wanted to say. I was reconsidering the outing, the entire endeavor. I had worked for two years to face my fear of moving water. I swam laps, learned to dive off a diving board, ventured into the ocean with a boogie board, and what happened? The ocean spat me out and broke my foot. What was the point of getting hurt doing something that was supposed to be fun? I grew up reading encyclopedias for fun, and I turned out mostly fine. Let's just go home.

"This is how she'll learn," Kent said, as if sensing where I'd gone in my mind. He, unlike me, grew up playing baseball and tennis, soccer and ice hockey. "She needs to fall down and get knocked around and realize she's okay. Like you. You got knocked around and broke your foot. You had the worst thing happen and you're okay."

This is not the worst that could have happened, I wanted to say. In *Change Your Brain, Change Your Life,* psychiatrist Daniel G. Amen calls these reflexive doom-and-gloom thoughts ANTs (automatic negative thoughts). ANTs now swarmed over every millimeter of my brain. *The ocean is indiscriminate. It could have broken any bone. It could have broken every bone. It could have broken my neck. I have only one neck. What if it broke Gigi's neck?* I swallowed, hard.

Gigi was back in the water, struggling to stay upright. The waves were breaking at her hip. She looked so small. I opened my mouth to speak.

"Let her figure it out," Kent said. I closed my mouth and shivered. I felt the warm sand under my feet and imagined cold wet sand under Gigi, giving way. Imagined her in too deep. The way I was, the day I fell into the Esopus Creek.

≈

I WASN'T SUPPOSED TO FALL IN. I was eighteen years old, Kent and I were dating, and a group of us converged on a friend's country house in the Catskills. I was wigged out already by the size of the mosquitoes. If I had known falling into a river was a possibility, I would have stayed safely indoors reading *Glamour,* with Cyndi Lauper on my Walkman for company. But the town was known for tubing—riding down the

river in the black rubber inner tube of a truck tire—and it was supposedly easy, even for nonathletic, indoorsy people like me. "You'll lie
back and get a tan," my friend Iris, who'd done it the summer before,
assured me. "Piece of cake."

From the moment the outfitter dropped the tube down into the
churning water two or three feet below us, and told me to drop myself
into it, I knew something wasn't right. The tube looked like it was cir-
cling the drain. That should have been a sign. As soon as my body
landed in the tube, the tube flipped over. *Oh!* I gasped, taking cold
water into my body like a sponge. It flooded my mouth, nose, and ears.
I felt the tops of my bare feet brush against river rocks below. *Bare feet?*
I thought, deeply confused. *I was wearing shoes a second ago.*

It's not like I'd worn REI trekking sandals, designed to stay on in a
river, but Chinese girls from the Bronx do not normally ford rivers. I'd
worn Keds knockoffs I'd bought at the Korean sundries shop for $10,
no tax, and now one sneaker whacked me in the ear and zipped away as
if on a Jet Ski, followed by the other.

The guy from the tube rental place was yelling something at me.
"What?" I yelled back over the roar of the water. Why was it so loud?
Wasn't this supposed to be peaceful? It was a *creek*. Nobody dies on a
creek, right?

"STAY TO THE RIGHT!" He was gesturing toward the right
bank of the river. "GET IN THE TUBE AND STAY TO THE
RIGHT!"

Seeing my friends dropping in and sailing away spurred me to action. I didn't want to be left behind. I hauled my body into the tube,
which popped out of the eddy it had been twirling in, and then I, too,
was sailing quickly and dizzyingly down the river.

"Seats are for wusses," my friend the local had said. They cost extra. So now as my bottom plunged into a stunningly cold bidet, I
pushed down hard on the tube with my armpits to keep from falling in.

I tried to steer. I tried to paddle. But my arms and legs were too short to reach the water. I was an upturned turtle, waving limbs uselessly, until the tube hit a rock and flipped again. This time, the river tore the scrunchie right out of my hair, and two feet of bad home perm plastered my face.

I reached for the tube blindly with one arm, pushed hair out of my eyes with the other, and then saw exactly why I had been told to stay to the right. Just ahead, the river split. All my friends were bouncing merrily down the main thoroughfare to the right.

As my tube and I hurtled left.

I tried to kick my legs and paddle one arm toward the right, but the current tore into me, pushing me back and dragging me where it wanted me to go, which was away from everyone I knew.

I screamed, as loudly as I could, but around the slaps of cold water hitting my tonsils it was more like gargling. *This river is full of people,* I thought. *Surely somebody will help me.* I waved frantically at my friends, but the action and noise of the water around me was like rush hour in Times Square. I couldn't make myself seen or heard.

No one saw me get sucked down the other branch of the river. My friends' laughter, which had sounded close before, came faintly through the trees, then faded away. And then I was alone.

Where am I going? I clung to the tube with both arms, my legs trailing behind like kite streamers. The water was so cold, so fast. Why was it so fast?

Later, I would find out that the overflow from the dam upstream had just been released, joining snowmelt from the Catskill Mountains and spring rain, and voilà: tourist-eating whitewater. But I didn't know that then, as the river spun me around, churning me over its rocky bottom like dirty laundry on a stone washboard.

The tube stopped, pinning me against the land separating me from my friends, the riverbank a solid, slippery wall of roots and mud. I held on to the tube with my left arm while grasping at a tree root with my right hand. I tried to see where the root led, but I couldn't see the base of the tree. I'd have to climb a few feet at least, to get up onto land.

The current continued to rush underneath me, banging the length of my body against the riverbank and river bottom. I was horizontal, one hand clutching a soggy branch about the width and firmness of an old lady's wrist, and the other on the tube, which pulled insistently downstream. *I'm going to be drawn and quartered,* I thought, shoulder muscles straining. *I can't hang on.* My whole life everyone had said I should be a hand model, so dainty, so pretty were my hands. *So useless!*

The branch snapped. I yelped as the river took me, over and under and around, until the tube stopped again, caught up in a wayward tangle of vines.

When I was nine years old, at the end of fourth grade, my family had moved from a quiet Canadian suburb to the Bronx. I remember entering the city school, with bars on its windows and an air of rowdy hostility coming out of every classroom. I remember walking the length of room 4-301 past thirty-six pairs of eyes to find a seat in the back, as the teacher yelled at the principal in the hallway, "Not another one! I can't take any more!" I remember stepping toward the "China doll" snickers of the kids who would eat me for lunch. That was as exposed and out of my element as I had ever felt.

Until now.

I screamed. I wanted someone to come crashing out of the woods above me and reach down and pull me out. I wanted to be home, safe and sound. I wanted to go to college and get married and have children. I wanted to pick a religion—why hadn't I done that already? I wanted to kill Kent and all my stupid friends, who make everything look so easy, when these things always happen to me. *Why do these things always happen to me?* I stopped screaming. Nobody came.

I'm going to die, I thought, *right here on this river.* I closed my eyes.

Several seconds went by, during which my heart kept beating. I wasn't going to die right then and there, I began to realize with hope. And then dread. Other things were going to happen first. I opened my eyes and looked at the tree root in my hand again. If I let go and floated down the river, all sorts of things might happen. Maybe this offshoot would meet up with the mother river again! Or maybe I'd go down a waterfall and get smashed to smithereens. Maybe I'd be saved by a fisherman. Or maybe I'd drift on and on to—where? Ohio? Pennsylvania? Which states bordered New York?

The next thought erased everything that came before. *What will I do when it gets dark?*

I had to get the hell out of the river.

Which meant I'd have to climb up. *All I have to do is get across this land and I'll be back in my life, back where I'm supposed to be.* I tried, feebly, to pull myself up with one hand, but it was no use. I'd need both arms and that meant letting go of the tube. If I let go of the tube and fell back in the river, I'd be totally screwed.

I looked down the rushing river again, searching for a way out. I couldn't ford it. I couldn't maneuver the tube down it. Could I swim? It was froth, punctuated by big rocks. How deep was the froth? How big were the rocks underneath? *I had no idea.* I have never had no idea the way I had no idea at that moment.

Oh hell. *Choose.* I let go of the tube. It tore away from me like a wild horse. I felt suddenly very small, a Borrower scaling a mossy tree, seemingly a mile high.

I wish I could say that I then mustered the strength to haul myself up out of the river, bushwhack barefoot across untamed forest, and conquer my fears of everything that had happened up to this decisive moment in my life.

But no. I slipped and scrabbled, trying to get a foothold here, a handhold there, and slid again and again. I tried hanging on to fistfuls of tiny roots, as fine as hair, almost hearing them tear away from the earth under my fingers. My arms, which I'd only ever used for raising my hand in class, burned. The time we had to climb the rope hanging from the ceiling of the high school gym in PE I hadn't made it to the top.

I can't do it. I let the realization wash over me. I wouldn't get to the top of this riverbank. I had no tube to get me down the river. *I have no good options.*

For a moment, my entire body went cold and quiet, except for the sound of my breathing, which was shallow and quick. Then the breaths came faster and faster until they caught up with each other, choking my throat closed.

"I'm freaking out!" is something I used to say all the time, about boyfriends, about tests, about getting into college. But this time, I really was freaking out. I could hear the freaking brain tissue tearing in my head.

Hot tears sprang to my eyes. It was the heat that brought me back to my senses. *I need heat.* The water between the muddy bank and me was warmer than the water rushing down my back. Hanging on with my hands, I pulled my body toward the mud to get warmer, panting and resting in a little pocket just out of the river's flow.

Looking downriver, through blurry tears, I saw a patch of green I hadn't noticed before, down a ways on the opposite bank. I squinted to get a better look. It was sunny and flat, unlike the vertical wall of foliage I was hanging on to by a thread. In an environment that felt as foreign to me as science fiction it took me a second to realize why this horizontal swath of green looked so familiar. It was *grass*.

Get there. It was a singular thought; it obliterated all else. I didn't wait. I let go of the roots, pushed off the muddy bank, and threw myself into the river. I don't know if I swam, or if the river carried me, but I felt propelled at great speed across space that suddenly contracted. One second I was flying through water, arms outstretched, and the next the water was land. *Oof!* Solid, dry, beautiful, land. Facedown in the grass, I laughed.

I lay there, coughing and retching, my body trying to squeeze water out of all the wrong places it had gone, the warm ground under my belly and the sun's rays on my back making me feel like everything was going to be just fine. And then I had a strange sensation that I was not alone. I lifted my head and saw two sets of bare feet in the grass in front of me.

I stopped, midcough, following the legs, slightly hairy legs, up to see the people they were attached to. *Please.* I prayed. *Please don't be ax murderers.*

They were teenage boys. Sitting in lawn chairs. They had long scraggly hair.

I was wearing a one-piece swimsuit, with skinny straps I had imagined untying so I could sunbathe without tan lines as I floated along. Now, in front of these Wayne and Garth lookalikes, I realized the river had untied the straps for me. I wiggled to pull my suit up while still lying on my stomach. *Please don't hurt me,* I thought, weighing whether I should just roll myself back into the river.

Then the blond, the Dana Carvey of the two, leaned his head back in the direction of a house. *"Ma!"* he called, without taking his eyes off me. "Ma! We got another one!"

"Ma" came running out of the house, and when she saw me, screamed. "I can't believe this!" She threw her hands up in the air, waving them in the direction of God. "Why are they sending people down the river on a day like today?!"

I started trembling. I tried to stand up, and then—as if everything that had been held in by cold and shock erupted—tears flowed down my cheeks, and little lines of blood ran out of cuts I didn't know I had.

My feet did not look like my feet. My feet have ten toenails. These feet had seven? Six? I didn't want to look too closely to see.

"Oh dear," Ma said, looking at me. "Are you okay? Can you walk? Let's get you a blanket. What are you staring at?" she yelled at the boys. "Get her a blanket! I'll pull the car out."

Ma drove me back to the rental company, fuming all the way. "I am going to give them a piece of my mind," she said, filling me in on why the river was so rough today. I wasn't the first person to get washed up in her yard. "And it's a good thing you did, too. There's a low bridge downstream. It would have clonked you good." I still see that bridge in my dreams.

Back at the rental place, Ma gave the man in charge that piece of her mind, at top volume. "She could have been killed!" Ma yelled, words I wished I hadn't heard. I looked around the shed, musty and dark, crammed full of black tubes. Today, I'm told, rental places along the Esopus also house wet suits, helmets, and life vests; seats come standard with every tube; USGS water level reports are checked daily; and rentals are cancelled after storms or when there's debris in the water. Proprietors assess whether customers are physically and mentally capable of handling themselves in the river and turn away those expecting an amusement park ride. Maybe the shift toward safe adventuring started with me, the poor city chick, almost drowned, sitting on that stool in 1988.

Or maybe not. The man in charge looked at me, and asked, flatly, "Where's the tube?"

⋙

I HAD BEEN SERIOUSLY SHAKEN that day on the Esopus. I had wanted to sue the tube rental company for reckless endangerment and emotional distress. "I could have died," I said to Kent. It was objectively true. I pointed to my many bruises. What if any one of those hard knocks had been to the head?

"But you didn't die," was Kent's reply.

Twenty-five years later and Kent and I are still having the same conversation, I thought, watching Gigi wading back into the surf.

Because our brains are wired for survival, "one thing happens to you that is potentially life threatening and you'll never forget it," says psychologist Michael Davis in *Nerve,* by Taylor Clark. Self-protection is a good thing, and if the lesson I learned was to avoid tubing in fast-moving rivers when I don't have a helmet and don't know how to maneuver the tube, that would be putting fear to its best use.

But for me, the fear didn't stop there. Open water unnerved me after that incident, and although I continued to go to the beach, it became harder to enjoy it. And once the kids came, my anxiety went up tenfold. It's called *catastrophizing,* when you take every situation to its worst possible outcome, and *generalizing,* when you apply the lessons of one experience to unrelated situations.

I did plenty of both.

"I just don't want Gigi to panic," I blurted out. "What if she panics and forgets everything, forgets how to swim, how to breathe? She hasn't been to the beach in years!"

Even as I said it, I knew it was an ANT, the kind Daniel Amen said I should step on before it breeds. "Do not accept every thought that comes into your mind," he writes in a chapter optimistically titled "Mastering Fear." "Thoughts are just thoughts, not facts."

Or, as my therapist says, "Stop making shit up to worry about."

Just then, the bottom dropped out from under Gigi and she slid away from us. I sat up in alarm as her surprised face went under. The wave took her for a moment, and then carried her back in to shore. She scrambled to her feet, looking disoriented at first, and then extremely pleased.

"Did you see that?" she called, waving both arms overhead. "I was part of the wave!" She strode toward us, cheeks aglow. "The ocean liked me, so it gave me a kiss!"

It was the old Gigi, the one who as a preschooler wanted to trade her legs for Ariel's *Little Mermaid* tail. Now she bubbled on joyfully, as if a dream had finally come true.

"My butt still hurts, but I'm glad I went in again. I'm proud of myself, Mama!" She shook like a puppy, sending a shower of water over us. "I love the ocean!"

"I'm proud of you, too," I said, standing up to wrap her in a towel. I was so relieved that Kent's *See, I told you so* moment didn't even bother me. I turned to fold up my chair. "And now we can go home!"

"What about me?" Ruby asked, hopping from one foot to the other. "I didn't get to go in! I don't know how to swim!"

"You're learning," Gigi said. "And one day you will be able to go in, and, oh, Ruby, you're going to love it!"

WHY SOME PEOPLE LOVE water and others don't is often a mystery. Some can trace a fear of water to a traumatic experience of near drowning or feeling out of their depth (for this reason it's not a good idea to drop a kid into the pool to "sink or swim"). Others, who never had the opportunity to learn to swim, or to practice enough to swim well, are quite reasonably afraid of drowning.

Perhaps as many as 12 percent of children have sensory processing difficulties, meaning the brain does not absorb sensory input—water, noise, light, temperature, smells, tastes—in a way it can regulate properly. What might feel soothing to one child (splashing around) could feel like an assault to another. Sensory delays often resolve as the brain matures. But for many who had bad early experiences with water, the aversion remains.

Evolutionary scientists might say your DNA holds the legacy of your ancestors' fears, while psychologists might cite unresolved emotional issues from the life you're in right now. In the book *Swim: Why We Love the Water* (a royal "we" if I ever heard one), Lynn Sherr quotes a psychiatrist who says, "People who can't float often have trust and intimacy issues. For some, if they're arrested in development, they hold on to the side of the pool, or can't let their feet leave the bottom. It's an aquatic version of apron strings: they can't take chances."

Yogis tie water to the second chakra, called *Svadhisthana* in Sanskrit, or the "dwelling place of the self." It is the energy center housed in the lower abdomen that governs creativity, passion, and emotion. When it's balanced, our lives flow. If you're deficient in this area, you might have a fear of pleasure or resistance to change. If you're excessive, you may display frequent emotional drama or sexual addictions. No comment on the state of my second chakra.

For many, fear of water comes down to fearing a loss of control. Paul Lennon, founder and owner of the Adult Aquaphobia Swim Center in Glendale, California, says that being weightless in water is like if gravity were suddenly turned off. You'd float out of your chair and "your heart rate would go up dramatically, because you'd be taken by surprise." Dealing with the fear means acclimating to both the fear and the sensation of weightlessness until they become predictable.

But for the majority of those who avoid water activities and swimming lessons, according to aquatic therapist Jeff Krieger, the founder of Strategies for Overcoming Aquatic Phobias (SOAP), the fear is visceral and has no clear explanation.

"Most people can't point to a particular reason they're afraid, and that makes them more afraid," he said. "They may be educated, fit, capable people on land, but in the water they lose any sense of competence and think, 'What's wrong with me?'" Jeff's interest in teaching swimming to fearful kids and adults started when he was a camp director and got into the pool to work with the kids who refused to go in. "I went home each day, plucking out fingernails from my neck and back where they'd held on to me in the water, crying," he recalled. "It wasn't because they were having a hard day. It wasn't because they wanted to give us a hard time. They were terrified. My heart broke for them."

Typical swim lessons teach a prescribed set of skills, beginning with "Put your face in the water and blow bubbles." Most instructors aren't trained to handle the students who hear this and run away screaming. In Jeff's experience, well-meaning parents often respond by making two mistakes. "They push too hard too fast, or they give up." Kids dig their heels in, parents consider how much lessons cost, and, "Before you know it, Bobby's doing martial arts instead and everyone has accepted he doesn't swim." In urban and poor areas where access to pools and lessons is limited, it's even harder to try to learn.

Sherr quotes John Ryan, Sr., founder of the Junior Lifeguard Program in East Hampton, New York: "I believe that between forty to fifty percent of the school age population cannot swim—that they cannot tread water for five minutes at the deep end of the pool. Yet they will go into the ocean with a boogie board. And that's dangerous."

The Centers for Disease Control and Prevention (CDC) reports that every day, about ten people die from unintentional drowning. Among children ages one to fourteen, drowning is the second-leading cause of unintentional injury-related death, behind motor vehicle crashes.

For a mother with an all-consuming fear of any kind of death happening to my children, the choice was clear. "You're going back to swim lessons, and that's all there is to it," I said to Ruby the next week.

"But what if I drown at my lesson? I don't know how to swim!" she wailed.

"The way you won't drown is by learning to swim!"

"But what if I drown at my lesson? I don't know how to swim!"

"The way you won't drown is by—Oh stop it! Just put on your swimsuit!"

We'd tried this, off and on for three years, starting with mommy-baby swim class, where she squeezed me so tightly I barely had enough air in my lungs to sing "London Bridge Is Falling Down" as I carried her under the dripping noodle held over our heads in the shallow end. The water hurt her eczema-prone skin, and when she cried to get out, we usually did.

As a preschooler, Ruby would stand poolside, in her gray-and-white shark-teeth swim cap with her own teeth clenched, and suddenly squeeze her legs together, gasping, "I have to go to the bathroom!" Ten minutes later, she'd be back, no sign of having been relieved of anything. *We're paying for her to use the locker room,* I'd think grimly.

But this time would be different, I thought. Ruby was familiar with the pool and trusted her teacher, Jennifer Paolicelli. Jennifer, a swim teacher for more than twenty years, is the founder of Aquabilities With Jennifer, a swim school that teaches over five hundred students a year. She is also an occupational therapist who works with children and adults with special needs and aquaphobia.

Jennifer had been fine with Ruby taking it slow up until now. But when I registered her and Gigi for lessons this time, Jennifer said, "Ruby is making progress, but she needs momentum. She needs to know we're going to stick with it." *She's right,* I thought. Ruby was in kindergarten; she wanted to swim like her friends and was worried she would never be able to. I wrote the check with purpose. *We're not giving up this time.*

I led Ruby to the edge of the pool and put her between two other girls. One cannonballed in, the other leaped, their smiles as bright as their orange and pink frilly bikinis. *They're like an ad for Club Med,* I thought wistfully, urging Ruby to follow suit. Jennifer was waiting for her in the water.

"What if I get water *in my eyes?*" Ruby asked.

"Blink it out, Ruby." Jennifer blinked her brown eyes purposefully. "Use your windshield wipers and blink it out."

"What if I get water *in my mouth?*"

"Spit it out, *bleah!* Spit it out."

"I can't do it!"

"If you say, 'I can't,' then you won't," Jennifer said, lifting her gently into the pool. Ruby craned her head to keep her face dry. "Let's say *I'll try.*"

"I hate back float!" Ruby protested, as Jennifer rested Ruby's head against her chest.

"Are you kidding?" Jennifer replied. "Back float's awesome! You can breathe, can't you? And your face is out of the water!"

Just then, a woman about my age walked past me to get to the shallow end. She was in a bright pink cap and a brown tankini, with a warm smile and a curvy figure. She laughed and waved at her daughter, sitting a couple of chairs down from me. As soon as she entered the water, though, her energy contracted. She stopped on each step to pull her arms close across her chest, to cover her mouth with her fingers, containing all her body heat and maybe her nerves into as little real estate as possible.

"Hi, Marisa!" Jennifer greeted her, walking slowly through the water with Ruby in tow. "Be right with you."

The adult was the one here for a lesson, I realized with surprise. A trembling child waiting for a swim class is a much more common sight, the cure as plain as day. Other parents, looking at Ruby's face screwed up tight, smiled sympathetically. Of course Ruby should learn to swim.

If she didn't learn now, eventually the peer and parental pressure to do so would go away, and then chances were that she would give up trying to learn. According to an American Red Cross survey of more than a thousand adults in 2011, two in ten people planning to swim, boat, or fish that summer could not swim well, or at all. The National Swimming Pool Foundation, an aquatic education and research nonprofit that trains pool operators on the safe handling of pool equipment, estimates that about half of Americans have a fear of swimming pools. That fear ranges from those who are afraid to swim in the deep end to those with severe aquatic phobias, including taking a bath or looking at a river.

Jennifer began demonstrating arm strokes, and it was a study in contrasts between Marisa's narrow, tight stance and Jennifer extending her limbs like taffy, owning the pool as she showed the kids how to "scoop" the water. "You scoop ice cream with a spoon, not a fork, right?" she said, cupping her hands. "Now, streeeetch your arm! Slooooowly! The last one to finish is the winner!" The couple of kids who could move slowly looked so relaxed. Ruby and the rest churned the water frantically. The faster they scooped, the more they splashed the faces they so desperately wanted to keep dry. "Shhhhhh," Jennifer said, holding a finger to her lips. "Quiet down." They calmed down a bit before panicking and thrashing again.

When Ruby's lesson finished, Jennifer brought her over. "Did you see Ruby's back float? She's a star!" Ruby smiled shyly as I breathed a sigh of relief. Another class done, meltdown averted.

"Okay, Marisa, your turn!" Jennifer said, going back into the pool. "Show me what you've been working on."

Marisa had started warming up with another instructor, kicking with a kickboard, and seemed to have more energy now. "Watch this!" She took a deep breath, bent her knees, and submerged her head under water. She came up beaming.

"Wow!" Both teachers cheered.

"I could cry, I'm so excited—I can put my head under without holding my nose!" Marisa said, wiping water and maybe a few tears off her face. "I know, I'm so dorky, but I was never able to do it before."

"Look at her," I whispered to Ruby, as I wrapped her in a towel. "Isn't she brave?"

As I helped Ruby get dressed I watched Marisa practice arm strokes and breathing. At one point she stood up, coughing. "I'm sorry," she said.

"Don't apologize," Jennifer said. "Just breathe."

After a while Marisa called over to her daughter and her husband, "Look at me!" I think everyone turned to watch as she edged her way down the side of the pool to the six-foot mark. Then she pushed herself away from the wall and started to tread water.

"Look at me!" she called out again, wonder and delight bouncing off every echoing surface in sight. *"I'm not touching the bottom!"*

Her family clapped for her as I walked by with Ruby. "Your wife's amazing!" I said to her husband. "What made her decide to learn how to swim?"

He put his hand on their daughter's shoulder. "Josie here is learning," he said. "Marisa wants to be able to help watch over her, God forbid anything should happen."

"I'm learning to go in the deep end now, too," said Josie, a pretty girl about ten years old. She waved at her mother. "It helps me to watch her. She works hard and keeps trying."

Marisa waved back, happy as a clam. "I'm very proud of myself!" she called over, splashing the water playfully.

Her smile was contagious. It reminded me of the day I'd learned how to dive into the deep end, two years ago. I *surprised* myself, and everyone who knew me. It was such a good feeling. *I miss it*, I thought, as I hugged Ruby and wished for the day she would feel the same way. I wanted everyone to feel the same way.

When Ruby was a toddler, I took her to a Gymboree class that ended with parachute time. At the sight of the colorful cloth parachute coming out of the supply closet, the kids started screaming in excitement. By the time the music started and the grown-ups lifted the chute above them, they were delirious. And then came *bubbles*. I turned to a dad holding the chute next to me and said, "They will spend the rest of their lives searching for this kind of happiness." This is why people try drugs or have midlife crises, when nothing they do ever compares to Gymboree.

But every time I faced a fear, it came close. Every sense came alive. My scalp tingled at the memory of diving. I scratched my foot in its brace and sighed as I packed up the swim bag. I couldn't do anything about my fear of rivers or oceans for the moment. Nor did I want to. But I was itching for an endorphin hit, and watching someone else face her fears could be almost as exciting. Maybe I could help someone else get over the fear of putting her face in the water.

I picked up my notebook. I'd been doodling waves up and down the margins, and the swoops and loops made shapes like the letters A, J, L, and I. *Anjali*, I thought, the effects of Marisa's smile suddenly spreading through my body all the way down to my toes. *Maybe Anjali is ready to try.*

≋

ANJALI, A FORTY-FOUR-YEAR-OLD MOTHER of three and a program director of a national nonprofit, had told me a while back that although she'd been hauling her kids to swim lessons for years, she herself didn't swim. "I grew up in the Third World," she'd explained, meaning near Sri Lanka's capital. "It's a very conservative culture. Back then it was hard for girls to even find bathing suits. It's not like I was missing out on a big part of the social life there." She'd recently texted a picture of her kids playing in the pool on their vacation, while she lounged nearby. Now, over lunch, I snuck it into our conversation.

"Do you ever think you'd like to swim with your kids?" I asked.

"Not really. I can go in the shallow end with them, and then come out and read my book. It's a lot of work to take swim lessons! Every session I register the kids, I think about it and then decide I don't have time. I used to feel guilty, sitting by the side of the pool and hoping the lifeguard was good because I didn't know how to help them if there was a problem. But now—" she leaned in, smiling "—all three of them know how!" She lowered her voice. "I kind of feel like I got away with not learning."

Facing a fear for the sake of your children is a powerful motivator, as I had discovered for myself. Jeff Krieger of SOAP once had a client, a young father who shook like a leaf at the prospect of submerging himself in the shallow end of the pool but was putting himself through the ordeal so he'd be able to save his son if he fell in.

"Give me three seconds of your life," Jeff asked. Whether it's putting her face in the water or jumping into the deep end, when a student hits a wall of fear she cannot get through by herself, Jeff asks her to trust him for three seconds. For 97 percent of Jeff's clients, those three seconds are like a baptism to a new life.

Jeff helped the man kneel down to put his head under water, and then lifted him up. "He started crying hysterically," Jeff remembers. "I thought he was traumatized!" Jeff felt terrible and apologized.

"'Are you kidding?'" the man replied. "'Apart from the birth of my son, this is the happiest day of my life!'

"That initial barrier, those three seconds, are so hard for people to get through," Jeff told me. "I wish I could just flip a switch for them, pat them on the back, and have them be okay. But I can't. The student needs to get through it, and for that, you need motivation, like doing it for your kids or realizing it's important to do for yourself."

Doing anything for someone you love makes it easier to justify the time and expense, and harder to quit. But with Anjali's kids so self-sufficient now, what was there to draw her into the water?

"What about exercise? It's great resistance training," I said, parroting what I'd read in *Women's Health* magazine, that water is almost eight hundred times denser than air, and any activity you do in it burns calories, builds lean muscle, and boosts metabolism. According to Thomas Lachocki, CEO of the National Swimming Pool Foundation, just standing immersed in water forces more blood to the central organs, increasing cardiac stretch, which improves the health of the heart. And it's gentle on the joints, making it an ideal exercise as we get older.

"It would probably help my back," Anjali said thoughtfully.

"Oh! I have the best story!" I said, remembering Robin, the best example I know of someone whose life changed the day she decided to put her face in the water. "I'll tell you."

≈

ROBIN GORMAN NEWMAN IS the founder of MotherhoodLater.com, an international organization devoted to those parenting later in life. She'd never learned to do more than the breast and backstroke, because she was not comfortable with the idea of putting her face in the water. One day when she was forty-eight, however, she was watching some senior citizens do laps at her community pool, and she had an aha moment.

How cool, to have that skill, she thought. *I want to do that.*

"What was I thinking?" she asked me rhetorically. "I think maybe I was delusional! This meant I would have to *put my face in the water*, first of all. Not to mention overcome my fear of going into deep water. And then learn to breathe."

There were so many steps. But as she watched the elderly lap swimmers calmly cutting their way through the water, she was filled with admiration. "Younger people often swim with this freneticism," Robin said. "But these older swimmers would just do their thing without self-consciousness. With no worry about *What do I look like?* or *How well am I doing?*"

How good they must feel, Robin thought. *I want to know what that feels like.*

The first step, to her surprise, was ridiculously easy. She got together with a friend who also hated the notion of putting her face in the water, and together, they got in a pool, counted "One, two, three, put your head in the water!" and did it. For the first time, Robin wore goggles, and what she saw through them shocked and delighted her.

"I discovered an underwater world, a completely different zone," she told me, her enthusiasm brimming over the phone line. "My friend felt the same—what we thought would be complete discomfort turned out to be the opposite: I loved it! I never could figure out why I thought putting my face in the water would be so awful. I never had a terrible experience I could remember; I had no experience, just my preconceived notions, which turned out to be wrong."

Because Robin felt most comfortable in her small community pool, she chose to practice there instead of taking swim lessons. She spent the summer watching the other swimmers, copying their motions in the shallow end, asking the lifeguards for advice and watching instructional videos at home. She was used to working out at the gym and "never thought twice about my physical ability to do it. It was mental, my fears—my desire to be in control, to be on firm ground—that stood in my way."

It was hard work. Starting at the deep end so she'd be in the shallow end when she got tired, Robin paddled her way down the pool, telling herself "a lot of stories" to keep panic at bay until the five-foot mark, where she could put her feet down with relief. With Robin's anxiety about the water, learning to breathe while doing the crawl had presented a particular challenge. "It of course meant swallowing half the pool and choking all the time," she recalled, adding, "it was exhausting."

Over the course of the summer, with the help and encouragement of the lifeguards and the regular lap swimmers, she worked her way toward her goal of swimming one lap before the pool closed for the season. But with closing three days away, she thought it wouldn't happen. "It's when I let it go that I could do it." Robin had been struggling to breathe on her right side, and she switched to the left. "I don't know why, but it worked for me."

Now, two summers later, swimming has become a favorite activity. Recently, Robin was able to swim for an hour, breathing properly, without counting laps. "I realized that for the first time, the anxiety was gone. I had no fear of the deep water at all. In fact, swimming clears my head, it's good for me on every level."

A year ago, Robin fell on a wet floor in a restaurant and tore two ligaments in her knee, an injury she may have to cope with long-term. Swimming is the only exercise that helps her knee feel better. In the water she can do leg lifts and use ankle weights and jog in place. "After all the work I did to overcome my fears, who knew I would wind up having an injury where swimming would be the best thing I could do? There may be a higher purpose to that aha moment, I believe."

Those who become parents later in life are often shocked out of old ways of seeing themselves by the surprises that go along with raising children. Just when so many settle into the predictable routines of midlife, Robin had opened herself to a new world. "I never thought I would discover an ardent passion, especially *this*, given all the discomfort I brought to it. I not only took on something new, I conquered something I thought I hated. What that means is the thing that's not even on your radar—*that thing* could be your next passion. I am still in awe."

The sense of triumph has carried over to other areas of her life. The author of two dating books, including *How to Marry a Mensch*, Robin is no stranger to taking on challenges. "My mantra is: *Tell me what I have to do today.* If it seems daunting, I break things into steps." When a theatrical producer asked her if she could turn her books into a musical, at first she balked. *I can't do that*, she thought. *I don't know how.*

"It can be easy to get stuck where you are, to question whether you can take on something huge and different, or to wonder *Are my best days behind me?* but then when I think of things I've accomplished, like with swimming, *who's to say that there isn't more in me?*"

Robin hired an accomplished playwright to offer feedback on her work, and has finished the first draft of her play. "I still have major editing to do and my moments of self-doubt," she said. "A musical would be such an unbelievable dream for me that it's something I can't fully fathom. But that's why you have to aim high and believe it's possible. If it means that much to you, as challenging or unfamiliar as it seems, wouldn't it feel worse not to try?"

"THAT'S A PRETTY AMAZING STORY," Anjali said, and for a minute she was quiet. "But, Patty, it's a huge endeavor to learn to swim! I can't even imagine finding the time to go once, let alone to practice. There are so many things I want to do that I don't have time for. And really—" she leaned back in her chair and stretched "—I am not naturally an active person. It's hard to get me moving." Another pause, as she looked down.

"And anyway, what if I did try to learn, and I couldn't? What if I put in this big effort and failed?" She raised her eyes to look at me, and I knew exactly how she felt.

When I started facing my fears, I didn't have time or energy or belief in my own ability to take on anything as challenging as learning to swim. I would have seen Robin—an entrepreneur, author, go-getter—as cut from different cloth than me. The fear of failure kept my ambitions small.

For me, facing fears was not about accomplishing major feats, it was about trying things I'd always avoided, whatever the result. One dive takes a few seconds. In half an hour, I tried a dozen times. That's the scale of where I started.

I pointed to my foot. "Look, I'm not exactly a billboard for things going well when you face your fears," I said. Anjali laughed. "No one can guarantee a straight up trajectory! But if you do anything that you've never done before—any *one* thing—it's exciting. What's something you're nervous about in the water? Something basic."

"Putting my face in the water and breathing. Everyone says it's easy, blowing bubbles, but I could never do it without getting water up my nose," she replied. "But what's the point of learning it if I don't have time to learn how to swim?"

"What was the point of me learning to dive?" I asked back. "There was no need to—no one was asking me to, it didn't help society, it didn't further my career. There aren't even diving boards at the town pool—I don't use the skill of diving at all. But facing something scary and believing I can get through it? *That's* the skill I use. That has changed my life." I was starting to get excited.

"Just think, Anjali—what if, like Robin, the thing you resisted your whole life was actually something you could *love* to do?" I could see it now: Jeff would be the perfect teacher for Anjali, *she can do this.* "And if it's horrible and you hate it, then it's a half hour out of your life."

"You mean just take one lesson?" Anjali asked. I nodded.

We looked at each other across the table. I could guess what was going through her mind. She was imagining all she'd have to do to make this happen, calculating if this endeavor was sitter-worthy or if she could stay an hour later at work and do it during lunch. She'd have to buy goggles, a swim cap, pay for a lesson. She'd have to go somewhere new and deal with a locker room (hello, who doesn't have a fear of public restrooms?); she'd be seen in a bathing suit, get cold and wet, and do something she was scared she couldn't do. And then she'd have to shower, get dry, and change her clothes and do her hair. Or she could just say no now and avoid the whole thing.

Once, on *The Amazing Race*, a woman with a fear of heights and water balked at the top of a six-story waterslide called the Leap of Faith at a luxury resort in Dubai. Wearing a pair of pink water wings and on the verge of hysteria, she shouted, "I can't do it!" at her teammate/boyfriend, who could not believe they might lose their chance at the million-dollar prize over this. He tried everything, up to and including calling her a moron and trying to physically push her down the slide as she screamed for her life. She did not go down the slide, and they were eliminated. Fans across cyberspace howled for her to dump his sorry ass.

I'm not going to push Anjali into this, I thought, softening my posture and sitting back in my chair. I didn't want to traumatize her. Or even make her too uncomfortable. Our friendship was more important. *It's up to her.*

"Whatever happens, I'll buy you a drink after," I said. No harm in throwing in a carrot.

"I'll think about it," Anjali replied.

≋

MEANWHILE, I was privately balking at going back to the pool myself. My physical therapist had suggested "Swimming would be good for your foot" so many times, I started bringing headphones to our sessions, to tune her out. After weeks of allowing my spirit to atrophy alongside my foot, my entire being ached and sagged. Even taking a deep breath hurt, and for the first time in years, I'd stopped doing yoga. I could feel myself expanding under my housedresses. I had no desire to be seen in a swimsuit or to get wet, much less haul myself up and down a pool lane. And what would be the point, if I was too scared to go back in the ocean anyway?

When I'd asked Jeff Krieger how he works with people with a fear of open water, he said, "Open water is a whole different animal. It's where anyone could get hurt at any time. If you're not a competent swimmer, you have to start in the pool."

I couldn't call myself a competent swimmer, exactly. I mean, I could swim. I could forward crawl and tread water, and I had enough body fat to float for a long time. But "competent" suggests a level of keeping your wits about you that I did not have once the water started moving.

When I got tired of moping about my dilemma, I began surveying everyone I knew. What should I do, I asked, go back in the ocean and face my fear again, or quit while I was ahead?

"With so many people counting on us, this is not a time when we can afford to be incapacitated," said Iris, my longtime friend and a former gymnast, who'd once told me tubing was a piece of cake. She'd gotten more cautious with age and motherhood, I thought, until she added, "so no skydiving for me for another decade or so, but trapeze is safe enough." *Trapeze?*

A yoga student of mine named Amy replied, "I vote for more adventures! You have a great story to go with your broken foot."

"Only you can decide what's right for you," a psychologist said. "What do you want to do?" *I want to face my fear and have everything turn out okay.* How could I make that happen?

"Visualize success," a personal coach I met at a friend's house said. "I wonder if your fear got in the way last time—you lost confidence and gave up in the wave. What if you go back in and imagine yourself just rocking it?" That sounded a bit like magical thinking to me. Didn't we just get done teaching our kids that they don't control the universe?

"You can't control the ocean," Patrick the surfer said. "I'm all for visualizing success, but what you need is strength and stamina, so when a wave rolls you, you can go with it and know you'll come up okay. Real confidence comes from experience, and that means swimming laps. *Get off your ass.*"

I groaned. There was no way around it. I'd have to get wet.

≋

"OKAY, MOM, SO YOU'RE A SUPERHERO, and your name is Elastic Kitty-O!" Ruby, in the tub, made her Playmobil kid take a flying leap into the water. I wiped my face. Although I was sitting outside the tub, I was pretty much soaked through. "And you have superpowers, like being elastic and poison ivy and other things I can't talk about."

"Ooh, I would love to be elastic," I said, smiling. "Then I could reach everything without getting up! But what are the powers you can't talk about?"

"I can't talk about it, Mom!" Ruby said. If she knew to roll her eyes, she would have. "My name is Hippy, and I don't have superpowers. Except my cuteness."

I was so happy I could hardly stand it, seeing Ruby playing in the tub. Jennifer had recommended playing with Ruby in warm water, having her try out goggles, wet her face, blow bubbles, where she was comfortable. "Make it fun!" was our homework.

Except that for so long, Ruby was never comfortable. When we brought her home from China shortly after her first birthday, she was covered with eczema from head to toe. For the next four years, we brought her to doctors, allergists, dermatologists, and homeopaths. We tried everything—at one point she had six different topical ointments that each had to be applied twice a day. Still she got skin infections and boils, and baths were torture.

My heart bled for her. The first year after an adoption is supposed to be about bonding, forming attachments for life, but every mothering instinct I had to cuddle, kiss, or tickle her, to bathe her or treat her sores, made her scream. Even our attempts to feed her turned out to be all wrong, as we slowly and painstakingly identified food allergies that made her skin worse. Sometimes when she cried, I wanted to cry right alongside her, over not knowing how to make it better.

"You want something to fix it," an allergist said, "but what you really need is time. Hopefully this will get better as she grows."

It was hard to know if it was time or the antihistamines or the restricted diet or the latest creams, but it has gotten better, I thought, running a hand along Ruby's smooth upper back. Her eczema was now mostly on her legs and arms, and mild enough that she could enjoy her bath.

"You are extremely cute," I said, sliding a pair of goggles into the tub. "How do you use that as your superpower?"

"I make bad guys look at me, and think 'Oh, she's so cute! We can't hurt her!'"

She flopped down on her belly, sending more water into my lap.

"I know a great superpower," I said, adding some toys to the bath. "Seeing underwater! Want to see what you can see?"

"Seeing underwater?" She sat up, allowing me to put her goggles on, and then dipped her face in and came up holding Crush, the sea turtle from *Finding Nemo*, with a wide, wet smile. Over the next couple of baths we added blowing bubbles to the list of her superpowers in the tub.

She didn't transfer the enthusiasm to the swimming pool for a while.

"Are they ever going to teach her how to swim?" Kent asked.

"It's a process," I replied, even though I, too, wanted to see some progress after schlepping her to lessons every week.

But then, on a cold and rainy November night, it happened. "Hey, Patty! Look at this!" Jennifer called from the shallow end. The pool is in a glassed-in atrium. With the sky black outside, every surface inside shone as if lit by a floodlight. Ruby was holding Jennifer, but not the way she usually did, close to her body as if for dear life, but with arms extended. Only their hands were touching. Ruby made sure I was looking, then took a breath and put her face in the water. She lifted her head quickly and looked for me.

"Hooray!" I gave her a big thumbs-up. And then Ruby did it again and again. With no one asking her to, just to show she could.

My early memories with Ruby hold so many moments of her discomfort and my helplessness that every smile she ever gave imprinted on me deeply. I never took a single one for granted. Her smile now, beaming across the pool, shot arrows straight through my heart.

Later, after the hugs and congratulations, when she was dry and dressed, we sat watching Gigi's swim team practice. The entire pool looked like it had been taken over by sperm on Ritalin, scores of frantically flailing bodies charging ahead in orderly lines. Gigi, in her own world, swam slowly and steadily. The other children were faster. But Gigi was the one who looked most at home.

Without taking her eyes off the action in the pool, Ruby asked, "Did something happen today? Something different?"

"Yes!" I said. "You put your face in the water over and over!"

She turned to look at me, cocking her head.

"Am *I* different now?" she asked.

I reached over to touch her face, to see if she had changed. She was my Ruby, peeking out from under straight bangs falling over her suddenly serious brown eyes. She has such a way about her, fierce and funny, more like Mowgli from *The Jungle Book* than a stereotypical China doll. I could pick her out of a crowd anywhere, but I almost hadn't recognized her in the pool just now. My Ruby didn't do that. My Ruby was afraid of water. But, oh, how she proved me wrong!

"You look more grown-up now," I said, gently brushing the hair out of her eyes, and then cupping her face. "You look like you're on your way to being a swimmer."

Ruby smiled and pulled away with a shrug. "Well, that's the way it is with swimming," she said in the voice of one who knows. "You have to get your face wet."

≋

ANJALI WAS MIA. It was understandable, what with the fall school madness, then the end-of-year crunch at work and the holidays at home. I sent her links to Jeff's website, with an occasional encouraging e-mail. I knew she was thinking about it; friends from our book group told me she was. In fact I hoped that the extra peer pressure of them knowing about her dilemma would help set her in motion. "At what point does resistance turn into readiness?" I asked a psychologist friend. "What more can I do to help her along?"

"There's no answer to that question," he said. "Each person is so different, you'll just have to see."

I hate waiting to see.

I apply every delay tactic myself, researching, thinking through every angle, envisioning every possible outcome, all in the hopes that eventually I'll feel better, braver, ready to go. But for some reason I want everyone else to take on their next challenges *now*.

In *Feel the Fear and Do It Anyway*, Susan Jeffers says: "The only way to get rid of the fear of doing something is to go out and do it. . . . The 'doing it' comes *before* the fear goes away." If Anjali got to her lesson, she would learn how to calm down her fear enough to make the task in front of her doable. But she had to go to the lesson, even if she was afraid. The fear was not going to go away first.

I sent one more e-mail. "When you tell this story, do you want to say you did the lesson, or you didn't?" I typed and hit Send. *That's enough*, I thought. *I've done what I could*.

Ten days later, while yelling at Ruby to stop giving me a heart attack on the monkey bars, I got an e-mail: "Been so busy at work I forgot to tell u I scheduled my lesson for today at 3:45. Just heading over. Sorry—just scheduled it this morning. Thx, maybe c u? Love a."

My "woo-hoo!" turned into a "What the . . ." when I realized the time. It was 3:16 p.m. My mind reeled. The pool was two towns away, a twenty-minute drive with traffic. I had to find someone to watch Ruby. I had to gas up the car. For crying out loud! Why hadn't Anjali given me more notice? Did she not want me there? I dialed her number and started walking toward the car. "Ruby! Get down from there," I called across the yard. "We have to go!"

Voice mail. Damn it.

"Hi, Anjali, I want to come cheer you on, but not if it makes you nervous—I'll head over, but call me and tell me what would be better for you." I tried to make my voice sound light, low pressure.

I called my sister. "HI SANDRA!" I shouted breathlessly into the phone. I was racewalking now, with Ruby trotting by my side. "Can you watch Ruby? Like, right now?"

"Sure," she said. "Are you okay? Are you having a heart attack?"

As I zipped down the Henry Hudson Parkway, the phone rang.

Anjali's voice came over the speaker, "Uh, I don't have a problem with you coming," she said. She sounded tense. It was 3:45 p.m. "I'm heading in right now."

I was still one town and five exits away. "Good luck, Anjali! I'll get there as soon as I can!" I tried to keep the disappointment out of my voice. This was like watching a whole reality show and then missing the reveal. And this wasn't a character on TV, this was *my friend.* I wanted to see Anjali change from her everyday clothes into her *I'm doing something completely different now* clothes, and then do it. I wanted to see if she greeted the teacher with excitement or wariness. I wanted to see if she took the stairs from the locker room to the pool level fast or slow. The big moments in our life often happen in a blur. I wanted to remember them for her, so she would never forget how brave she was.

Traffic near the pool ground to a halt. It was 3:55 p.m. Oh, hell. I wondered if Anjali was in the pool. Maybe not yet. What sets apart teachers and therapists who specialize in working with fearful students is the time they spend getting acquainted, building trust, talking about how fear plays out in our bodies, before they get anywhere near the water. Most of Jeff's clients are fifty to seventy-five years old, coming to the pool after injury or arthritis because their doctors told them to. They've had a lifetime of thinking *I can't swim, I'm going to drown,* and putting them in the pool would be the worst way to start.

So perhaps Jeff was with Anjali by the side of the pool, explaining how the panic response is an early alert system that in most situations kicks in well before it needs to. The amygdala is part of the limbic system in the brain that houses our most primitive instincts and regulates emotions and memory. This so-called lizard brain gets danger signals superfast and processes them furiously, setting off a heart-pumping, breath-quickening, muscle-tensing fight-or-flight reaction. The brain's prefrontal cortex, which processes rational thought, developed much later in the course of evolution and gets messages slower. We're wired, therefore, to feel fear first and then assess what to do.

He could be asking Anjali to hold her breath, to show her how long she could, with plenty of time to right herself in the water and get to air. Perhaps he was teaching her to breathe out through her nose with her mouth closed, so that when she tried it in the water it would feel more natural. This exercise does double duty because a long, conscious exhale, as every yogi knows, relaxes the nervous system. Perhaps Anjali was feeling calm. *I hope so. I hope she's not cursing my name.*

Once I parked the car, I ran, thinking about how I'd missed the birth of my twin niece and nephew while I was sitting in traffic and how one person's wasted half hour can be the turning point of another's life. I blew past the doorman. The elevators were up on high floors and I needed to go down to the basement. It was 4:05. The lesson would end in ten minutes.

Jack Bauer in the face of a suitcase bomb couldn't have felt the minutes ticking away any louder than I did, as I ran down one hallway after another trying to find a staircase down. The doorman came over, looking concerned. "What are you doing?"

"I need to go downstairs," I panted. *Good lord, woman*, his expression said, *you need to go to the gym that badly?* He opened a door and I flew down the stairs. A lady buzzed me into the gym, asking, "Do your kids have lessons today?"

"No—my friend—I'm going to see her teacher," I babbled incoherently, taking the stairs up to the pool level two at a time. At the top, the final barrier, I peeled off my sensible sneakers, one sock then two, and stuffed them into the Street Shoes Here cubbies, ran past the No Running sign, slid to a stop just before falling in, and there I was, looking down at Anjali. In the pool.

She looked beautiful.

She was all in blue. With her navy cap and goggles, the turquoise straps of her bathing suit bright against her dark brown skin, black strands of escaping hair wet against her forehead and neck. *They were wet!*

She was holding on to the edge with both hands, standing in the shallow end, nodding at Jeff, whom I'd never met in person before now. I took him in: a kind-looking man with a white beard emanating calm. She was in good hands. *It's all good!*

"Look at you!" I exulted, dropping my purse, raising my arms high and clapping for Anjali.

"I'm doing it," she said, looking pleased.

I searched for a dry patch on the deck and sat down cross-legged. When I looked up, Anjali's face was in the water.

What? I blinked hard, scrambling to process what I was seeing. She was still holding the deck with both hands, but now her face was in the water and she was blowing bubbles. The very thing she feared. One by one, her legs floated up. I sat, gaping, unable even to search for my camera. At the end of her exhale she stood up, and with the rest of her face obscured by cap and goggles she emerged like the Cheshire Cat, nothing but her big, beautiful smile.

"I can't believe you!" I cried. "That was so great!"

Jeff high-fived her, asking how it felt.

"It was okay," she said, nodding.

"Now," Jeff said, "since you're doing so well, and we're at the end of your lesson, I'm going to push you a little bit. Let's step away from the wall and do it again."

Her face froze. "I don't think I can," she said, at the same time that Jeff led her, holding both her hands, away from the wall. "Okay, I guess I can," Anjali said, a hint of humor washing over her anxiety.

"There are three degrees of separation in learning to swim," Jeff said. "First, the wall, then the floor, then me. You still have me." He squeezed her hands, demonstrating how he would signal to her when it was time to stand up. She nodded, blowing air out of her mouth in an effort to settle herself. "I have to figure out how to empty my head."

"You gave birth to three kids, right? I'm sure you had something to help you focus for the pain."

"Not really," Anjali said wryly. "Just drugs."

But she took a deep breath, put her face in the water, and let her feet float up. Her arms outstretched, *one, two*—he squeezed—*three*, and her feet found the bottom of the pool. She stood up.

"That was good!" Jeff said. "Next time, we're going to let go."

The muscles around her mouth and chin tightened. It's the look Gigi gets when she realizes how high she is on the monkey bars, the look my father gets before he gives a toast. The moment between *oh, no* and *ah, what the hell*.

She put her face down. Her feet came up, Jeff let her hands go, and there she floated, free. Anjali blew bubbles by herself for five seconds, by my excited count. Then her hands found Jeff's as her feet found the floor; and when she stood up, Jeff gave her a double high five and Anjali's thirty-minute lesson, dreaded for months, was over.

In the locker room, Anjali changed back into recognizable form, taking her wavy black shoulder-length hair down and putting on a white peasant blouse and dark trousers. Her energy, though, was completely different, her actions brisk, her voice excited and proud.

"I can't believe I did it!" she said, toweling off her hair. "I've always been afraid to breathe out underwater, and I did it, in the first lesson!"

"The very first lesson! Tell me what I missed—tell me everything!"

"We talked for the first part—I wasn't in the pool that long before you got there. Jeff is amazing at explaining things. Do you know how many people have tried to teach me to blow bubbles? And every time—water up the nose! I didn't think it could be any other way. Jeff told me to start exhaling through my nose *before* I put my face in—if air is pushing out, no water can get in. No one ever told me that before!"

She brushed her hair quickly, talking all the while. *"And* he taught me to keep my mouth closed, so I don't swallow water. That sounds so simple, but it's not! It's counterintuitive."

"Really?" I asked, trying it for several breaths. Ha! It *was* an effort to keep my mouth closed.

"He said every adult he works with is afraid of getting water up the nose and in the mouth. That made me feel better, I'm not alone."

Anjali marveled that she was able to talk her brain and body into doing things that did not come naturally. "My first try, I got chlorine up my nose. We kept practicing and I didn't really like it. I was resisting. But then I told my brain, 'My body is panicking way before I need to panic, I'm really okay'. He had me practice holding my breath with my mouth closed, above the water, and showed me I could do it without struggling. So when I felt tense and my mouth wanted to open underwater, I didn't let it. I told myself, 'It's fine, I can hold my breath for a long time. I can keep my mouth closed'."

Anjali was exterminating her ANTs, I thought with delight. This freed her up physically, emotionally, and mentally to learn the techniques she was being taught.

"I was able to do it in thirty minutes!" She checked her watch; she had kids to pick up. We started walking. "I can see how this could become normal, I could never imagine that before."

Her happiness was intoxicating. I wanted more. "Tell me about the moment you floated free—what was that like?" I asked, wishing I could step into her body and experience it all for myself.

"That was a wild moment! I just emptied my brain and put my face in the water, and I felt my legs float up and I was blowing bubbles, and I was, like . . . Wow . . . this is so cool! It's not just me and some pathetic failing on my part. *I can do this!*"

We arrived at her car. I wished I could get in with her and keep talking.

"Tell me, Anjali," I said, "what made you decide, in the end, you were ready to try?"

"Well, a couple of things," she said, opening the door and putting her bag inside. "When you said, 'When you tell this story, do you want to say you did it, or not?' I realized that I didn't want to be the person who was too afraid to even try one lesson. I didn't want to think of myself that way. And when we were on vacation, I saw how much the girls enjoy the pool, and it brought home to me that this is an experience most human beings have that I could never have."

We all want to be under the parachute at Gymboree. "A child who's afraid to swim knows she's missing out on something," Jeff says. "She wants to be part of the fun, but she can't, and that has emotional consequences. An adult who doesn't swim carries all those experiences of feeling left out and embarrassed. It takes great courage to come forward and try to change. At first, it's just tiny steps. But then, when they get it, when they feel that giddy pleasure of simply being in the water, it's like they're a kid again. They *play*." For Jeff, this is the most gratifying part of teaching adults. "No matter how old they are now, they get to have that piece of childhood back. It's wonderful to see."

"Anyway, Patty, it is so much less scary to me now. I feel empowered!" Anjali said, getting in her car. "I'm so glad I did it!"

After she drove off, I stood alone on the curb, trying to remember where I'd parked my car. My left foot was throbbing. I wiggled my toes inside my sneaker. I had run from the car to the pool in a full-fledged sprint, I realized. And the foot was still in one piece. Maybe I'd babied it long enough. It was time to get back in the pool.

※

I WAS SO OUT OF SHAPE. If you were to see me in the pool that January, you would have thought I was drowning on each and every lap, for all the spluttering and coughing I did. On two occasions, you would have seen me run headfirst into the end of the pool as I attempted the backstroke. Me holding my head. Me calling it a day.

But, guided by the image of Robin slogging across her community pool every day for an entire summer until she could swim a single lap, I kept at it, and by February, I had my sea legs back.

Freshly scrubbed after my best pool session yet, I clicked off the hair dryer and looked at myself in the locker room mirror. For months, my sedentary body thought the trace amounts of endorphins you get by eating chocolate and sitting on the sofa was all it was entitled to. Bruised and vulnerable, my reflection had barely shone back at me. When I thought of the beach, I could see myself only as an onlooker while everyone else frolicked in the waves.

But now, flushed and happy, I looked like a new person.

I'm going to try to surf, I thought. Maybe it was the endorphins talking.

Are you crazy? the Greek Chorus protested. *You can't surf! You're scared to even go back in the ocean!*

I could almost feel the sand slide under me. Surfing was crazy.

Okay. Maybe I won't surf.

Or maybe I will.

CHAPTER 4

BEING HEARD

Public Speaking

lease stop spinning, I begged the bathroom. I leaned the top of my head against the door of the stall. *Nice door. Please be cool.* Fear of public toilets be damned, I would have lain down on the floor if I thought it would help. No such luck.

Through the crack in the door I saw a stunning woman standing by the sink in a crisp dress and shiny shoes, putting on lipstick. A soprano hummed scales as she waited outside my stall for me to finish whatever I was doing that was taking so long. The swish of dancers' feet going through warm-ups vibrated through the floor. So many hopefuls trying out for so many shows. *What am I doing here?*

Prickly heat spread across my scalp and down over my body like a swarm of fire ants, or what I imagine anything with a name like *fire ant* would feel like touching my skin. My turtleneck trapped the heat around my neck and throat. *Water.* I needed water. I burst out of the stall, arms full with my coat and bag, and awkwardly washed my hands, taking a sip of the lukewarm water while trying to keep from splashing the stunning lady and staring too hard at her exquisite face. *Her* hair wasn't on fire. Not a strand was even out of place. *How could anyone say no to you?* I thought. *I hope we're not auditioning for the same thing.*

I was hoping to land a spot in *Listen to Your Mother 2012*, the first New York production of a nationwide series of staged readings started by blogger Ann Imig that was, as the tagline proclaimed, "Giving Mother's Day a microphone." The original show, performed in Madison, Wisconsin, in 2010, had been such a success that now ten cities wanted to host their own. The show's logo, a woman speaking through a megaphone with her head thrown back, was a cri de coeur that spoke directly to my heart. "Listen to me!" I said out loud to the casting call in my e-mail inbox, shaking my fist for good measure. "I, too, have things to say!"

It sounded simple enough, to read a five-minute original piece in front of a couple of producers. I had nothing to lose, apart from a morning when no one would normally be listening to me at all. *Plus, my chances must be pretty good,* I thought. *How many Asian-American blogging mothers of children adopted from China could be auditioning for this? They'll remember me. Especially if I wear my lucky red turtleneck.*

That was all before I stepped through the elevator doors into the Ripley-Grier Studios in Manhattan's Garment District, and took in the buzz of a million dreamers looking for their big stage or screen break in one of twenty-some rooms on this floor alone. And before I found the door marked *Listen to Your Mother* Auditions and met the woman waiting to audition right before me—a lovely Asian woman. In a red turtleneck. We looked at each other, mirror images of surprise, then panic. Cue sweating.

I'd excused myself to find the bathroom, and when it got too crowded in there to hide any longer, staggered like a drunken freshman back down the hall to wait on the bench next to my twin.

It was like Marilyn Kang all over again, I thought, closing my eyes and trying to breathe in to a count of three and out to a count of six, remembering that a long exhale settles the nerves. Marilyn had been my best friend and archrival in fifth and sixth grades at PS 95 in the

Bronx. Best friend because we each knew what it was like to have Tiger parents, who expected us always to be number one. Archrival because only one of us could be number one at a time.

Marilyn would practice piano, going over tricky passages until tears fell onto the keys, just as I'd study the multiplication tables until tears splashed down onto my study card. Let's pause to note that the plastic study card, made in Taiwan, was waterproof. As if especially created for crying on.

Like many Asian kids we knew, our job was to prepare for, and ace, tests. "Drill, drill, drill, that's the only way you'll learn," Ba believed. "Stand up! Speak up! What's six times seven?" he would ask, and my mind would spin helplessly as he drilled a fear of math, spelling bees, and Alex Trebek into my brain.

Because 6×7 (and 7×8 and anything $\times 12$) made me cry, I usually wasn't asked to do math for company. But gatherings of family and friends often meant being called up in front of assorted Chinese "aunties," "uncles," and "cousins" (we were all related even if we weren't) to recite Chinese poetry or sing a song, with our family honor on the line. My parents, like all Chinese parents, would cluck afterward, saying I would have been better if I had practiced harder.

I suspect they were hoping to prepare me, at age six, for defending my future PhD thesis. That turned out to be a waste of time, since I never pursued a doctorate. But it did prepare me for standing up in front of any audience—to this day, no group of VIPs is more intimidating than the Joy Luck Club gatherings of my childhood—and trying to win it over.

Kids like Marilyn and me were praise-seeking missiles. We got so little of it at home, we fought for it from teachers and other kids' parents and anyone else who would say "good job" or, even better, applaud.

We competed in everything except sports, which I ceded to her. With the unfair advantage of a brother at home, she had a mean kick, and she was always chosen for teams ahead of me. In fact, she was often just the slightest bit ahead of me in other areas, too, the 102 extra credit girl to my 100. But in sixth grade, I got the lead in *Mame* and Marilyn the second lead, a distinction that felt as significant as winning Olympic gold versus silver.

Someone walked past me just then, brushing my leg and bringing me back to where I was. When I opened my eyes, I saw a series of plaques on the wall, given by the United Stuntmen's Association. I sighed. Wouldn't life be great if we could call in a stuntman for all the really hard parts?

The door to the audition room opened, making me jump a little. The other Asian lady was called inside, and I wished her good luck. I sat up straighter on the hard bench, pulling out my script to study as the other red turtleneck disappeared behind the door. *Let the games begin.*

≫

MY FATHER ALWAYS SPOKE his mind. As a graduate student in Canada, he sought housing with other Canadians rather than with other foreign students, so that he could practice English. At home Walter Cronkite was always on the television so we could hear proper pronunciation and be conversant in issues of the day.

In English, his second language, my dad wrote his PhD thesis, taught classes, cursed out other drivers, argued with anyone trying to cut in line, made toasts, and made friends with coworkers and neighbors of all ethnicities. He never let having an accent stop him from expressing himself. He believed what he had to say was important; he had faith that more often than not, people would try to understand him.

My mother, on the other hand, didn't say too much in group

gatherings and often apologized for her poor English. I thought she was simply shy. In my twenties, however, I went on a trip to China with her and saw what she was like when she could speak her first language, confident that she would be understood. It was like watching her pop out into three dimensions for the very first time. She was funny, lively, often the center of attention. I knew she was smart, but in Chinese she was more than smart, she was *respected*.

We moved to the Bronx when I was in fourth grade. On my first day at PS 95, Ma brought me to the office to register me. It was April, late in the school year, and hot that day. The school administrator looked at us irritably across his desk. Another immigrant family, he probably thought. For his school that already had more children than chairs.

Ma, in halting English, explained that I had attended school in Canada. As if he didn't believe Canadians spoke English, he tossed a copy of *The New York Times* toward me. "Read it," he said. "Out loud."

My cheeks burned. This man thought we were stupid.

I picked up the paper and asked, "Any article?"

"That one," he pointed. *Stand up. Speak up.*

"'Koch Plans to Keep the Measures That Cut Congestion During Strike,'" I read out loud. From the moment I'd started kindergarten, my parents had encouraged me to read and speak English better than the natives. "You want people to respect you," my father said, and I had not done extra homework every day of my life to stand down now. I read and read, until I ran out of article.

"It continues on another page," I said, looking up. "Shall I keep going?"

He sat there, stunned. "Tell me what it means," he said.

I told him.

To this day, Ma marvels at how nice he became to both of us right then and there, welcoming us to the school, ushering us to the class-room like VIPs.

We are all VIPs. I think maybe this is why I went into communications, why I want everyone to know the power that comes from speaking up with confidence.

〽

"SO HOW'D IT GO?" my girlfriend asked over the phone as soon as it was over. She was deep in full-time parenting and enjoyed getting dispatches from the outside world.

"Apart from almost fainting when the producer pointed her iPhone at me and said, 'You don't mind if we film you, do you?' it was fine," I replied. I was standing by the elevator banks, gawking at all the gorgeous people coming and going. "The camera took me by surprise— I was afraid if I screwed up it could be posted to YouTube and on the Jimmy Fallon show before I had a chance to change my name!"

"Oh my goodness, I would have died," she said. "I would have left. Well, I wouldn't have been there in the first place."

Somehow, I'd made it through.

I had done my usual fifteen-second routine before starting.

I took in my surroundings. There was no mic. The space was small, but there was someone in another audition singing behind a curtain next to me. I'd have to project to be heard. There was no podium to hide behind or hang on to, just a few thin pages of script on a music stand. "Make believe you're brave," I whistled the lyrics from *The King and I* to myself and stood up straighter.

I took in my feelings. Without my heavy coat and bag, I felt so light I might blow away. I told myself why: I'm light-headed because my lizard brain thinks the unsmiling producer in front of me is going to eat me alive. And then tweet about it. So it's diverting blood flow to my heart and gut. My brain needs oxygen. *Luckily, there's plenty of oxygen here.*

I took a deep breath, relaxing my belly and puffing up with air, making myself take up space. *I am here.* I stopped floating away. With my next breath, I let the nerves go through me. Bring it on: the chills, the tingling, the dry mouth, the tight throat, all fight-or-flight reactions to feeling threatened, completely predictable. *Let them come, let them go.*

I set my feet slightly apart and turned out, with one foot in front, to make a stable platform that prevents (or minimizes) trembling and, with your best foot forward, projects *I'm glad to see you!* to your audience. It also gives you something to think about other than running out the door.

"It's all just energy," the poet Patrick Donnelly said at Bread Loaf in a talk about how to give an effective public reading. "Take any nervous energy you feel and turn it into energy for what you want to say." Remembering why you're in front of the audience makes how you look to them secondary. I thought of Gigi and Ruby, of how their childhoods were going so fast and how I wanted this one sublime piece of it to be on the record somewhere, forever. That's why I was there.

I smiled, acknowledging the two producers and the camera, thanking them for listening. Then I did my best. I saw one producer wipe away a well-timed tear. The other never looked up from the script she was reading. The camera gave no feedback at all. They said thank you, they would let me know. The outcome was now out of my hands, and I wouldn't learn what it was for weeks.

"It was fun, actually. You should try out next year," I said to my friend. From the sounds of her kids fighting World War III in the background, she had loads of material.

"Oh no," she said. "It was bad enough when I had to give reports at work. Getting up in front of people is not my idea of fun. You're probably a born performer."

I'm not sure if I was born with whatever it takes to enjoy public speaking or if the emotional and professional rewards of doing it are what make it fun for me, but I love it, in spite of the nerves I always feel. I love communicating ideas and connecting with others, and I love watching other people do the same.

When I was a book publicist, I trained writers to speak into the mic about their work with the same clear voice their words held on the page. Every time I saw expressions of interest or delight in the audience, or heard a gasp of recognition, I felt something magical had transpired. Laughing or crying as they left an event, or standing in line to thank the speaker for touching their lives, listeners seemed different from who they'd been when they'd walked in. Each of us holds the power to affect so many others when we get up to speak. It's a skill I'd like everyone to have.

And what better time to explore this subject, something I actually felt competent at, than now? It was November and starting to get too cold for outdoor adventures. My foot was finally out of its brace, and I had no desire to break it again. I was eager to sit back, relax, and watch other people face their fears for a change. Screw rock climbing. Bring on the heated conference room!

But where would I find people afraid to speak in public but brave enough to be written about by me? They'd have to be pretty committed to face both those fears at once.

≫

"MOST PEOPLE ARE AFRAID of public speaking because they haven't been trained in it," says Rick Frishman, a media trainer, coach, and publisher. He and I go way back as publicists, and we share a passion for helping people with good ideas get them out to the world. "Most people have been trained in how to handle numbers or work a computer program, or whatever their jobs are. If they trained to speak in public the same way, there would be much less fear."

But most people don't, so public speaking routinely ranks as a top fear; in some polls it outranks the fear of death. Which sounds ridiculous, until you start meeting Marines and firefighters who would rather go into a war zone or a burning building than to the front of a classroom. "My husband was a wreck for days before reading to our daughter's second-grade class," a manicurist confided. Her husband was a Force Recon Marine, a certified skydiver. "He made me bake brownies so they would like him no matter what."

Whether it's an evolutionary drive to hide our vulnerabilities from potential enemies or an existential longing to be understood, speaking in public is freighted with a lot more meaning than goes into the bulleted lists we put in our PowerPoint slides. The underlying emotional fears of rejection or humiliation or failure, plus the hope and ambition that fuel the pressure to perform, are a potent combination that hypercharges every public speaking event.

Since it can be easy to avoid the whole situation by not volunteering to get up and at 'em in the first place, those who decide to face this fear are usually highly motivated by a professional obligation or opportunity, or something they can't get out of (like their own wedding toast). Fortunately, lots of help is available, from professional media coaches to web tutorials to books. And for 280,000 people and counting, there's Toastmasters International, "the world's largest nonprofit organization dedicated to teaching public speaking and leadership skills," according to its press materials.

Toastmasters started as a club in a YMCA basement in Santa Ana, California, in 1924. In searching for a chapter near me, I discovered it now has 13,500 clubs in 116 countries, which speaks to the overwhelming need people feel across cultures to become more comfortable in front of an audience. Twenty-seven clubs met within ten miles of my house—I'd have my choice of where to begin my search. I picked one that looked to be well within a half-hour drive.

⋙

A HALF-HOUR DRIVE, my eye. "Address not found," my GPS said calmly. I cursed, not so calmly. I was so late. And of all the appointments to be late for: my first Toastmasters meeting. This chapter met at lunchtime. I had planned to arrive early and introduce myself and my intention to observe the meeting. I wanted to be as nonthreatening as possible to people who were already plenty nervous.

By the time I finally found the turnoff, huffed and puffed across the football field–size parking lot, and found the conference room, I was sweaty, breathless, and a half hour late. I paused at the closed door and considered not going in, but the officers were expecting me. I opened the door.

A petite Asian woman was speaking haltingly in accented English in front of the room. She wore glasses and was looking at papers in her hand as she spoke. *Please don't lose concentration,* I begged her in my mind. *Don't look at me. I'm not here.* She looked up then, directly at me, and paused midsentence. Seventeen men and women sitting around a horseshoe arrangement of conference tables turned to look at me, too. *Crap.*

She smiled at me and said, "And welcome to our guest. You are right on time!"

Tension broken, everyone laughed and then turned back to her. Sighing with relief, I sank into a chair on one side of the horseshoe. She finished her report without further interruption and with aplomb. With a handshake, she passed us over to Dana, the club's president, who said, "Thank you, Yumi," as she sat down.

Yumi—good host, I wrote in my notepad. Part of being a great speaker is making your guests feel welcome. A fear many people have of public speaking is how to handle the unexpected. Yumi had just done so graciously by focusing not on how my late arrival made her look but on how it might make me feel. As a result, the entire room warmed up and drew closer together, safe in her hands.

Dana, an older woman whose short light hair floated softly over her head like a halo, spoke in an assured, elegant way, enunciating clearly without condescending. She invited us guests to introduce ourselves.

I had just sat down, but now I was up again. "My name is Patty Chang Anker," I said, "and I'm a writer who's interested in how people face their fears." Having outed myself, I wasn't sure if they would want me in their midst anymore. I spoke a bit about how wonderful it was to see so many courageous people and how I looked forward to getting to know them, and then I sat back down, hoping to stay down.

The meeting was already half over—glancing at the agenda I saw they had finished the club business and the main speakers before I got there. Goodness, what was left to do?

"And now, Table Topics!" Dana said. An excited rustling went through the room. In Table Topics, the host asks the kind of question that might come up at a dinner party or around the office water cooler, and then speakers riff on it for a minute or two apiece. *There is no right or wrong response/answer, just your best attempt!* the agenda read encouragingly. Still, impromptu speaking is not for the faint of heart.

First topic: "How do you exercise?" Leo, a young and energetic Asian man, jumped right in. "I do a program called Insanity," he said, with a slightly crazy smile. *Great opening,* I thought. Out of a banal subject, Leo was promising conversational gold.

"You may have heard of interval training, where short bursts of intense activity are followed by rest?" He was involving the audience by asking a question. We all nodded.

"Well, Insanity demands *loong* intervals of intense activity followed by very brief rest. And it's *insane.* I would demonstrate it for you, but I'm actually afraid I might split my pants." We all laughed, because pants splitting is always funny and perhaps because Leo was playing against expectations. He was in business attire, and the thought of him splitting his dress pants had us rolling.

"He is so funny!" the woman sitting to my right mouthed, patting my arm. Her name tag said Natalie. Her thick auburn hair, cut in a long bob, shook as she shook her head in admiration.

Leo was now jumping up and down to demonstrate how Insanity annoys his neighbors. Wrapping up, he called his workout "audacious," using the word-of-the-day posted with its definition on the podium behind him—"Audacious (adj.): 1. Daring, bold 2. Original"—and sat down to claps and cheers.

Next topic: "How do you clean your house?" Seamus, a lanky man with slightly mussed hair, volunteered to take it on. His style, quiet and wry, was completely different from Leo's. He looked out over our heads thoughtfully as he spoke. When the punch line came—"How do I measure a good enough job when it comes to cleaning? I guess it's that I'm not too disgusted to use that pan again"—we all laughed in surprise, as he sat down, grinning ear to ear.

"He's so funny, too!" Natalie enthused next to me. Yes, I agreed again. Seamus's indirect style of humor was effective and attention getting in its own way.

I noticed, amid the whooping, how many flashes of color people were sporting in the typically gray-toned conference room: an orange scarf here, a bright blue blouse there, two men in purple shirts. *You have to want to draw attention to yourself to wear a purple shirt,* I thought, looking down at my own gray sweater and black skirt, happy to blend in with the carpet and walls.

Back at the front of the room, Dana said, "Our last Table Topic is one I was asked in a competition." Imagine enjoying public speaking so much you'd do it competitively! "And I hated it. So I thought I would share it with you."

The topic: "If you were to turn your life into a sitcom, what would it be like?"

Wow, tough one! The other topics—exercise and cleaning—were about direct experience. This would require thinking about one's life and then imagining it as something else, something entertaining. The speaker would have to highlight which aspects were funny, who the characters would be, what story lines would play out. This would require another level of thinking on one's feet. *I'm glad I'm just a guest,* I thought.

Dana looked right at me. "Perhaps I'll offer this to our guest," she said diabolically. My heart and stomach, which had only just recovered from the agita of my late entrance, collided and fused, an imploding star. *She can't be serious. I just got here. I'm here to watch other people sweat!* But there she was, smiling angelically (how could she look so sweet and be so evil?), and people were clapping for me. There was nothing to do but get up again.

When I was media coaching, I would tell clients that in live situations they actually had time to think. In the time it takes to nod, sip some water, take a few steps, or pause to acknowledge someone in the audience, they could plan what to say. Now, in the maybe five seconds it took to put down my pen and walk to the front of the room, my thought process went like this:

I can't freaking believe this. This is a disaster. I'm going to look like an idiot! I'm going to have to start over with a whole new club next week. For crying out loud! What was the question? Oh hell.

My five seconds were up. Everyone was done clapping and was now looking at me expectantly.

Deep breath. *Think. Sitcom . . . physical comedy . . . I'm a klutz!*

"The situation comedy of my life would have a ton of physical comedy," I began. "Pratfalls, mortal danger, bodily fluids going everywhere, because I am a klutz. I'm a klutz because . . ." I paused.

I can't believe I have to do this. Don't look dumb! Don't be annoying! What am I talking about? Oh, why I'm a klutz. "I'm a klutz because . . ." *Say what you know.* "Because I was brought up by Tiger parents." *Find Leo, he's Asian, see if he's nodding . . . Yes! Talk to Leo.* "Parents who thought getting into an Ivy League college was a lot more important than learning how to hang off the monkey bars without a head injury."

Leo's laughing! Okay, this is good. Relax, Patty, this is a group for people afraid of public speaking—you're fitting in. What now? I needed an anecdote. My aching foot provided one. "I broke my foot trying to face my fear of the ocean. I said, 'I'm not afraid!' and the Atlantic Ocean answered, 'You should be!'"

Who are the characters? What's the point of the show? "My daughters would be great characters, because they're always up for doing something that will make me look ridiculous. I'm trying to teach them it's okay if people laugh at you, as long as you're able to laugh at yourself."

Warmed up now, I told more stories, until I noticed people beginning to break their gaze from me. *How long have I been talking? Wrap it up, woman. Bring it back to sitcoms. Oh, and use the word of the day!* "My sitcom would be very audacious because every week we would try something new. We'll have way more than fourteen episodes' worth of fun. I hope it gets renewed season after season."

Everyone clapped. Tipsy with relief, I made my way back to my seat and collapsed next to Natalie. "You were great!" she exclaimed. Given her rave reviews of every single speaker, I might have taken the compliment with a grain of salt but I didn't. We *were* all great, just for stepping into the ring and opening our mouths. *Thank God it's over.*

Then came the evaluations. Seamus, the Ah-Counter, got up to call out those who littered their speeches with filler syllables while vamping for time or trying desperately to disappear. "I'm the nitpicker, the police officer who tickets the jaywalker," he said. After naming a couple of offenders, he gestured at me. "Our guest had some *um*s and *ah*s, and *you know*s," he said. I felt myself flush. I did?

"Remember," Seamus said, "try to minimize, not eliminate." Ah, good advice that keeps speech sounding natural. On second thought, strike the *ah* at the beginning of that last sentence.

The timer stood up next. It's hard to overstate how important a social skill it is to fill the time you're given with interesting and entertaining content, and then *stop*. Many a political campaign, sales deal, legal deposition, or wedding proposal have died on the vine, thanks to a person who wouldn't stop talking. The rule in PR has always been: Never say anything or write anything that you don't want to see on the front page of *The New York Times*—which, in the age of viral media, has never been more important.

"Expect that people are recording what you say," Rick Frishman says. "Once it comes out of your mouth, in a tweet, or on Facebook, it could be anywhere. If you're too frightened that someone might record something and put it out there, then you haven't prepared enough." Rick's adage is: "A closed mouth gathers no foot" and its follow-up, "When in doubt, *shut up*."

The converse is also true. Running short, all headline and no story, is just as problematic. In my eighth-grade communications class, poor Evie Lu got up to speak on the subject of pet peeves for three minutes. "Don't you hate it when you go to eat a grapefruit and juice squirts in your eye?" she said. That was it. She had nothing else. But the rule was that you had to stand there for your allotted three minutes. One hundred and sixty-nine excruciating seconds later, Evie was finally allowed to sit back down, and we all silently vowed always to have something more to say.

Perhaps that's why, as the timer informed me, I went over my allotted time by a third.

People started passing slips of paper toward Dana, who tallied them and then announced, "Today's winning Table Topic speaker was . . . Patty Anker!" *Oh my goodness! They voted for me!* It got even better. Dana presented me with a certificate. Certificates are crack for praise-seeking junkies. I wondered, for a moment, if I'd gotten the mercy vote, for the newbie who couldn't even get to the meeting on time, to encourage me to come back. No matter, it worked. *I am totally coming back here next week.*

It also worked on Natalie, who was also visiting that day. "Everyone who knows me can't believe I have a fear of public speaking. *'You?'* they say, because I'm so gregarious. I don't have a problem talking to people, but this?" She gestured at the scene around us and froze her face into an eye-popping, teeth-clenching universal expression of fear. "I can't do *this*. But watching everyone else do it is getting me excited. I'm going to sign up."

It *was* exciting to be in that room. I had expected it to feel awkward and painful, full of uncomfortable pauses, foot shuffling, and throat clearing from people who did not want to be there. Instead, it was full of energy as earnest speakers and attentive listeners entered new territory together.

Many of the members of this club worked as computer specialists or accountants. ("We're numbers people!" one told me. "There should be a club for people with a fear of numbers and technology," I responded.) Their reasons for joining ranged from desiring career advancement to needing to recover from past poor performances, and their levels of confidence varied. But one thing they had in common: Each of these smart, accomplished people could have decided they weren't cut out for the spotlight and retired to the back office of life. But they hadn't. *If you spend your lunch break here,* I thought as the meeting adjourned, *how can you not go back to your desk more awake and alive?*

~

"WHAT ARE YOU AFRAID OF when you get up to speak?" asked a seasoned Toastmaster named Elaine Rogers from the front of a different conference room the next week. Dressed in a pretty green suit with gold buttons, Elaine looked calm and in control as she smiled at us encouragingly. "Take the Terror Out of the Talk" read the PowerPoint slide behind her.

I was munching on pizza and salad along with a couple dozen other people in business attire who had come for the special workshop and the free lunch. A number of those present were curious about Toastmasters but had never come to a meeting before. Of course, most of them were there because they were afraid to speak up in the first place, so the silent chewing went on for a while. Eventually, some experienced Toastmasters piped up.

"Forgetting the words."

"My voice shaking."

"People judging me."

Then others started chiming in.

"Losing my train of thought."

"Boring people."

"My heart pounding."

"Having an asthma attack."

"Feeling dizzy."

"My stomach doing flip-flops."

"Sweating."

"Yes," Elaine said. "Ever notice that when you're nervous, you get a dry mouth and sweaty palms? Why couldn't it be the opposite, dry palms and a lubricated mouth?" Everyone laughed, and then we all wiped our hands on our paper napkins and took a sip of soda. "All these are valid feelings when you come up here. They happen to everyone."

The crux of her presentation came next: "The number one antidote to fear is experience. Say it with me!"

"The number one antidote to fear is experience."

Which means not hiding under the radar until called upon but volunteering to speak in a variety of settings again and again. Practicing, rehearsing, getting up, and doing until the feelings of nervousness become familiar and the belief in your ability to get through them is strengthened.

Toastmasters members shared their techniques for rehearsing without pressure—one did it in front of her puppy, who would love her no matter what. Patient or indifferent ears seem to work best. Another person said she rehearsed in front of her twenty-three-year-old niece. "I can tell how I'm doing by the number of times she checks her text messages," she said.

Apart from making speeches, just learning to use your voice is a good life skill. Hope, a high school classmate whose voice I rarely heard in class, reconnected with me on Facebook and told me that volunteering to read to children at a library when she was in her early twenties helped boost her confidence, and she's more outspoken now.

Over the next few months I attended various Toastmasters events (including a regional competition that was inspiring for both the quality of speeches from experienced Toastmasters and for firing up my lust for medals), and I became a regular at the club near me.

At one meeting, a youthful-looking woman named Rosa was presented with a Table Topic: "You have eighty dollars to spend in Chicago. How would you spend it?" As topics go, it's pretty tricky, because you have to do math (*gah!*) and draw on any knowledge you have of a city you may or may not have visited.

Rosa was tentative. "Um, I'd call my friend on the phone," she said softly, making her hand into a little phone and cocking her head. "I would have to hitchhike in Chicago, because I only have eighty dollars," she said, thinking out loud. A pause. Then more confidently: "I would enjoy the architecture in Chicago . . ." Her voice trailed off. "I would spend about thirty dollars on lunch." Everyone laughed, wondering how much this little woman could possibly eat.

Rosa had come to Toastmasters because, she told me, "I'm painfully shy." I had been surprised to hear that. Rosa is a pretty brunette who often wears her hair pulled back. Her thin, dark eyebrows arch over dark-rimmed glasses, giving her a serious demeanor. You could imagine her starring in a romantic comedy where the heroine doesn't realize how beautiful she is until she lets down her hair and is transformed into Selena Gomez. She looks like someone who could assume the world would like to know her better, yet while she sounded fine, she gave every appearance of wanting to hide. "What else would I do? How much money do I have left?" she asked. I wished I could slip her a note: *$50, Art Institute, Wrigley Field.* But she was on her own and running out of steam. "I wouldn't have to spend much money to walk around and enjoy the architecture," she repeated, and we clapped as she sat down.

The next speaker was Natalie, who had joined the group after her initial visit. She got $20,000 to spend in Madrid.

She started off strong: "I'm a photographer, and I could buy a lot of great equipment with ten thousand dollars, so that's what I would do first off!" But as she reached around for her next thought, it was as if an inner dimmer switch was getting turned down. She began to stand back on one leg, her weight shifting away from us. She looked down at the floor, thinking. When she spoke again, she tried to steady her voice.

"I'd take the train out of Madrid and go to Portugal," she said. *Good job*, I thought.

"You don't have to answer the question as it's asked" sounds like something only political spin doctors say, but it's true. When you're stumped you can often redirect the discussion. Remember that *you do know stuff*. You have something to offer, so offer it without feeling lame or apologetic for not knowing everything at all times. I've seen countless experts in their fields answer questions out of left field with an energetic: "Good question! And do you know what I find interesting?"

And it's okay to be honest if you need to do some research before answering. Rick Frishman says if he's not sure he'll say, "I don't know. That's a great question. I know more about fill in the blank, but this is something I need to look into. If you send me an e-mail, I'll find out the answer for you." The benefit, Rick points out, is "Now you've got an opportunity to forge a relationship with that person. You can turn a negative into a positive. If you try to make it up, you'll say something stupid."

Natalie clearly knew more about Portugal than Madrid, and, now on comfortable terrain, she spoke fluently of Lisbon's museums and restaurants. A minute later, she finished to applause.

Natalie was on a roll. In the next couple of months she would make several speeches and volunteer for officer positions in the club. She was ready to make a change in her life, she said. "I feel like I have nice ideas and I should share them. It's important for me to get past the fear so my voice can be heard."

In addition to giving impromptu talks, Toastmasters members complete ten prepared speeches designed to practice different aspects of public speaking before attaining Competent Communicator status. After that there are advanced degrees and loads of certificates, ribbons, and medals to be won.

Everyone starts with an Ice Breaker, a four- to six-minute speech about oneself. Before she went up to do hers, I asked Natalie how she felt. "I'm riding on so much energy I'm pumped up. I'm focusing more on my pumped-upness than my nervousness," she said, clasping her hands. "Ooh, my hands are cold! When they call my name, I might fall on the floor! Will you catch me?"

"Your hair will not touch the carpet," I promised. So much of the Toastmasters experience is about holding space for each other, knowing that when you open your mouth others are listening, with the intention of helping you and also helping themselves. Any mistake is a public service in a way, because other members can learn from it. Evaluators give feedback on each speech, and assigned mentors help the speaker prepare for the next speech. Allowing your weaknesses to be addressed lets you improve far more efficiently than just praying to get your moment in the spotlight over with so that you can forget about it. Until the next time.

Trying to come up with some reassuring advice for Natalie, I remembered comedian Craig Ferguson's riff on public speaking and started to laugh out loud at the memory. "What you want to do is break the ice, tell a joke [or] a humorous anecdote," he said on his *Late Late Show*, in the Scottish burr I'm mad for, along with his dark wink-wink-nudge-nudge delivery. "A good ending is something like: 'And that person wound up being my spouse!' A bad ending is: 'And that's how I tore my scrotum!'" Hmm, maybe not the best anecdote for this midday meeting in a place of business. I straightened my face.

"Remember, you're breaking the ice from the moment your energy begins to interact with others," I said. "You're wearing clothes that say, I'm a creative person." Natalie was wearing a black turtleneck with a bright yellow necklace and a yellow skirt. "If you smile and look interested in your audience, and invite them into your space, that's breaking the ice. You'll have done half your job just standing there, before you say a word."

Many people fear public speaking because of what others may be thinking of them. The truth is, while many people won't pay any attention to what you say, pretty much everyone will look at you. And fortunately, you have a lot of control over how you appear.

"What three words do I want people to think when they see me today?" Style consultant Bridgette Raes says to ask yourself this question every time you get dressed. If the words are *confident, smart, powerful*, you'll dress a bit differently than if you're trying for *artistic, fun, free spirit*. And if your clothes are in line with your personality and your message, you'll project authenticity, and more than any specific things you say or do in the spotlight, people will remember *you*.

Natalie was dressed to impress, and her Ice Breaker—which included slides of her photography, artwork, and family—did, too. For those who are comfortable running AV equipment, having a focal point and built-in outline can help keep things moving, and pictures personalize presentations. We all felt we knew her so much better after.

≈

FOR MANY, learning techniques and getting experience and feedback are the ticket to speaking in public more freely. For others, who know their material cold and have performed perfectly thousands of times but freeze up (or live in fear of freezing up) when the stakes are high, more practice may not be what's needed. Understanding our underlying fear of failure may be more illuminating.

Barbra Streisand stopped giving live performances for twenty-seven years after blanking on song lyrics in concert. Even megastar Adele battles stage fright, telling Touré of *Rolling Stone* that she escaped out the fire exit at one show and has thrown up from nerves more than once. How does she cope with all the live performances she has to give? "I just think that nothing's ever gone horrifically wrong," she says in the article. She also cracks jokes and draws upon Sasha Carter, an alter ego she created to pump herself up that is Beyoncé's Sasha Fierce and June Carter combined.

The stories of celebrities with stage fright are legion, but even with much lower stakes, we all get that jolt of fear: *This is the day everyone discovers I'm an idiot, and my life will be over.*

Ivette felt unbearable pressure whenever she had to speak in public. "My heart's pounding right now," she said, both legs visibly shaking even though she was wearing two sweaters over pants up onstage in a stuffy lecture hall at New York City's Albert Ellis Institute. And even sitting in the front row, I strained to hear her quiet, tight voice.

Ivette was petite, and with her brown hair in a ponytail and her eyes downcast, she looked more like a teenager than a thirty-year-old college student with responsibilities. She had just that day white-knuckled her way through a report about Albert Ellis in her psychology class, she said, and had recently blown a job interview because of nerves. Despite her fear of speaking up in front of strangers, her frustration had driven her to volunteer to have licensed professional counselor John Viterito, diplomate and faculty member of the Albert Ellis Institute, shrink her head in front of this audience of about sixty mostly psychologists in training at the institute's Friday Night Live public watch therapy-in-action session.

John, wearing a dark sweater over a collared shirt, had many hats to wear for the evening. He greeted her warmly like a therapist, welcomed the audience like a talk show host, and then turned professorial, looking out at us through round spectacles to explain how to work with a fear of public speaking using the institute's approach.

Albert Ellis was a psychologist who believed we can control our feelings by retraining the brain away from its irrational thoughts. In an NPR interview he relayed how as a shy nineteen-year-old he forced himself to face his fear of speaking to women he found attractive by going to the New York Botanical Garden every day and chatting with those he encountered. "If I die, I die. Fuck it." In one month he met about 130 women and made one date, who never showed. But "I saw philosophically, cognitively, that nothing happened, nobody cut my balls off. I had a hundred pleasant conversations."

Ellis founded Rational Emotive Behavior Therapy (REBT) in the 1950s and it became a precursor to the family of therapies known as Cognitive Behavioral Therapies (CBT), which are now first-line treatments for anxiety, panic disorders, OCD, and phobias. REBT seeks to solve problems by challenging the beliefs that lead to self-destructive behaviors, and it propagates psychology's outsize love of acronyms by using, you guessed it, an ABCDE model.

A is the *activating* event, which in this case is speaking in public, John explained, to the sound of pens scribbling on notepads throughout the audience. "Activating events affect people differently. I don't have the same reaction to public speaking that Ivette does. That is in part because we have differing *belief* systems." (Those would be *B*.) He turned to look at her. "What do you think, when you get up to speak?"

She cleared her throat. "I think, 'Am I gonna say the right thing?'"

"Assume you say the wrong thing. What then?"

Ivette didn't have to think long to answer. "Embarrassment. Shame."

"Embarrassment and shame are *C*'s—emotional *consequences* of activating events, but more important, beliefs," John said. "Now, you have a thought that leads to that feeling. What is it?"

Ivette grasped the armrests of her chair as if she were trying to keep herself from disappearing. "My thought is 'It's bad to say the wrong thing,'" she said. A number of listeners nodded their heads sympathetically. We could all feel the same sick feeling in our stomachs.

"It may feel bad to say the wrong thing," John said, "but can you follow it up with 'It's okay to be human'?"

He was demonstrating *D—disputing* irrational beliefs—in this case, the idea that we have to be right, or else. Most of our unhappiness derives from beliefs we have constructed, he explained.

I must do well—

You must treat me well—

XYZ must happen—

OR ELSE I CAN'T STAND IT.

These are what Ellis called "musterbation" thoughts, irrational beliefs that we choose to peg our identities and realities around. When we talk back to them with more realistic thoughts, we have the opportunity to experience *E*—the *effects* of revised beliefs, which usually involve feeling a heck of a lot less miserable.

"Let's think about this," said John. "When someone else is giving their crappy PowerPoint presentation that has no power (and no point), are you thinking, 'I'm going to scrutinize her! And condemn her!' Do you think your classmates really care about how you speak, or are they thinking about when they get up next?"

"People expect older people to know more," Ivette said. "I'm the grandmother of the class, I should do better." The pressure she was putting on herself was palpable. She sank farther down into her seat, making her sweaters look empty.

"It would be nice to know more, but why do you feel you have to?" John continued. Musterbation thoughts, especially those built up over a lifetime, do not go away easily. "It's like a two-year-old with a cookie. He'll scream, cry, bang his head as if his life depends on getting that cookie. But it doesn't. He wants the cookie, that's all."

"It's not the same!" Ivette protested, sitting up a little. "Getting a job is important."

"The idea is the same. Whether it's a cookie, a spouse, a car, a job, a speech—the thing that we define as necessary changes. It's when we define a desire as an absolute necessity that we make ourselves crazy. Yeah, it's important to do well at a job interview. But 'I must do well at all times under all conditions' is not true. If you make a mistake, it's not the end of the world."

I almost laughed out loud. I grew up eating fear of failure like a breakfast of champions. Once, when I brought home a B in high school and my mother was upset, I said, "You know, I'm human, I'm allowed to make mistakes." Wanting to give her a reality check, I added, "Do you even know how much worse it could be? There are kids out there who get Cs!"

I had forgotten for the moment that we lived in the land where, as Tina Cohen-Chang on the TV show *Glee* put it, an A minus is like "an Asian F."

Ma's response? "If you ever get less than a B, don't come home."

So I, and maybe Ivette as well, was raised to fear failure more than the end of the world. The end of the world might be preferable, actually.

"The idea 'I need their approval *or else* I'm no good, therefore I have to do well' makes your survival contingent on both your performance and their approval. Two things you cannot guarantee," John pointed out, touching something in my heart that felt like a tightly wound string.

The strain of doing well enough to impress bosses, parents, friends, and the nameless masses when you can't control other people, and when you yourself are fallible, is a setup for a nervous breakdown, or at least chronic fatigue.

"Have you ever objectively done poorly in public speaking?" John asked.

"I don't know—no one would tell me," Ivette said.

"Have you ever died from it? Gotten kicked out of school?"

She shook her head.

"So you've survived. 'I want their approval so I want to do well' is different from 'I need their approval so I must do well.' There are no musts, no shoulds, only wants," John stated. Ivette looked a little shell-shocked. Softening, he asked, "Can you remember my mellifluous voice telling you this?"

"Yes," she said quietly.

His parting message to Ivette was that the most important thing she could do now to challenge these life-limiting beliefs was to practice public speaking. Getting up there repeatedly would show her she could survive. This is the exact mission of Toastmasters, and it is exceedingly effective. But until she understood that the beliefs that drove her fear of public speaking were false gods to begin with, any attempt at it risked reinforcing the fear. Deactivating the power of the thought "I have to do well" frees us up to spend less energy worrying about doing well and more focusing on doing our best.

So much of what John said applied to so many areas of my life that I approached him after the formal event to see how he would dispute one of my irrational beliefs. It was hard to pick just one. I didn't want my kids to become anxious about everything and to avoid trying things, the way I had, I explained.

"Oh, don't put that on yourself!" he exclaimed, stepping down from the platform stage to speak to me. "How many parents teach their kids to smoke and overeat? None. But they do it anyway. And then we model bad behavior that many of them never pick up on. We are not brainwashed by anyone else," John said. "We brainwash ourselves. We pick things to believe in and then turn them into our truth. If you're anxious, it's because you decided to be. And if your kids are anxious, it's because they decided to be."

My thoughts, normally trafficking in the parenting advice of a half-dozen experts at a time, skidded to a place they'd never gone before. A place full of music and maypoles and singing "It's not my fault!" But then they screeched to a stop.

"I hear my mother in everything I do," I said. At the moment, she was saying she couldn't believe I was talking about my problems with a stranger. "Her voice, saying, 'Don't do that! You could get hurt!'"

"That's because you thought to yourself 'Mom is right.' If there had been a hundred other kids in your family, many would've thought 'Mom is wrong.' It's your choice to buy into her story."

My choice. That made it sound so simple. But it wasn't like I was choosing which pair of black pants to buy (which, if you ask anyone who's gone shopping with me, is hard enough). Chinese culture is like its own religion. It worships ancestors and respects elders above all. Choose whether to listen to your mother—was that even allowed?

John's words rattled around in my mind all the way home. I had gotten the great news that I'd been cast in *Listen to Your Mother*, one of fifteen readers, and I was both thrilled and terrified at the prospect of reading my own words onstage. It was one thing when I was publicizing other people's ideas—I could talk about them all day. But writing and reading my own stories for others to take in and judge was a level of exposure that made me tremble inside. I wasn't sure if I was more afraid of not being heard or of being heard and deemed a disappointment. Oh, and did I mention my parents would be in the audience? Forget the cameramen, the press, the countless strangers, and the professional reputation I was supposed to be building by not sounding like a fool. What if I lost face for my family?

When I decided to start a blog in which I chronicled my attempts to face fears in areas where I had no past track record of success, I had to accept the possibility, nay, likelihood, of humiliation along the way. I was going to try to learn how to dive into a swimming pool when I'd only ever done belly flops before, for example. I had no idea if I'd be able to "succeed" by anyone's measure but my own.

So in an act of spin-doctoring James Carville would have approved, I redefined "success" in my head to include "failure." This didn't come naturally to me. Losing face is about the worst thing a Chinese person can do to herself and her family, and public embarrassment is the very thing a public relations professional is hired to prevent for clients. Putting myself up for ridicule went against every fiber of my being.

What freed me up to do it? Something I read in a book that I needed to read again. As soon as I got home, I found my copy of *The Art of Possibility* by Rosamund Stone Zander and Benjamin Zander and found my favorite chapter, "Giving an A."

In it, Benjamin Zander, the conductor of the Boston Philharmonic, writes about how difficult it was to teach graduate music students the art of performance. Performance involves taking risks and allowing oneself to feel a range of emotions, but in the hypercompetitive world of limited first chairs and solos, the students were consumed with anxiety about how they performed compared to one another.

So Zander decided to alleviate the anxiety by telling them at the outset of the academic year that all they had to do to earn an A from him was to write a letter. It would be written now, in September, but dated May, and it would describe how they had changed during the year to become "that person who will have done all she wished to do or become everything he wanted to be." He told them he wanted them to "fall passionately in love" with the person they described in the letter.

Reading them now for the umpteenth time, the letters still made me cry. Wrote a Korean flute player: "I used to be so negative person for almost everything even before trying. Now I find myself happier person than before. I couldn't accept my mistakes about a year ago, and after every mistake I blamed myself, but now, I enjoy making mistakes and I really learn from these mistakes. . . . I used to play just notes, but, now, I found out about the real meaning of every pieces, and I could play with more imagination."

"I have found a desire to convey music to other people, which is stronger than the worries I had about myself," wrote a student named Giselle. "I have changed from desiring inconsequentiality and anonymity to accepting the joy that comes from knowing that my music changes the world."

And what really made me bawl: A Taiwanese student told Zander that in Taiwan "I was Number 68 out of 70 student. I come to Boston and Mr. Zander says I am an A. Very confusing. I walk about, three weeks, very confused. I am Number 68, but Mr. Zander says I am an A student . . . One day I discover much happier A than Number 68. So I decide I am an A."

The difference between a 68 and an A is like the difference between how the school official treated my mother and me before and after he heard me speak. It is like the difference between Ivette's downcast eyes and John's level, thoughtful gaze. Imagining this student walking into a room as an A instead of a 68, the enormous burden lifted from his shoulders, gave me chills.

Because I got Bs in high school science, I grew to hate the subject for what it did to my GPA. I assumed the anxiety I felt before every test meant I wasn't good at science. I avoided it in college almost entirely, thereby closing off any number of career options.

But when I went to work in book publishing, I was assigned to publicize all kinds of books—including books about physics, biology, and psychology. Each time I encountered one of them, I worried whether I would understand it, but given no choice, I dove in, and eventually became the go-to publicist in my department for books in those categories. I studied anatomy as a yoga teacher, nutrition and neurology as a parent. And I loved it.

"This is what happens in life. You're in the eighth grade and you get a B, and someone tells you that's not good enough," I once heard a motivational speaker say, like a gypsy reading my life story in my palm.

"And then what you take away, for the rest of your life, is *I'm not good enough.*"

How would life be different if we all knew we were earning As? That our process of learning, which includes making mistakes, was not something to be ashamed of but to be celebrated? What risks would we take? How excited would we be to try?

I'd written my own letter, of sorts, when I started *Facing Forty Upside Down.* I was not in love with the person I was then at all. I wanted to become the kind of person who would be fun to be around, who could laugh at her mistakes and then get up and try again.

"I don't want to hear myself say 'One day, I'd love to' or 'Of course, if I had all the time in the world I would' or 'If I weren't so sleep-deprived/busy/chicken, I would . . .' one more time," I wrote in my inaugural post. I was going to say yes to experiences that scared me, for the sake of my children, "who face new challenges every day without hemming or hawing and perhaps deserve a mom who can do the same."

I was going to be proud for trying, regardless of outcome, I promised myself. I posted a picture of me looking happy and more confident in a swim shirt than I'd ever felt. But just seeing me look that way had made it feel possible. *That's the kind of person I would fall passionately in love with,* I'd thought. *That's who I am on my way to becoming.*

Much of what I'd declared back then had indeed come to pass, I realized with amazement, flipping through the dog-eared pages of *The Art of Possibility.* The book had come recommended by Tony Smith, a professional coach to many CEOs and public figures. Tony was a church acquaintance who would tell me during coffee hour that each of us has the power to transform the world, if only we would step out of the confines of our thinking, which is almost universally mired in the past. It was a lot to take in on a Sunday morning while chasing Gigi and Ruby away from the cupcakes. *But I should tell him the book made such an impact on me,* I thought. Maybe he'd have something to say about facing a fear of failure as well. Boy, did he ever.

≋

"I THINK THAT YOUR COURAGE goes as deep as the center of the earth," Tony said, speaking in a slightly strangled voice that registered a ten for intensity but was dialed back to a volume of eight for my sake. I always get the feeling with Tony that if he were to really express himself, we would both explode.

I had told Tony about my Greek Chorus and my aversion to taking risks and my fear of looking stupid. He had taken off his shoes, displaying eggplant-colored socks, which said quite a bit about his opinion of what others might think of him.

"I think you buy into this story of your upbringing as a way to let yourself off the hook from the power of your own power," he said, boring into me with his eyes, seemingly inches from my face. "You say you had these parents who raised you a certain way, this culture that taught you a certain way, and many people would say, 'Oh poor you, of course you're the way you are.' But I say, bullshit. You've made this work for you. This way, you don't have to be responsible. And you can go on your whole life not owning your power. You are as afraid of success as you are of failure." I tried to duck his gaze. Success meant more expectation, more risk, a farther way to fall. It also meant more work, and I was *tired.* Tony's eyes followed mine wherever they tried to go. "But there's a cost to that," he continued. "To not living your life fully, to not giving everything you can give, until what? Until you die?"

I sat there, looking at Tony, feeling dizzy. We'd only started this conversation two minutes ago. There is no preparing yourself for Tony. He doesn't waste time warming up. If you're here, he's *RIGHT HERE, RIGHT NOW,* 100 percent. I swallowed. My stomach was empty. I'd had no dinner, and now I had no story of my upbringing to wrap myself around either.

"The only way to access your power is to stop living in the past and start speaking to yourself from the future," Tony said, leaning in farther. Any closer and he'd be in my lap. "Do you think the Founding Fathers had any reason to believe in democracy? No! Monarchy was all around them. But Thomas Jefferson said *I believe in the United States of America, and I am willing to stake my life on it*. That's where the exciting stuff happens."

I was terrified. I just wanted to be brave enough to go onstage, to go back in the ocean, to write a book. I wasn't looking to start a revolution.

"Tony, do you think everyone is meant to be Thomas Jefferson?" I mean, maybe some of us were meant to be Betsy Ross.

"I do," he said, nodding. "In their own way, in their own lives, yes."

He tapped my notebook. "But this note-taking, this being a good student, observing the world as it is, is not the way there," he said. "All this needs to go out the window."

I reflexively pulled my notebook toward me, its spiral binding warped from use. It, or one like it, had become my companion, my reason for being in any given place—a bar, a pool, a party, or RIGHT HERE, RIGHT NOW. I was going outside my usual footprint constantly these days and my notebook was my lovey, my wingman, my excuse to start or end a conversation. It was my way of never being alone.

"Truth hurts, huh?" Tony asked. It sounded more like an answer the way he said it, though.

≫

"WOOF! WOOF! You have to go to work! If you don't, you won't earn any MONEY and then you won't be able to PAY THE BILLS and then you're going to GO BANKRUPT!" Psychologist Joseph Rhinewine made the little stuffed dog named Keats bark into the camera. I giggled at the video, titled *Living from Fear or Values*, part of a series Joe was developing to explain Acceptance and Commitment Therapy (ACT). Joe is an old classmate of mine who now runs Portland Mindfulness Therapy, a counseling and mental health practice in Oregon. Keats continued in a frenzy: "AND THEN you'll lose the house and then you'll be HUMILIATED and then you'll be OUTCAST, your relatives will HATE you and then you will DIE ALONE AND UNLOVED."

Joe cleared his throat, then said in his normal voice, "And that is a life driven by fear."

While REBT practitioners might challenge Keats's thoughts ("Will you really die alone?"), Joe, who practices Acceptance and Commitment Therapy, takes a different tack. "Let's not concern ourselves with disputing Keats," Joe explained over the phone. "We're not going to fight mind with mind. That's exhausting. Instead, let's *accept* the fearful thoughts and *commit* to doing the things we value that are worth some pain and suffering along the way."

ACT was developed by Steven C. Hayes, a psychologist who in the late 1970s suffered from panic attacks that worsened when he tried to control his thoughts. In a profile of him in *Time*, John Cloud writes that when Hayes started drawing on his experience with meditation he discovered that "accepting that his panic would happen allowed him to be able to distance himself from it." His anxiety lessened, and over the next decade or so he built an approach that takes attention away from the things we fear and puts it toward the things that matter to us. The first paper mentioning ACT was published in 1991; as of 2006 roughly twelve thousand students and professionals have been trained in it and it's now used to treat issues from anxiety, depression, and addiction to psychosis.

"Keats is one voice, but he's not the only voice," Joe said. "When you tune in to your values you may raise the volume on the part of you that says 'Work is important to me because I get to . . . be creative . . . help people . . . make money . . . support my family . . . even if it's difficult at times, even if bad things could happen, I'm going to go to work.'" Of course, that's likely to make Keats bark louder as well.

"Keats is never going away," Joe explained. But he doesn't have to control your destiny. "You get to choose what you actually do." Joe encouraged me to imagine holding the stuffed dog and patting it while walking across the room. "Let's hold Keats lightly, while at the same time *commit* to moving our arms, legs, mouths in the direction we want to go."

Joe and I went to the same ultra-competitive school in Manhattan for one year, but then his family moved away. For those of us who stayed, the word *acceptance* had only one meaning, and that was with the word *college* in front of it. We were our SAT scores: Failure was never an option. I told Joe about the pressure to perform I still felt in so many areas of my life, the pressure Ivette and Rosa and anyone who is afraid of public speaking feels whenever people might be judging them.

"If someone's been told their whole life 'Don't look dumb, don't let people down, don't fail,' it's pointless to try to convince them that looking dumb would not be the end of the world," Joe said. "And have you ever noticed the more you tell yourself not to think something, the more you think it?" Yes. Telling myself *Stop stressing out!* is the quickest path to stressing out. "So we accept that our mind gives us all kinds of thoughts that cause us discomfort. What I would ask is, 'Does the way your mind speaks to you help you achieve your goals?'"

"Well, it makes me work hard and do my best," I said.

"Okay, it can help you get a lot done, but is that a satisfying way to live? I mean, it's kind of like living like a hunted animal, isn't it?"

"Uhhhh . . ."

"What if I told you or Ivette or Rosa that the way to get the things you value, like being able to communicate what you know, being able to help and connect with others, *what if THE TICKET IN was heart palpitations and cold sweats?* Could you say, 'Although I am uncomfortable now, it is worth it to me. I have things I want to convey'?" The first sentence of Steven Hayes's book *Get Out of Your Mind and Into Your Life* is, "People suffer." But suffering can be a conduit to joy. "Let's not worry about getting rid of anxiety," Joe said. "That's a dead man goal, meaning dead people do that better than you ever will. Instead, let's make your top five *life* goals and then go for them whether they cause discomfort or not. Let's make your life about *that*."

THE DAY OF THE *Listen to Your Mother* show, I stood in front of my closet, paralyzed by choice: heels or flats, lipstick or gloss, Spanx or sucking in. Which kept my mind off thinking of all that could go wrong.

"Things going wrong" is its own category when it comes to reasons people dread public speaking. Things go wrong all the time in life, but when it's in front of other people, it feels exponentially worse. And because there is no end to the number of ways things could go wrong—up to and including tripping and falling off the stage, getting the hiccups, and God choosing this moment to grant you the gift of speaking in tongues (see? I've thought of them all; this is why I hide in bathrooms)—it's much better to spend your time rehearsing your speech and doing your hair.

Rick Frishman gives as many as twenty speeches in a year and has pretty much seen it all.

"I've had times in the middle of a speech where the whole Power-Point went away," he told me. "I just went on because I knew my material. If you don't, you're a little screwed. You've got to know your stuff." And a printout of your outline, for backup, is good, too.

"Once, I realized partway through a big speech there was a slide coming up I didn't want to use. When it came on the screen I said, 'See this slide? Now you don't!' and scrolled right past it." Rick did this so smoothly, a blogger in attendance posted it as an example of how to handle skipping ahead when short on time. It's also a great example of the Toastmasters adage: *Never apologize for minor mistakes.* Apologies take attention away from your main points and draw it to unimportant glitches. Rick kept things moving in the direction he wanted to go, and the audience trusted it was where they were supposed to be.

"There've been times where the mic's gone off. I hope that the AV people will get it on, but in the meantime, I keep going. I've got a pretty loud voice. But here's the main thing," Rick said. He said it in bold and italics, just like this:

"People know that you're just human and that shit happens."

"What if the audience looks bored?" I asked Rick. This is the beginning of the end for many people. Having finally worked up the courage to get up there, looking out and seeing unimpressed faces can feel devastating. The instinct is to look away from the audience and down at one's notes, and to speak as quickly as possible to get things over with. This instinct, however, makes for a self-fulfilling prophecy, as it ensures that the rest of the presentation is as boring as it can be.

"I go into the audience a lot," Rick replied. *Brave man,* I thought. *He goes swimming with the sharks.* "I am always moving around, asking people questions. If somebody is nodding off or I can see they're zoning out, I purposely walk by them and then they wake up, thinking, 'Don't call on me!'"

I laughed. Rick wasn't the swimmer, he was the shark. "So, you terrorize your audience into paying attention?"

"Ahem. It keeps them very involved," Rick said demurely.

"Hang on, I'm just writing a note to myself," I said. "'Do not go see Rick Frishman live.'"

Joking aside, what Rick said brought the question of fear—the speaker's, the audience's—to a head. How could we get past all that, I asked him, and just enjoy the time we spend together?

"The reality is, be real," he said simply. Each of us has a reason for wanting to be heard. Rick calls it our noble intent. And it's not to make more money. It's to teach something, share something, to make a difference. When we tap in to that energy and put it into our work and our words, the people we're speaking to sense it. "Then the audience will be real with you, and you'll be in sync," he said.

That's the groovy, juicy, fun part of public speaking, the *communicating*. And who doesn't want to be a part of that?

"You gotta have fun," said Rick, wrapping up our talk with my kind of conclusion. "Don't take yourself too seriously."

≋

MY DECISIONS WERE MADE. Heels. Gloss. Sucking in.

I had practiced my reading on friends, I'd taped myself, and given myself my own stinging critique. I had connected with my noble intent, which was twofold. I wanted to tell the story of my daughters with love. And to do my job well.

I was first in the lineup. The way I saw it, my job was to assure the audience that they were in the right place. That their money had been well spent. That they wouldn't be trapped in their seats for the next hour and a half with lunatics—or bores—at the mic. The producers told me they wanted to open the program with "warm and funny," and, dammit, that's what I was going to be.

I arrived at the performance hall full of positive thinking and good energy to spare. I even meditated with Estelle Sobel Erasmus, another reader, in the green room as we waited to go on. Joe Rhinewine would have been proud of us.

Joe once said on his Portland Mindfulness Therapy blog that every time he's about to go in front of a camera, the image of Cindy on *The Brady Bunch* freezing up on a quiz show flashes through his mind. ("Oh, thank you, Mind!") Not helpful. Then, he practices mindfulness, which is.

He observes his feelings without criticizing himself. "If you are nervous, you need to be aware of that and accepting of it, in order to do your best," he writes. "When we are gentle with ourselves, when we are compassionate with our own feelings, we can show the world who we really are."

Next to Estelle, I sat with my eyes closed and let the butterflies come. *This is it! This could be great! Or it could be horrible! Ugh! That's an automatic negative thought!* Just as I was about to whack the ANT with a shoe I stopped myself. *Those are nerves talking. Accept the nerves. It's okay to be nervous. Commit to what I care about.* And then, just as there are no atheists in foxholes, I covered my bases by adding an REBT touch: *And anyway, whatever happens it's not the end of the world.*

In the movie *The King's Speech*, George VI, who has a stutter, gives an important radio address in the culminating scene, and we get to see him use every technique he has learned from the vocal coach who became his friend along the way. Breathing; using silences; pushing through consonants; thinking "God Save the King"; and, fundamentally, understanding at last that he is no longer the neglected boy who was never listened to growing up but is now the king who deserves to be heard because he has a voice and something important to say. Whether the blockages are physical, mental, emotional, or primal, there are ways to overcome them.

I was starting to smile even with my eyes closed. *I'm about to do something exciting.* The butterflies morphed into diving swallows and then shrank down into no-see-ums. *Isn't this exciting?* I squeezed Estelle's arm. We opened our eyes and took in the flurry of primping and picture snapping in the dressing room around us, and then each took a turn autographing blogger Kirsten Piccini's high-heeled shoe.

"If you're not nervous before you go onstage, you're not doing it right," Rick Frishman says. We must have all been doing it right. Some of us were writers, nervous about the stage; a few were actors, nervous about their writing; some were worried about making people laugh; others were worried that they themselves would cry. I found out later that one was afraid she'd start lactating, another was not carefree about her feminine hygiene products, and one had actually peed herself onstage in high school and almost held up our show running to the bathroom one last time.

Amy Wilson, our director, had us all hold hands in a circle. "Before you start speaking, take it all in," she said. "Look around, be in the spotlight. This is your moment." We squeezed one anothers' hands. Yes. We were ready to go.

I couldn't wait to start. The moment your energy comes near a live mic, something ignites—you can feel electricity in the air. If you know what you want to say, it's the most excited you'll ever feel.

I had, as Toastmasters instructed, visualized success. It all started off as I had envisioned. René Syler, former host of *The Early Show* on CBS, introduced me and I stepped up to the podium, feeling tall and proud. *I'm so glad I wore my heels*, I thought. *I'm accessing my power.*

I took my stance, relaxed my belly, breathed in oxygen, let the nerves go. I greeted the audience with a warm smile, beaming all my good energy to meet theirs. *I have a voice*, I thought. *God save the king!*

The first line went well. I think the next sentence or two were also fine.

Then what was it that Rick said might occur? Oh, yes.

Shit happens.

The spotlight on me turned off. Either that, or I was having a stroke. Then the lights went up. On the audience. Standing by myself at the podium in the dark, I thought, *Oh hell.*

It's just a glitch, I told myself. I continued reading, not wanting to break the flow.

Audience lights down, up, down, the random flickering continued. I slowed my pace, teetering in my now too tall heels.

How long is this going to go on? I fretted, telling the story of when Ruby came into our family. *Maybe I should stop.*

Suddenly, my brain was taken over by a two-year-old on a rampage for a cookie. *I only have five minutes. FIVE LOUSY MINUTES TO SAY WHAT I WANT TO SAY! IS IT TOO MUCH TO ASK? THIS IS RUINING MY YOUTUBE CLIP!*

Grown-up Patty tried to contain the tantrum. *Welcome! I'm warm and funny! Everything is fine! Pay no attention to the darkness around me!* I focused on the words, trying to smile reassuringly, as I spoke about how the girls fought like the WWF meets *Crouching Tiger, Hidden Dragon*, how life in our house had become wall-to-wall noise and chaos.

It felt very familiar, this sensation of trying to act in control when things were actually spinning away and bursting into flame all around me. Why?

Oh, yes. *It's just like being a mother.*

It was just like the time I blew a tire on the highway with an anxious nine-year-old Gigi in the car. "We're okay, honey," I said, over and over, getting us off the road safely. My meltdown could wait. I wanted her to be okay.

I relaxed. *This is not the end of the world. This is actually pretty exhilarating.* What was it Tony had said, tapping my notebook? Being on the sidelines observing others was not the way. Center stage, flying by the seat of my pants, must be closer to what he had in mind.

I remembered how at Elaine's Toastmasters workshop a woman had said she was afraid of blushing conspicuously, and Elaine replied simply, "Not everyone can see what you feel." In the book *Nerve*, the clinical psychologist Paul Salmon talks about the "illusion of transparency" that comes with stage fright: "When your heart is pounding, you think everyone can see it," he said. "When you're physiologically activated, your senses become more highly attuned and you magnify the impact of these things. It's like you're under the microscope."

"And even if they did see you blush, it's not a big deal," Elaine added. "They probably understand. Some people may be looking to criticize you, but most people want you to do well."

My hand is quivering, but it's no big deal, I said to myself as I launched into the next anecdote in my reading, about how Kent and I had been stealing a kiss in the backyard when Gigi interrupted us. I realized that the lights were on me again and not on the audience. The way they were supposed to be. *Success is being here and enjoying it.* I smiled now, for real, as I set up the punch line: "'*Heeeey.* Whatcha doin'?' Gigi asked. She was suspicious. Mom and Dad don't usually stand around doing nothing.

"'We were having a moment,' Daddy said.

"Gigi looked us over. Then a lightbulb went on. 'Oh, I get it,' she said, snuggling her way between us. 'Were you guys thinking about . . . back when . . . it was just the three of us?'"

The audience roared.

After I finished, I sat down in a chair onstage, right behind the podium. One by one, the other brave souls stepped up and told their stories. There were tales of an Italian mom's cooking, more than one mom's craziness, and a mom growing older and needing care. There were stories of toddler mayhem and vomit on a toothbrush, miracle twins after infertility, and a baby that was wanted but never came to be. And there was a bittersweet reminder that motherhood ends all too soon when the child becomes an adult.

I thought of my friend Hope, whose job reading to children helped her overcome her shyness. She told me she became truly outspoken when she had to speak for her autistic son. "He is my biggest reason to have a voice," she wrote to me. "I want people to know that when I tell my story about him, I'm not looking for pity but understanding, patience, a chance to show how autism can look."

I thought of the woman at Toastmasters who told us how she spoke up to a teenage gang member to tell him to leave her son alone, with both conviction and charm ("You're so good lookin'! Why do you need to be in a gang?").

And I thought of Rosa. She had stopped attending meetings for a few months, citing other commitments, and we had all missed her. But she'd come to the club's end-of-season party. Each person was asked to the front of the room to declare his or her goals for the coming year. One by one, members went up, not letting anything—self-consciousness, an accent, a past failure, a fear of rejection—stop them. When Rosa's turn came, she declared, "My goal is to make at least one speech and to become more comfortable speaking in public, to be a little more, um, fluid and less nervous." A few months later she completed her Ice Breaker. After a frenzy of drafting what she would say, she recorded herself and realized: "I was trying to do too much, I was making it too complicated." She simplified, and she got through the speech.

"I survived," she'd told me with a smile. I'd congratulated her, thinking, *What's different about her?* And then I realized: She was wearing her hair down.

Up onstage at *Listen to Your Mother*, there was a shaky voice here, a tear shed there, a leg that trembled which the audience could not see. And fifteen unforgettable stories. Everyone triumphed. No one died.

In the happy milling about in the auditorium after the show, my father slapped me on the back many times and said, "Wonderful job!" My mother gave me a squeeze and we took pictures together. In my heels, I tower like Mulan Barbie with her adorable Polly Pocket parents.

My old high school boyfriend, Danny, was there. He told me that Ma and Ba looked a lot less intimidating to him than when we were in ninth grade. Until he said to my mother, "Mrs. Chang, you must be so proud of Patty." Apparently, she replied, "Well, she can read and write. So I guess that's something."

"Ooooh." Danny, a former naval officer, shivered comically in the retelling. "Yup, she's still scary."

Not really, not anymore, I thought, looking at them greeting my friends and in-laws. I never stop admiring them for stepping out in a culture and language not their own. My mother was probably being modest. And whether she ranked my work as an A or an Asian F was beside the point. Ma and Ba both would probably grade their own English skills below an A but it was never an excuse for them not to do their jobs or to shy away from navigating the English-speaking world on our behalf when we were young. Every job interview, every parent-teacher conference might have provoked anxiety, but they went through with these challenges anyway, because they knew why it was worth it. And, standing on that stage, regardless of how it went, or what anyone else might have thought of my performance, I knew why I was there.

I believe in the power of stories to change minds, open hearts, connect people, and create a better world. We imagine something and then we do not keep it to ourselves. We declare it, in front of others, and then progress is possible. This is why cavemen did not stay hiding by themselves in the dark. They built fires and came together, told stories, and advanced civilization. I had told Tony that I was no Thomas Jefferson, but I also believe each of us is more powerful than we know.

I once asked Victoria Ramos, the yoga teacher who taught me the handstand, how to contend with the voices that say "Don't do it, it might end badly." In return, she asked three questions worth asking oneself every day, several times a day: "Why do you think you're here to hide? What if you being out there was a gift to the world? And what if what you thought was dangerous was a lie?"

The part of me that is afraid of being ignored and afraid of being heard, that seeks a path of least resistance and greatest comfort, the me that whispers "Don't bother, why risk anything, no one will notice if you sit this one out" is the dead man talking, seeking an anxiety-free life.

But the life worth living is the one worth the effort, the discomfort, the throat clearing and soul baring. We all speak for someone or something. Whom do I speak for? For all the people who think they can't. Come out of the bathroom! The world needs you. And I know you can.

CHAPTER 5

GROWING UP
Biking

am going to eat cake tonight," I whispered to Kent, surveying the scene in front of us through tears of joy. Gigi's fifth grade workbooks, full of her writing, were neatly stacked on her desk, her most recent spelling test taped to the wall. It was parent night at the special education program we had moved Gigi into starting in fourth grade, and what we were seeing was what we had hoped and prayed for—a place where Gigi could learn, grow, and belong.

I don't know of any parent who can sleep well if her child is struggling at school, and for several sleepless years while Gigi was at the local public school we agonized over what to do. The move from the imperfect-fit-but-known school to the unknown-but-hopefully-better-fit school was nerve-racking. But now, a year and a half later, Gigi was thriving, and I felt triumphant. At last, I was going to enjoy an open house.

Who knew if this feeling would last? Gigi would be graduating from here at the end of the school year and going to a different middle school in the fall. The idea of more change, more uncertainty, made me feel faint. But for tonight, everything was perfect. I was going to nibble on cookies and hear how well our daughter was doing. I was going to relax.

"Excuse me," I said, squeezing past other parents to get to the knee-high refreshments table. I took a slice of coffee cake from its super-market box and popped it in my mouth, turning to smile at Kent across the room. It tasted marvelous.

Kent was chatting with Michael Star, the school's occupational therapist (OT). A thin, soft-spoken man in his late forties, Michael was dressed in a polo shirt and khakis, comfortable clothes for working with kids on mats and swings. According to the American Occupational Therapy Association, the job of an OT is to "help people across the lifespan participate in the things they want and need to do through the therapeutic use of everyday activities (occupations)."

Michael's job is to help kids with disabilities function better in school. What that means varies greatly depending on the needs of the child. For some autistic kids, expanding their ability to tolerate light, noise, or movement is a priority. For kids with emotional difficulties, it may be to teach ways to calm down, or to focus. Like Anne Sullivan to dozens of Helen Kellers each year, his job often entails pushing kids to move past limitations, frustration, and fear of failure, to bring a child to greater self-sufficiency.

When Gigi arrived in the program in fourth grade, her handwriting, after a history of hand tics, was illegible. "Teach her to type" was the advice we were given before. Michael, patient and tenacious in equally ample amounts, started her from scratch and taught her to write. Ever since, every time I saw him I had to repress the urge to throw my arms around him and start blubbering tears of gratitude.

I smiled and waved happily, my napkin sending forth a little cloud of powdered sugar like confetti. Michael smiled back and then left Kent with the speech therapist to make his way over. Compared to most of the kids in Michael's caseload, Gigi's goals were relatively straightforward. Perhaps he would tell me she was doing well and we'd pat each other on the back for all her gains. That's that! Enjoy your cake!

But, no. After a warm how do you do, he switched gears.

"Mrs. Anker," he said, his voice announcing a new subject, a new agenda, "does Gigi know how to ride a bike?"

I tried to swallow the cake in my mouth. It was stuck.

"Uh, no." I coughed. *Please, please don't ask me to teach her to ride a bike.*

"Really?" He raised his eyebrows. "You should really teach her how!" He said it like we didn't know what good times we were missing out on.

I moaned inside.

He must have seen panic in my face because he started using his soothing voice, as if talking me down from a tree. "It would be good for her to work on balance, coordination, being smooth and steady."

I bit my lip, squeezing my napkin into a sticky ball in the palm of my hand. *We taught her to tie her shoes. To read and write. To do multiplication. She knows how to calculate a tip. Real-life skills! Why does she need to know how to ride a bike?*

"It's good exercise, fresh air." Michael was still talking, as if what he was saying was perfectly reasonable. "It's something you could do as a family. She's almost eleven years old—it'll be harder as she gets older . . ." His voice trailed off. A little awkward silence followed.

"Um . . . is there a reason you haven't taught her yet?" he asked, looking unsure of whether he wanted to know the answer.

"I don't ride a bike!" I blurted. Once upon a time, I did, a little sparkly number with a banana seat, back when I was nine years old and our family lived in Canada. Oh, Canada! So glorious, so free of muggers. But once we moved to the Bronx, riding a bike was like singing "Bike-jack me!" with every ring of the bell, and I gave it up.

It didn't help that I knew people who had been hurt badly, getting hit by buses and trucks, while biking in New York City. I blame New York. The song should really go "If I can make it there, I'll make it anywhere, as long as I don't have to bike. Or drive." No one was asking me to take Gigi into the mean streets of Manhattan, but still.

Not that my fear of bicycling was limited to the city. A family resort in Vermont, where we'd vacationed ten years before, was closed to cars, so you had to get around by bike. What a lovely, bucolic idea, pedaling in the country air! Until my hurry to make the champagne cruise from the lakeside dock collided with my lack of ability to pedal and steer at the same time, and I ended up in a ditch. I walked everywhere for the rest of the vacation.

Of course, I blamed Kent. Because he's a great cyclist, and I'm not. So there must have been something he could have done better.

I couldn't blame Megan, the wonderful yogini who gave me a bike lesson when I started blogging about facing my fears. She calmly talked me through my anxieties going up and down a long driveway, and if I could have kept her by my side and stuck to long driveways, I might be okay.

But I would not be anywhere near as calm teaching Gigi. I hate the sensation of gathering speed. I hate the idea of my children in harm's way. Plus, I have a fear of children on bicycles falling on top of me. All I would do is scream *"Slow down!"* and *"Stop!"* which might be counterproductive to the task. I did not want to teach Gigi to ride a bike.

Michael was looking at me inquiringly, so I tried to explain.

"Gigi's dad is the cyclist in the family, and he works so much he's rarely home in daylight. He also has a bad back." *And a very low threshold for whining.* "We did try to teach her a couple of times, but it was really stressful." I think "Never again" were the exact words used by everyone involved. I paused. Did I sound as lame as I thought? What kind of parents can't teach their kid to ride a bike?

They must teach empathy skills in OT, because Michael said all the right things.

"It *is* really hard to teach a child to ride a bike. You're pushing her to do something where she could get hurt. You can't really explain how to do it—how can you explain how to balance? She just has to feel it. And Gigi has some small motor delays, maybe some anxiety, too, that make it harder."

I breathed a little easier. Maybe his next sentence would be "Never mind, let's teach her to play Boggle instead."

Of course it wasn't.

"Whatever difficulties Gigi has should not prevent her from riding a bike," he said. "This is something she can do. It would give her a sense of independence." My throat tightened. I wanted nothing more for Gigi. The familiar anxiety that accompanies daring to hope began welling up in me.

"She should learn to do it." He was unequivocal.

Michael had said that when it came to handwriting, he didn't give Gigi a choice. She had to do it. He made sure she was in an "optimal state of arousal" for learning—that sweet spot of being both alert and relaxed—by having her warm up with an activity she liked. He made the process of writing as enticing as possible, with interesting pens and paper. He incentivized her with rewards when she was done. He did a lot of work to set her up for success. And then she did the work to learn to write.

"I knew she could do it," he said, when I asked him how he had broken through. "She just needed to know we weren't going to give up." The key word there was *we*.

Now, he looked at me, as if to say *Am I making myself clear?*

He was.

≋

"UGH," GIGI GROANED, when I told her I was signing her, Ruby, and myself up for bike lessons. She looked over my shoulder at the Bike

New York website I had up on the computer screen. I had spent their winter break praying for someone, anyone, to teach our kids to ride, and when a friend told me to try Bike New York, the not-for-profit organization that produces the TD Five Boro Bike Tour, I thought I heard angels descending. Apparently, there are people out there who love bicycling so much they will teach you or your kids for free, and lessons were starting up again in the spring.

Gigi did not view this as a gift from God. "Another thing you're dragging me to," she said, sounding morose. The pictures of happy, smiling cyclists did nothing for her. To her, bicycling was all about falling, skinned knees, looking dumb. I felt her pain, a little too much.

"You need to get your own fear in check," Kent had said to me many times, about many things. "It's rubbing off on the kids. You have to believe it's going to be fine—if you don't, they won't buy in."

So I selected an adult class scheduled a few weeks before their kids' class. If mine went well, I'd feel more confident making them go to theirs. There were lessons all over the city, but the ones in Van Cortlandt Park in the Bronx, the very park I grew up *not* biking in, caught my fancy. The opportunity to go back and rewrite history with my daughters felt right somehow.

The only hesitation I had was the clever way Bike New York makes you commit to a free class. The class is free if you show up. If you don't, fifty dollars gets taken off your credit card. Was I ready to commit?

Gigi had been waiting to use the computer, and upon realizing it wasn't going to be available for a while, she turned to go. "I don't have to know how to ride a bike, you know," she grumbled, stomping downstairs to watch TV. "You drive me everywhere anyway."

That did it. I hit Enter. Registration received.

≋

WHEN I WALKED THROUGH the southern entrance to Van Cortlandt Park, I barely recognized it. Back in the eighties, this part of the park, bordered by Broadway and the elevated subway tracks near 242nd Street on one side and the ramps to the Major Deegan Expressway on another, was a "park" in the city sense of the word. The grass knew it didn't belong. The litter and broken glass did.

The park was close to where we'd lived in Kingsbridge Heights, essentially our backyard. The boys in the neighborhood often chose to go farther up the hill to Riverdale, to use the ball fields at the posh private schools, Horace Mann and Fieldston. Van Cortlandt was the place kids went for a pickup game before heading to Burger King while it was still light out. You didn't want to be in the park at night.

But now, I walked under a decorative wrought-iron archway, by a statue of a coyote erected in 1998 in honor of "the first confirmed coyote sighting in New York City since 1946." It was surrounded by plantings that looked like they were put there on purpose. There was a brand-new playground on one side, a new running track on the other.

In the distance, I saw a fenced-in concrete yard, probably a holdover from my childhood or before, with a couple dozen bikes lined up in one corner. Ah, this was more like the Bronx I remembered. As I approached, seeing the weeds sticking up through cracks in the asphalt, I felt like I was coming home.

A woman passed me, looking lost. "Are you going to the bike lesson?" I asked, catching up to her. "I think it's over there." I pointed to the yard with the bikes.

"*Ohhh!*" she exclaimed, with a lovely, lilting laugh. Her face relaxed. "I was worried I was in the wrong place!" She spoke with a slight Indian accent and introduced herself as Jaya.

"Will this be your first time on a bike?" I asked, as we made our way toward two men wearing blue Bike New York T-shirts.

"I took a lesson a couple of years ago, but then I didn't practice and got scared all over again," she said, echoing my own experience. With each passing year since that bike lesson with Megan, I'd felt less confident about getting back in the saddle. "I love to travel, and basically anywhere you go in the world, you would be able to enjoy it more if you rode a bike," Jaya explained. "I really want to learn."

A young, serious Asian woman fell in stride with us. She introduced herself as Jenny. "Is this where we're going to ride?" she asked, scanning the yard nervously. "It looks hard. Hey, are my pants okay?" She was wearing loose athletic pants. "I'm worried they're going to flap around and get caught in the bike. Should I tuck them into my socks?" I didn't know. I was wearing close-fitting yoga pants, which, I was beginning to realize with each step, were starting to lose their stretch.

It was thirty-seven degrees out, according to my phone, a sunny but chilly spring morning, and I was feeling jumpy and cold. *I should have worn another layer between my shirt and my windbreaker*, I thought, tugging the pants up and the jacket firmly down.

When we approached the bike station, an avuncular man with a white beard named Ross asked us to sign a waiver and try on helmets. I signed the waiver without reading it. Reading waivers is a good way to lose your deposit. A man in dreadlocks named Clyde sized us up for bikes.

More people came, some in pairs. "Bernard is riding," a blond woman said, smiling at her companion, a big, lovable-looking Asian man, made bigger by the thick, brown, fuzzy zip-up jacket he had on. I envied him his warm apparel and demeanor. He looked cheerful, and his friend gave him a squeeze, saying, "I'm the moral support."

For a moment, I wondered if I should have brought someone to cheer me on, witness the moment. But then another spectator, a self-professed "serious cyclist," set up a lawn chair, sat down, and started calling out instructions to his female friend, who was tentatively sitting on a bike. She smiled wanly. *On second thought, I'm glad I came alone.*

Helmets and name tags on, our group of fifteen straddled our black-and-orange Schwinns, looking similarly ill at ease. We were all over the map in age and ethnicity, but there was no question we belonged together.

"How's everyone doing?" Clyde asked, scooting on his bicycle in front of us. "Apart from nervous?" We all tittered, shifted our balance from one foot to the other.

"You'll notice your bike is missing something," he said, pointing down. I'd noticed. "That's right—we took off the pedals so you can practice getting your balance and coasting. You're going to scoot with your feet." He demonstrated, pushing the ground away with one foot and then the other, the bike coasting easily along. "As you get comfortable, coast for longer." He leaned his head back serenely, looking like Brian Boitano, skating with the stars.

"Now"—he sat straight up—"if you want to slow down, you will not do it like Fred Flintstone. Never skid with your feet!" We imagined the prehistoric dirt flying. "Squeeze your hand brakes *very gently!* These are good brakes, they will slow you down very quickly. You do not have to grab them." He deepened his voice ominously. "Bad things happen when you grab the brakes."

I squeezed the hand brakes gently. Such a foreign concept. My last bike had foot brakes; the car had a foot brake; if I wanted to slow down while running, I slow down my feet. How was I going to remember to use my hands to slow down?

Clyde stopped and pointed to his hands on the handlebars, his butt on the seat, and his feet on the invisible pedals. "If you are in contact in these three places, you are *on the bike*," he said emphatically. "You do not need to look down to check if you're on the bike. What happens if I look down?" He looked down; you could see if he were moving he'd pitch head over handlebars in the next frame. "That's right—it wouldn't be pretty, folks. Where you look is where you go, so keep your eyes up."

Keep ur eyes up, I wrote in my notebook, while juggling my phone and trying to take video.

"Hey," Ross said, walking up next to me. "You can't bike and take pictures at the same time. Believe me, I had a woman who tried to text while biking and she fell over."

Putting away my phone, notebook, and pen was like disconnecting all my defenses. With nothing in my hands I had no choice but to wrap them around the handlebars and focus on the task at hand. The air seemed to get colder where we were waiting in the shade.

"When I point to you," Clyde said, "you will kick the stand back and go. You'll be like 'AAAAAAAAHHHH!'" he screamed. "That's okay. Give each other plenty of room." He indicated for us to go in a big circle around the yard.

Everyone squirmed. It was a *Gentlemen, start your engines* moment, except none of us wanted to turn the key.

"Okay, Pink Pants!" Clyde pointed at a lady in pink sweatpants. "Go!" She pushed off. The next lady had forgotten where her kickstand was. A third and fourth were sent on their way while she searched. Then it was my turn, and I pushed off. Almost immediately I wanted to brake. The bike was flying! Every pit in the surface of the yard felt like it was going to catapult me off my seat. But my feet were hardly leaving the ground. I looked around and everyone had the same look of intense worry or concentration as they shuffled around the yard on their bikes, barely moving.

"It's so weird," I muttered. "It feels like we're going fast, but we're

not at all." We looked more like old people pushing walkers in an outdoor exercise period.

It was actually hard work, pushing our bodies around the yard. After a few laps, the complaining started. "I'm out of breath," one woman
said, stopping to rest.

"My butt hurts," I said, stopping alongside her, "and my pants are
falling down."

"Your butt hurts?" Bernard called from across the way. He must
have been lip-reading from that distance. His formerly cheerful face
was contorted in a grimace. "My hips are *ON FIRE!*" he howled. His
voice got louder as he got closer to us. "I'm so *TIRED!*" He actually
looked like he was breaking a sweat in the freezing cold. "I'm in *PAIN!*
And we haven't even done anything yet! It's been *TEN MINUTES!*"
His voice faded in volume, but not in anguish, as he passed by, asking
the question on everyone's minds: "What's going to happen when we
have to *PEDAL?*"

A woman, whose name tag shouted KAT in big block letters, was
standing still, straddling her bike. As I pushed by her, she confided
in an undertone, "I don't know how to turn. Every time I try, I start to
fall over."

"I only know how to turn left," I said. I was gathering speed, coasting between strides, trying not to crash into anyone. So was everyone
else: We were starting to look less like geriatrics and more like circus
clowns.

"Red Jacket!" Clyde called. "Hello! You with the red jacket!" I
looked down at my red jacket.

"Do you mean me?" I asked, coasting by him in my never-ending
left turn. I was too scared to use the hand brakes, too good a student to
use my feet to stop.

"Yes, you," Clyde said. "I think we have our first candidate for pedals. You feel ready?"

"Well, as long as I don't have to turn right," I called back. *Or brake.*

Clyde cruised over. "Follow me," he called, leading me toward the right. I overshot it and wobbled. *I'm going to fall!* I yanked left, too far, wobbled again. Through the mists of time I heard Megan's calm voice on the driveway: "Every wobble does not equal a crash. Think of a wobble as a chance to get centered again." I pulled right, then left more gently, managing to stay upright.

"C'mon," Clyde urged. "Follow me. Don't look down, eyes on me." He led us into the center of the yard, then out to the perimeter, weaving me, still pushing myself with my feet, in a large figure eight that crossed and recrossed the slow and unsteady current of fellow students on their bikes. I strained to judge how much time and space I had to cross their paths. Interestingly, the faster we went, the easier it was.

"What's your name?" he asked. I told him, and we bantered for a moment. *You're trying to distract me from the terror at hand,* I thought, scooting within a hair of Jaya. "Sorry! Sorry!" I called out.

"Yeah, right!" I think she said, although all I saw was the back of her helmet as she teetered away.

"Guess what, Miss Patty," Clyde said, after a couple more figure eights. "You're turning right!" He led us back to the bike station, calling out, "Easy on your brakes!" I surprised myself by stopping before I hit anything. "She's ready, Ross," he said. "Give the woman pedals."

As I passed the bike over, I rubbed my aching hands. "Are your hands hurting?" Ross asked. "If you're nervous, you're probably strangling the handles. Don't hold on too tight—it doesn't keep you from falling."

Ross was right. My fingers felt like stiff claws. I put my hands inside my jacket to warm up and willed them to relax.

Pedals on my bike, Ross instructed me, a righty, to put the right pedal up at one o'clock, step down, and start pedaling. Nothing to it. It was actually easier than pushing off the ground. My knees came all the way up to the handlebars. I looked ridiculous, but I was upright and moving.

Bernard was really sweating now. "Dude!" I called, riding past him. "It is so much easier with the pedals!"

"Is it really?" he exclaimed. "Oh good, that's something to look forward to. God! *GIVE ME SOME PEDALS!*"

One by one, students were called to the side to get pedals; and as each reentered the fray, the excitement went up, the speed went up, and so did the casualties.

"Oh! Look out!"

"Fence! Fence!"

"Coming your way!"

"Oops, sorry!"

But they were, in the grand scheme of things, tiny accidents: bumps and bruises, scrapes and minor indignities. A few students went to the Band-Aid station.

And at the same time, smiles were breaking out all over the place. People started laughing. I saw Jaya pedaling steadily in front of me. "Jaya," I called, pedaling faster to catch up to her.

"Don't you run into me!" she called back over her shoulder. "I feel you there! I know you're there!"

"Thanks for the faith!" I laughed. "Hey, Jaya, where do you want to go when you travel?"

"Where? Everywhere! Before I die, I want to see—Uh-oh!" We weaved so close, I saw the whites of her eyes. I slowed down to let her go ahead. I wanted to hear her list, but I also wanted her to have a chance of biking somewhere beyond Van Cortlandt Park before she died.

Trying to stop was a mess. I kept trying to push the pedals backward, and when that didn't work, panicking and squeezing the hand brakes too hard. I stopped short with a squeak in front of the young blond woman, who was sitting on the ground, looking at her phone. I shook my head. "I don't know what I'll do going downhill," I said.

She looked up at me, shading her eyes from the sun. "Use your brakes from the beginning of the downhill—don't ride the brakes, but keep coming back to them so you don't gather too much speed." She spoke with authority but broke off abruptly, looking up over my shoulder. Bernard was pedaling toward us, a huge grin on his face.

"Oh my God!" She jumped up, scrambling to aim her camera phone. "Bernard! I am so proud of you! Keep riding, don't pay attention to me. Oh my God!"

"This is *SO GREAT!*" Bernard enthused, a bear of a man on a too-small bike. "Tracy, it's so much easier with pedals! *I LOVE THIS.*"

"Is that your boyfriend?" I asked. "He's so cute."

"My fiancé," Tracy said happily. "He has such unbridled enthusiasm! I tried to teach him, but it was not a good thing. He's doing great here!"

Bernard slowed to a stop in front of us, beaming.

"Honey, you're doing so well! I was just telling Patty here, when you're on a hill, you'll want to start braking earlier."

Uh-oh.

"We're up to hills already? Really, honey?" Bernard said.

It was a familiar dynamic: The enthusiasm of the experienced outpacing the readiness of the novice. I knew it well. In areas in which I feel least proficient, I always attract the most pointers from well-meaning family and friends. Which is great, until it starts to make me feel like an idiot.

Every time I rode by the guy in the lawn chair, he was calling out some other tidbit of advice to his girlfriend. "Stop it!" I wanted to scream. "You're distracting her! She's got enough to think about!" Not that I was projecting or anything. But it was striking to me how one of the aspects of bicycling that had always freaked me out—that you're on your own with no one to help—could also be a big plus: no backseat drivers.

Tracy, to her credit, took Bernard's hint immediately and let it drop. I asked Bernard if he'd grown up in the area, assuming city kid syndrome accounted for the late start bicycling. Actually, he told me, he'd grown up in Cleveland, where everyone rode bikes but him. "My dad was a pediatrician," he said. "He was scared of me getting hurt."

On my next lap, Clyde called, "Jaya! Patty! To the side!" I wondered if I had broken some rule of the yard. But instead he said, "You guys are ready to have your seats raised. Jaya, you first."

Jaya smiled. "At last! I am first in something! And it is not in falling!"

I felt similarly pleased, until Clyde said, "Of course, what this means is that your feet won't reach the ground as easily." Our smiles faded. Clyde demonstrated mounting the bicycle by holding the hand brake, swinging one leg over, stepping down on the pedal and sitting up onto the seat, and placing the other foot on the other pedal in one smooth movement. Jaya mounted and pedaled away.

"But, Clyde," I asked, "how is she going to get *off* the bike?"

"Oh dear. I have to show you guys that," Clyde said, pedaling after her.

The stopping and dismounting was my central fear. Ever since that champagne cruise ditch debacle, I kind of equated stopping with crashing.

Clyde brought Jaya over and showed us how to dismount. The key was to come to a smooth stop; then dismounting was easy. This probably sounds completely obvious to anyone who is comfortable riding a bike. But for those who aren't, the realization is profound: You can actually control your bike. Crashing is not a given. This was a sense of power you could learn to love.

About an hour and a half into the lesson, Clyde shouted for the whole class to gather around, and what had to be the happiest group of cyclists on the planet came pedaling in. We looked like an advertisement for Wellbutrin.

"You are the fastest-learning group I've ever had!" Clyde said. We all whooped for ourselves. "Now I'm going to explain gears."

Gears, it turned out, was one challenge too many for me to take on that day. I dutifully wrote down the information: *Gears help you exert the same amount of effort under changing conditions. In general, start out in a lower gear; shift up as you speed up and down as you slow down. Shift while pedaling, shift early and often, and adjust depending on how tired you are, what the weather and terrain are like.* But by the time we took to the yard to try out this new skill, my brain was not shifting smoothly anymore. My stomach growled, and my butt was so frozen I could no longer tell how low my pants were riding. Making decisions while pedaling was too much. Was it achievement enough for one class that I'd relearned how to balance, turn, and use hand brakes to stop? Could I save learning gears for another time? Yes, I decided. Feeling light-headed and slightly loopy, I brought the bike in alongside Jenny.

She looked like a totally different person. Her face was happy, her body relaxed. Her serious demeanor was gone. "I was so nervous when I saw the concrete yard!" she said. "I thought we'd be on a nice soft dirt path, maybe with some grass to fall on."

"Really?" I laughed. "Is that what you meant when you said, 'This looks hard'? I thought you meant 'This looks difficult.'"

"No, I meant it looks *hard*, like it would hurt to fall down on it!"

Jenny grew up in California, in an area "with plenty of bike lanes," she said, not giving herself the urban out. But she'd stopped riding when she was eight, after she crashed her friend's bike into a tree. "I wasn't hurt, but the bike was messed up, and my friend was, like, 'You can't borrow my bike anymore.' After that, I didn't want to invest in equipment I might destroy." After years of carrying that responsibility, she'd discovered in two hours that she could ride a borrowed Schwinn without destroying it. How much more capable are we than we give ourselves credit for?

As Jaya rode toward us, smiling serenely, I imagined her biking along the Danube or among rice paddies in Vietnam. I loved that she wasn't doing this for anyone but herself. "Send me a picture of you biking on vacation," I said, when we hugged good-bye. She looked like she was mentally planning the trip already.

Not everyone learned to ride that day. "Sometimes, people try but it's not for them. They're doing it for someone else, and they're miserable," Ross told me. "Some folks don't have the physical coordination to do it—you'll see that at times with people who are much older." There was an older woman in our group, who gamely pushed herself on her pedalless bike for the duration of the class but never balanced. I wondered if she would come back and try again.

"But most people get it, and when they do, the glee you see . . ." Ross's expression finished the sentence for him. Priceless.

Glee is what Bernard and Tracy were bathing in, as they returned Bernard's equipment and asked for advice on where to bike in the area. "We're going to go buy me a helmet right now!" Bernard said.

Ross and Clyde made a pitch for taking more Bike New York classes. "People are so excited when they leave here," Clyde said, "they want to get going right away. But there are a lot more skills involved when riding in traffic. You need a greater degree of control. You need to signal so that other vehicles can anticipate your actions. And to process a lot of information in real time and make appropriate decisions."

The National Highway Traffic Safety Administration reports that in 2010, 618 American cyclists were killed and an additional 52,000 were injured in motor vehicle crashes. Bicycling is a healthy, fun, relatively safe activity that's good for the environment and everyone should try it. But with statistics like that, it also makes sense to take classes on how to do it safely. Bike New York offers lessons in street skills, bike maintenance, buying a bike, and more.

"Tell me, Bernard, did you do this class for you or for your fiancée?" I asked.

"Oh, definitely for me," he said. "I really wanted to learn. And it's more fun to do it when you have a reason, someone to do it with." He smiled at Tracy, who smiled back in a way that made me a bit nostalgic.

"What a great way to start a marriage," I said to no one in particular, watching them leave arm in arm. *And what a great way to start my day,* I thought, as I walked toward my car to go home.

THE MORNING OF Gigi and Ruby's lesson was hot and sunny, and Kent and I woke up crabby. Despite my loading the car with what Michael would call "behavior modification techniques" (i.e., bribes), I was having trouble keeping my attitude in the realm of "positive reinforcement."

It had been a royal pain getting them fitted for bikes. The girls were between sizes, and I'd had to borrow and buy bikes and go back to the store three times, hauling the bikes in and out of the SUV each time, covering myself in grime. Ruby's feelings swung high and low—she'd prance down one aisle, exclaiming, "This is so cool!" and drag her feet down the next, whining, "I know it's too hard—I'll never learn."

Gigi's voice followed me over my shoulder in a continuous loop. "I could get scrapes, you know. I could fall. I'm bigger than I used to be. I'd be falling from higher up. That's gonna hurt. Do you think I need elbow pads?"

By the night before the lesson I had already indignantly declared to the girls that this whole enterprise was for their own good and complained about what an effort it was, how expensive it was, and how appreciative they should be. Kent was in even worse shape. He felt bad delegating this piece of parenting. Riding a bike should be as easy as . . . well, riding a bike! Why hadn't the kids been able to learn when he'd tried to teach them? What was wrong with them? What was wrong with him?

By the time the four of us entered the yard at Van Cortlandt Park, we were a hot, bickering mess of insecurity, self-loathing, and dread— not the optimal state for learning, I thought.

A young man with a messenger bag slung over his Bike New York T-shirt met us with an eager face and an easy smile. "Hi, there." He introduced himself: "I'm Dan Suraci." Dan had been a Bike New York instructor all the previous summer at Van Cortlandt, he told us. He rode his own bike forty miles a day round-trip from where he lived in Brooklyn to do it.

Feeling the youthful energy emanating from this twenty-something (*Forty miles a day! Across New York City! To teach city kids to bike!*) was like smelling the head of a newborn. Suddenly, I had no guilt whatsoever about delegating the job to Dan. He belonged in the hot, sunny yard with my kids. I belonged on the shady park bench, handing out snacks. "C'mon, honey," I said to Kent, inviting him to sit with me. Already I was in a better mood.

Volunteer instructors fanned out across the yard with a child or two each, and many moms and dads joined us on the bench, looking just as relieved as we did to abdicate responsibility and just take pictures and cheer. Other parents hung in there, gamely trying to help the process along. I watched as a little boy, mad at his father for trying to steer his handlebars, slapped his dad's hand. The dad time-outed the bike, looking like he wanted to kick it for good measure. Another child fell, howling, "You were supposed to catch me!" Her mother looked stricken. I felt sorry for them but glad to know other people struggled the way we did. Things sometimes look a lot easier than they are.

One boy went down with a clatter and his dad bellowed, "That's okay! At least you fell forward this time." I recognized the dad and waved at him. "Weren't you at the adult class with me?"

"I couldn't ask my kid to learn if I didn't know how myself," he said, as if for the both of us. "Back up you go!" he called to his son, who gamely got back on.

Doing something yourself gives you street cred with your kids. And knowing for yourself the tension of trying something new makes you respect your kids more as well, each and every time they get up and try again. It's so hard, making them do something that hurts, over and over. How will they not associate the activity—or you, for that matter—with pain? And if they don't pick it up right away, if their frustration gets the better of them, how can you keep your own impatience and disappointment from affecting their self-esteem?

Dan had none of that baggage. For the next three hours, he directed Gigi and Ruby—whether individually or together, while running alongside them or from a distance, with pedals or without—in the same encouraging voice. "Look at me—look at me—look at me."

Somehow, when a dad or mom says, "Look at me," it comes out "LOOKATMEPAYATTENTIONAREYOUNOTLISTENINGHOWMANYTIMES-DOIHAVETOTELLYOUTOSTOPLOOKINGATYOURFEET?" Even the most positive parent begins to lose heart if other kids are getting it and hers is not, and at that point even the gentlest "You can do it" goes through a scrambler, so the kid hears *"WHY CAN'T YOU DO IT?"* and thinks *There's something wrong with me.* And replies, *"NO, I CAN'T."*

"YES, YOU CAN!" the parent retorts, and off they go, to hell in a bike basket.

When Dan said, "Look at me," he meant simply "Look at me." That's all. The kids heard "Look at me" and that's what they did. He said it like a mantra, over and over, without judgment, without recrimination, without ever tiring or acting like there was anywhere else he needed to be.

My girls responded by doing what he asked, although they moved so slowly and carefully, putting their feet down at the slightest wobble, that they weren't getting enough speed to really balance.

Kent and I took turns with Dan, pushing them along and calling out, "Pedal—pedal—pedal!" until Ruby balanced on her own for a few yards before putting her feet down and turning to look at us, all smiles.

"That was great!" we all yelled, except Gigi, who frowned. All morning, the girls had been keeping tabs on who was learning faster. Ruby is a fierce competitor, and Gigi is five years older. Whoever learned first, it was going to be ugly.

Gigi pushed her bike over to the bench. "Can I look at Bonkey?" she asked.

Bonkey, a stuffed animal, was an extrinsic motivator (aka bribe) I brought for a successful bike lesson. Michael had suggested it. "Some kids are intrinsically motivated by an activity," he'd explained. "They want to learn to ride a bike because they think it's fun." We both knew this would not be Gigi and Ruby. "But if it's something you want them to do more than they do themselves, they may need an additional incentive to make it worth the pain."

Gigi longingly patted Bonkey, so named because it looked like both a bear and a monkey. "I'm tired. I want to stop. Do I have to keep going?"

"Yep," I said, gently taking Bonkey away. Gigi sighed and went back out. I sighed and patted Bonkey as well. The girls and I have something in common. We have all been told our entire lives that we're smart. Maybe because we're Asian, the stereotype follows us. But there are two problems with this. One is that, if you actually are smart in some areas (which most people are), and things come easily to you there, you don't get in the habit of working hard to figure things out. The second is that unless you really are gifted in *every* arena (and no one I know is), being told you're smart makes looking or feeling dumb intolerable. We're not supposed to fail. If we fail, it's the activity that's dumb, not us. Of course, underneath all of it is the ever-present fear that we're not really smart or capable at all, but we have to keep the world believing we are.

By sending Gigi back out there, I was making her work hard and telling her bicycling was not dumb, and hopefully not making her feel inept. Which her sister could really do if she learned this and Gigi didn't. Where was Ruby, anyway? I scanned the yard, and just then, Ruby, pedaling at a clip, tipped over and fell to the ground with a clang. I ran over and picked the bicycle off her, and she crawled into my arms, betrayed and bawling. Her pants were ripped, her knee was scraped. I administered a Band-Aid to her knee and a lollipop to her mouth.

"I'm done," she cried. "Can I have my Bonkey now?"

"Yes, of course you can," I said, just as her father came walking over, saying, "Oh no, you don't. You can't end with a fall. You have to get back on."

I gritted my teeth. *She's tired. She's done enough,* I said to Kent with my eyes.

Ruby protested. "I *knew* I was going to fall. And I did! And I ru- ined my pants. *I LIKE THESE PANTS.*"

"*So what?*" Kent said impatiently. His eyes said back to me, *Life is hard! Get over it! We didn't just go through a three-hour class for her to not like biking!* I felt our entire train derailing.

Dan came over. "It's okay, Ruby," he said nonchalantly. "I fall all the time. But then you get back up." We all cooled down, and after a cuddle and a snack, Ruby was ready to go back and try again.

Trying again was the point, Dan explained. A six-year-old's sense of balance is still developing. She may or may not get it today. But it was important not to let a fall stop her from trying.

Gigi, perhaps sensing all the energy building around Ruby, threw caution to the wind and pedaled hard—right, left, right, *splat*. Down she went, and I cringed, preparing for an angry outburst from her as well. But instead, Gigi popped up and threw her arms in the air in triumph, checked to see if we were all watching, and yelled, "I rode my bike!"

≫

MICHAEL STAR BEGGED TO DIFFER. "She rode how far?" he asked.

"Hard to say," I said. "She pedaled three times before falling." We had chosen to end on that high note, and at last the girls got to cuddle their Bonkeys. Kent and I made up, happily declaring it a successful outing as we left the park. I'd called Michael to report the news.

"That's not riding a bike," he said flatly. "There's something holding her back. I wonder what it is."

I thought of the time Gigi, around nine years old, spent an entire ice-skating lesson standing as still as an ice sculpture, in the middle of the rink. *What is she doing?* I wondered, for the first ten minutes. Then, as the end of her lesson approached and she still hadn't moved a muscle, I started to fume. This wasn't lesson one, two, or even three, mind you. Gigi had gone willingly to the class for five weeks, making slow but steady progress on her skates. So what the heck was she doing out there now? The skating season was almost over! How much did these lessons cost? The goal was to learn how to skate!

After the lesson, I'd skated up to her, all set to demand an explanation.

"Mom!" Gigi turned around with a huge smile. "I didn't fall once!"

So that's what she'd been doing for half an hour. Trying not to fall.

I hugged her hard, almost pulling us both down. My heart hurt with knowing exactly how she felt—how scary it is to go fast and not trust yourself to stop before hurting yourself or someone else in your path. How hard it is to fall and get up with your knees shaking and try again. It hurt knowing how many times I have felt paralyzed, physically and emotionally, hanging on to the little patch of steady ground beneath me. Like right then, when the only way my heart felt better was by holding Gigi and not letting go.

Gigi accepted the hug, and the next week went back to pushing and gliding slowly around the rink, teaching me that learning is seldom a straight path. That no one knows how much safety we need to absorb before we can dare to venture further on our own.

It was late spring now. Gigi only had a few more weeks before graduating to middle school. The idea of leaving her teachers and therapists was worse than letting go of training wheels. Michael and Gigi had a bond. Perhaps Michael felt the upcoming separation as well.

"I suppose I could teach her," he thought aloud. "I taught my kids, my neighbors' kids. I really want Gigi to learn this."

I held my breath. In all the years of working with so many therapists and teachers who could all be making more money doing other things, the generosity of spirit common to most practitioners in the field still caught me by surprise and touched me to the core.

"You know what, let's do it," he said. "I'd love to teach her."

Michael had commented before that my yoga teacher ways were good for teaching Gigi how to calm down but too soft for teaching her to do new and difficult things. I tend to emphasize acceptance. The world is a place where children are constantly being challenged. Yoga is a place to rest and be.

School OTs, on the other hand, measure performance by goals, stated in writing at the beginning of the school year. The ability to perform a task or skill is at stake. All efforts go toward teaching Janny to button and zip, Bobby to throw and catch, Max to organize his thoughts and write three legible sentences in a row. For each goal attained, a new goal is then set.

An article I'd once read in *Psychology Today* discussed the difference between self-esteem and self-efficacy. Self-esteem is about a person's sense of self-worth. It is an important feeling to instill in all children but especially in children with special needs, who get more reminders of the ways they are lacking compared to others. In yoga, the message is fundamental: All of us are valuable and worthy of love, regardless of what we can and cannot do.

Self-efficacy, on the other hand, is about believing you can achieve your goals. According to the article, people high in self-efficacy are more motivated, persistent, and empowered. They see tasks as skills to be mastered, setbacks as challenges to be overcome, failures as part of a learning process for future success. Every time we learn something new, we build a track record of success that builds self-efficacy, which means we have to keep trying things and not give up. Low self-efficacy breeds whenever we avoid things for fear of failing, and it has been linked to helplessness, anxiety, and depression.

I desperately wanted Gigi to have a sense of both self-esteem and self-efficacy. Heck, I wanted to have both. How much better to go through life thinking *I think I can* than *I probably can't, so can we just skip the pain and humiliation of trying and go eat ice cream instead?*

I was looking forward to watching how Michael taught Gigi to bike.

⤓

GIGI WAS STRUCK BY the novelty of meeting her OT's family, who joined us for her Saturday afternoon lesson at Harbor Island Park overlooking the Long Island Sound. She and Michael's nine-year-old daughter, Brooke, took curious peeks at each other, intrigued by this glimpse into their father/teacher's other life. Then they settled into comparing bikes and footwear. We promised them ice cream after the lesson, an extrinsic motivator that seemed to work for both of them. I thanked Marlene, Michael's wife, for taking time from their weekend to be with us. "He enjoys working with your daughter," she said. "He loves seeing kids make progress."

Michael took Gigi to a grassy slope, and established their familiar rapport. "This is going to be a thirty-minute OT session," he said, looking at his watch. "Just like school."

Gigi tried to pedal down the grass but fell, and after several more spills, Michael moved her to a paved path. The smooth surface was easier to pedal on, and she picked up some speed before veering off into a tree.

"That was awesome!" I yelled. It was awesome, in my opinion. She'd gone faster than she had ever gone before, and she was gamely getting up after every fall and trying again.

"No, it wasn't," Michael said. He called over to Gigi. "That wasn't awesome. That was good. Awesome will be when you're really riding and staying on the path."

Michael ran alongside her as she pedaled, with a hand on her back.

"Whenever he takes his hand off her back, she falls," Marlene observed. "She turns to look at him to see where he went. She's relying on knowing that he's there."

In OT and in special needs yoga, we do a lot of "scaffolding," using our own bodies to support students until they acquire the core strength to hold a position on their own. How much and how soon to back off is a delicate balance that a teacher has to remind herself to test, lest the student become dependent on the help.

And while Gigi might have been relying on Michael's presence, it was also making her push harder, to please him. She was going faster between falls. "Isn't it more fun when you go faster?" I asked brightly.

"No, it isn't fun," Michael answered for her. "Right now, it's just hard work." It was hard work for Michael, certainly. "I'm not as young as I was the last time I did this," he said, rubbing his back.

After a couple more falls, Michael gave Gigi the hard truth. He was going to stop running beside her. "I can't catch you," he said. "You have to do this yourself."

Gigi, who had been asking off and on how many more minutes until the lesson was over, immediately began pressing for early dismissal. "One more try, and then we stop," she said, setting her face as if preparing for a fight. She looked hot and tired. I knew Michael was, too. He checked his watch. It was about the end of the thirty minutes promised.

"Marlene's going to wait for you all the way by the water fountain," he said, sending Marlene about seventy yards down the path. "If you can pedal all the way to her, we can stop. Otherwise you have to come back and try again."

Michael gave Gigi a push and then let go, yelling, "Don't stop! Don't stop!" Gigi, seeing a strawberry ice pop in her future, did her level best, getting halfway to Marlene before wiping out. A deal was a deal, though, and she got back on and tried again.

This time, Michael sent her down the path toward me with a push, and walked behind her saying, "Pedal faster! Pedal faster!" almost more to himself than to her. Because Gigi was pedaling just fine. She first veered right, then left, then found center. She pedaled straight and true, away from Michael, her eyes up and looking into the distance, as if she knew she could do it. As if she had nothing to fear.

Except, perhaps, her mother. "Hit the brakes!" Michael called, as Gigi approached me. I was filming the moment, too excited to move out of the way. Gigi squeezed the brakes just right, coming to a perfectly controlled stop.

"*That's* what we're talking about!" Michael said, jogging to join us. We all congratulated Gigi this time, liberally—and sincerely—using the word *awesome*.

"How do you feel?" we asked her. Gigi's face was red, her eyes bright. She pressed her lips together and simply nodded. It seemed that the effort of not wanting to care, and then trying so hard, and the relief and pleasure of getting it after all, took away all her words. Almost all.

"Can we get ice pops now?" she asked.

Later, as we squeezed into a booth at the ice cream parlor and tried to slurp up our treats before they melted, Michael asked Gigi if she'd ever been Rollerblading.

I sucked in a breath. Brain freeze. *Please don't make me teach her that.* I thought, wiping my hand with a sticky napkin. The fifteen-year-old memory of the last time I bladed, speeding down 84th Street toward moving traffic on First Avenue and "braking" by crashing into two newspaper dispensers and a garbage can, flickered across my mind.

But here with this happy crew, in the afterglow of accomplishment, even getting back on those wheels seemed possible.

"No," Gigi said. "Would I like it?"

I sat and listened to them chat. Outside, children laughed as they rode by on scooters, flashing sweaty, dirty, happy smiles at us through the window. I let the ice pop melt in my mouth, enjoying its coolness and sweetness, for as long as I could.

CHAPTER 6

CONTROL

Driving

Y ikes! I thought with dismay, as I opened my car door. *I forgot to clean out the car!* I thought I'd thought of everything, but now, with the half-baked smell of our last three road trips wafting up at me, I realized I'd forgotten perhaps the most important thing. Quickly, I leaned in to pull fistfuls of snack wrappers, junk mail, and kids' socks from under the seats.

I didn't want to be late, but the car—a gray and looming Honda Pilot our kids named Storm—was a disgrace. I had dressed nicely for this appointment, not for cleaning, but it was more important that the car look good. I took the garbage out, gave the dash a dusting, and put provisions in (water bottles, power bars, fresh cookies). There. Storm looked more presentable now and, thanks to the cookies, smelled better, too. Was the music loaded? Yes. I wanted everything to be as comfortable as possible for my passenger today. About the only person I ever clean the car for anymore is my mother-in-law, but Carmen was a whole different kind of VIP.

Carmen, a human resources executive, a mother, and a young grandmother at age forty-seven, had stopped driving about fifteen years ago after a terrible car accident in which she was the driver and her then-fiancé and her daughter (eight years old at the time) were passengers. The three of them were badly hurt, and, although they all eventually recovered from the physical injuries, the memory of the incident sent Carmen into a cold sweat at the thought of driving again.

Today, I would be delivering her to a driving lesson, which felt like both an honor and a responsibility.

"You're driving her?" my mother had asked, looking horrified, when I told her the plan.

"Well, yes, Ma. She can't drive herself—that's the point. The school's all the way out on Long Island."

"You're going from Westchester? All the way to Long Island? In that big car of yours? You better be careful!"

"I know, Ma." I said what was on both our minds: "I don't want to get into an accident with her in the car!" We laughed—ha-ha! How ridiculous *that* would be!—and then looked at each other soberly. That would be just awful.

I tried to reassure her and myself at the same time. "It's not exactly the blind leading the blind—I drive all the time, you know."

It's true, I do drive all the time, everywhere, despite my roots. I grew up surrounded by New Yorkers ("If you can't get there by subway, why go?") and role models like Ma and my mother-in-law—smart, capable women who nonetheless delegated driving whenever possible to the men in their lives. I dug deep to become a driver, despite all my fears, and I'm proud of it. I've got a good track record, too. Just not with this particular vehicle.

We got Storm after our mini-SUV (named Clifford the Big Red Car) broke down on vacation in rural Vermont the previous summer.

"What does it mean if the little alarm light is lit?" I'd asked the mechanic on the phone. He was more than twenty miles away. "Is it okay to drive?"

"Oh, it's fine to drive on," he'd said. "You can bring it in after the weekend and we'll check it out."

"It's fine," I mouthed to Kent, who was driving as we spoke.

"Whew," he mouthed back.

There was no way to get around without a car where we were, and it was almost dark.

"Er, it's not flashing, is it?" the mechanic asked. It was an aside, like he'd only just remembered (or read in his manual) to ask.

"Hold on, I'll check," I said, looking over at the display. It was flashing.

"Uh-oh," the guy said.

Apparently a *flashing* alarm meant something slightly different: The car was toast. So, what happens when your negotiating position with the car dealer is "We have no way of getting home and our kids are freaking out because they thought they were going to Vermont to go on hayrides and see where milk comes from and instead all they have to play with is your Spin to Win Your Rebate spinner and—*Honey, leave the water cooler alone!*—we'll take any car we can drive off your lot *now*"?

You end up with Storm, an SUV much wider and longer than anything I'd ever driven before and not scaled for the tight spaces of the city or the winding roads of our town. After I had three fender benders within a month over the winter (don't judge, only two were my fault), I felt, every time I clambered up behind the wheel, like a rookie soldier mounting an army tank. Civilians beware.

At least I knew what to do if I got into an accident today, God forbid. I had our insurance and AAA numbers handy, and the friendly folks at GEICO know me by name ("Mrs. Anker! You again!"). Was the phone charged? Check. I plugged the GPS in, turned the old-fashioned road atlas to the right page, and then looked at the directions I had printed out for backup.

The plan was to pick up Carmen in New Rochelle, across the county from me, and bring her to Valley Stream, Long Island. The drive was going to involve traveling on five parkways plus the interstate and crossing the Throgs Neck Bridge, and could take up to two hours each way, depending on traffic. Every time I drive home from Long Island I want to crawl under the covers with a teddy bear afterward to recover.

I asked myself one last time whether this was a good idea. There were driving schools right in Carmen's town that could pick her up for lessons. Ten years ago, she had worked up the courage to try just that, and the instructor, who was used to simply telling students what to do ("Turn the key. Signal. Pull out.") put her in a panic. The last time she was pushed past her comfort zone she'd almost killed her family. This was too much, too fast, and she walked away fearing driving more than ever. The standard driving school that catered to sixteen-year-olds itching for the open road was not going to work for her.

Lynn Fuchs was worth the pilgrimage. Lynn had also once been hurt badly in a car accident where she was driving, with her daughter in the car. But instead of making her afraid to drive, the accident inspired her to become a driving instructor so she could teach others how to drive more safely. She opened her own driving school and also became certified in counseling and an expert in treating people with driving phobias.

Lynn estimates she has taught a staggering twenty thousand lessons in the past thirty-two years. In her office, the thank-you letters from students ("I just came home from driving in my neighborhood *all by myself*," "Thank you from the bottom of my heart for teaching my mother to drive, it has changed her life in more ways than we can say") cover a wall and overflow from baskets on her desk.

Best of all, she's a Long Island grandmother who gives big squeezy hugs and is reassurance personified. I took a class with her ahead of time to suss out her teaching style, which was gentle, careful, and clear. I, for one, have never been calmer in a car. Lynn probably has, though.

"You did very well today," she said at the end of our time. "But please, Patty, promise me this." She turned to me with her hand on her heart. "Promise me you will s*low down!*" *Yes,* I thought. *This is the right teacher for Carmen.*

I was starting to feel excited. This was a big day for Carmen! Her daughter, now twenty-four and with a son of her own, did not drive either. Carmen hoped to set a good example for her and her grandson. She was tired, she'd told me, of so many things. Of her two-hour commute each way to work (which would be thirty minutes if she drove). Of being a grown woman and dependent on others for rides. Of explaining why she didn't drive, which meant talking about the accident over and over. She wanted to stop being a victim, and today was the day everything could change.

As long as I could get us there and back in one piece.

I turned on the ignition, and the blast of cool air from the AC was instantly calming. With the car in park I took a deep breath and meditated for a moment, imagining a clear line of energy, a purple path on the GPS, from me to Carmen to Lynn. The engine purred reassuringly. I opened my eyes and slid the sunroof shade open. I had prayed for good weather, and there was nothing but clear skies above. The roads would be dry.

"Please God," I murmured, carefully checking every window and mirror for innocent civilians as I backed slowly out into the street, "don't let us get into an accident today."

≋

THE ONLY TIME I'VE ever run my car off the road was for a cinnamon roll.

Kent and I were vacationing in Glacier National Park, back before we had kids, when a long road trip was about blasting our music and gossiping about our friends, and not like being stuffed in a sack with five cats, a stick of beef jerky, and Raffi. Apart from worrying I'd be buried by an avalanche or get mauled by a bear, I was pretty carefree.

We stopped for cinnamon rolls in a town that was famous for them. I don't know why we thought they would be a good car snack. But we hit the road with a bulging paper sack of them, their warm, sugary fragrance filling our rented Ford Taurus. It was my turn to drive.

I didn't like the higher speed limits out West, but I couldn't argue with the conditions: The road was flat, the sky was clear, the river wound pastorally alongside the two-lane highway. We were heading north toward the Canadian Rockies, where the scenery and people were only going to get nicer. Kent held up a hunk of cinnamon roll in my direction.

I reached over, assuming he was handing it to me, but he held on, assuming I would tear off a piece. "What are you doing?" I asked, turning to him. *Let go of the cinnamon roll! Give it to me!* I don't think I said it out loud, because his horrified expression stopped my words midbrain. Following his gaze out the windshield, I saw the grasses of the Montana plains parting over the hood of the car. Rapidly. It took a second to process what was happening. Where was the road? Oh God! I had driven off the road!

You know the little round red reflectors stuck on thin metal poles at evenly spaced intervals all up and down the highway? Ever wonder what happens when you hit them at ninety miles an hour? They go "Ping!" and flatten to the ground.

"Ping! Ping!" *AAAAAAAAAAAAAHHHHHHHH!* we both screamed.

I don't know what possessed me to jerk the car back onto the road at such a high speed. Of course now I realize that at such a speed even a little turn of the wheel makes a big turn in the car. In this case, a big, violent turn careened us onto and across the highway to the side that bordered the river. I yanked the wheel again and spun us 180 degrees back onto blacktop, screeching to a stop in the middle of the road, pointing south.

Luckily, we were in Montana. The only people within miles were eating their cinnamon rolls at the diner we had just left. There wasn't another car in sight. So we sat gasping and shaking and howling at each other for a few moments.

"We could have ended up in the river!"

"We could have ended up in a ditch!"

"Why didn't you give me the cinnamon roll? That is so like you. *WHY CAN'T YOU JUST GIVE THINGS TO PEOPLE?*"

"Why can't you turn your head without turning the wheel at the same time? Is it too much for you to do *TWO THINGS AT ONCE?*"

"What are we doing sitting here? We could get hit by a truck!"

"Turn the car around!"

"I'm not driving—are you crazy?"

And so on, until we switched seats and Kent got us going in the right direction, and after a few miles of quiet when the twitching in my legs stopped, I was suddenly starving. "Want a cinnamon roll?" I asked. We laughed and laughed until we cried. Well, I cried, anyway. I rummaged around for the bag and, picking it up, realized it was empty, but for a slippery coating of sugar inside and out. "Where'd they go?" I asked.

The answer was "everywhere." The cinnamon rolls had gone flying—once we started looking we could see sticky gobs on the windows and doors, over the radio dials and in the AC vents. For the rest of the trip every time one of us reached to adjust the rearview mirror or flip the visor down, we stuck our fingers into another hidden pile of goo. "*Ew,*" I would groan.

"Yum," Kent would say, smacking his lips.

The truth is, as scary as it was, the only casualty that day was the cinnamon rolls. We were unscathed, and, although I was more careful to keep my eyes (and the car) on the road afterward, I did get back behind the wheel that trip. It became a funny story, in which Kent dubbed me Daisy Duke for the way I'd taken the Taurus off road, *Dukes of Hazzard* style. If I thought about how badly that episode could have ended I would've stopped driving. So I didn't let my mind go there. *All's well that ends well,* I told myself.

For Carmen, it was a different story.

≈

I FIRST MET CARMEN at a Toastmasters event, where she'd opened a speech by saying that years ago, she'd been badly hurt in a car accident. Attractive and well spoken, with big brown eyes framed by dark bangs and shoulder-length hair, Carmen instantly had our sympathy and our attention. We all instinctively prepared for a sad story, leaning forward with concern.

At which point, Carmen, standing at the front of the room in a well-cut blue suit and heeled pumps, began to demonstrate how impossible it had been to shave her legs with her various limbs in casts. Everyone watching burst out laughing, as Carmen, smiling with actual mirth, reflected on the ludicrous situation life had put her in.

That she'd survived something so major, sense of humor intact, impressed me. I asked to interview her, and a few weeks later she wrote back. We arranged to meet in the employees' café at the accounting firm where she works.

"I'm sorry I didn't get back to you right away," she said, leading us to a high table with tall, barstool-like chairs. "Every day I told myself, 'E-mail Patty back!' and every night I went home and said, 'I forgot again! Stupid me! Damn, damn, damn!'" Carmen punctuated each *damn* by pretending to hit herself in the head.

"No worries," I said, unpacking my laptop. "I appreciate you sharing your story. I know this isn't easy stuff to talk about." I perched on the stool, ready to get started. Carmen was on a lunch break, and I knew we wouldn't have much time.

Although we look completely different (I'm short and Asian, Carmen's tall and Latina) we soon discovered we have much in common: We both grew up in the Bronx, where having a car was an invitation to theft. Even worse, the thieves had attitude. In my neighborhood, burglars would steal batteries and tag the cars they hit with stickers, so they would know which ones to skip the next night. One guy had his car stolen and the only thing left in its space was the Club. Even if you could afford to replace your car, you could never replace your dignity.

In this context, lots of people we knew didn't drive. Carmen's mother didn't, which wasn't a problem since there was usually a bus or a relative to get them around. I didn't really start driving until my midtwenties, and Carmen didn't learn until her thirties. Like me, she was a nervous driver at first, sticking to local roads. And both of us, when we were still new to highway driving, had one crazy, dangerous thing happen to us on the road. But that's where our stories diverge.

It was 1997 or thereabouts, Carmen said, fuzzy on the date. Mark, her fiancé, lived on Long Island, where everyone drove. He wanted Carmen to learn, and at first, she was game. He taught Carmen himself, starting out on the streets of his neighborhood.

"But then," Carmen said, "he thought it would be a great idea for me to drive from his house on Long Island to my place in the Bronx." A great idea, if you're going for a Darwin Award.

This route had every challenge: bridges; tolls; city traffic; highway construction; and, worst of all, the LIE, the Long Island Expressway. On any given day, on any given stretch of the LIE, more than two hundred thousand vehicles travel on up to eight lanes of traffic, some of them sporting *I drive the LIE. Please pray for me* bumper stickers.

"I was terrified," Carmen said. "I didn't know anything—how to merge, accelerate, change lanes, nothing. I was looking for direction from him the whole time. It was like we were parent and child. 'What do I do now? What do I do now?'" In those days before E-ZPass, Carmen remembers not being able to get the coin in the basket at a toll booth, and almost crying as she got out of the car to find it on the ground. After almost two hours, she got them to her house in one piece, but her nerves were shot.

Was she proud? Had the ordeal boosted her confidence? I asked.

Not really, she replied.

"When I got to the Bronx, I was, like, 'Wow, I did this,' but I didn't feel at all comfortable or ready to do it again." But the following week Mark thought she should. "This is where I regret I didn't say, 'No, I'm not ready,'" Carmen said, shaking her head. "I was too passive. I'm not a pushover, I could have said no. But he'd been driving since he was fifteen, so I thought maybe he knew best. He was so strong in his opinions, it made me feel insecure about mine. 'Maybe this is how I can overcome my fears,' I thought."

Carmen took a breath, swallowed. "So the next week, we all get in the car. I'm driving, he's next to me, my daughter is sitting behind him. Seat belts on." She pantomimed clicking her seat belt and setting her hands on the wheel.

"I didn't even know how to get on the highway. I waited for him to say go. It was almost like I could close my eyes and just listen to what he told me to do." She closed her eyes, remembering. "I was in the right lane, which I don't like because of cars coming in. I tried to get into the center lane. I'm looking back, signaling, seeing the gap. He said it's good to go." She went. Just as another car in the left lane tried to move center, into the same spot.

I held my breath, part of me not wanting to know what happened next. How bad was this going to be?

"So Mark grabs the wheel and yanks it to the right to avoid that accident. And I—I lost control of the car. I didn't know what to do. All I could think was that we were going to crash to the right, the side my daughter and Mark were on, and all I wanted was to get the wheel to my side, so if we had an accident the impact would come to me. And so I must have turned the wheel, too much." It was happening in slow motion, she indicated, just like a movie.

The next part, Carmen doesn't remember. The car hit the cement divider. Her face hit the steering wheel. The car was a compact, a used silver Eagle, with no air bags. Carmen came to as the police pulled her out of the passenger side door. The driver's side of the car was smashed like an accordion. "That's when I realized I'd been in an accident," she recalled.

She paused a moment. We were mentally both by the side of the road, surveying the scene. I wished I had something to offer her—water, a blanket.

"My first thought was, 'Where are my teeth? My two front teeth were missing!' And, 'Where is my daughter?'" One ambulance took Carmen and Mark to the nearest hospital, which did not have a pediatric ward. Another ambulance took Carmen's daughter to another hospital that did.

Her daughter's pancreas and spleen were damaged. Mark had a collapsed lung. Carmen's arm, ankle, and kneecap were broken. She had head injuries and nerve damage; she didn't even realize at first that her nose had been flattened across her cheekbone. In the emergency room, people stared at her and she didn't know why. Days later, when she saw her reflection in a mirror for the first time, she started screaming. "I looked like the boy in the movie *Mask*," she remembers with a shudder. "I called my mom, hysterical, crying, 'I'm a monster!'"

Carmen had multiple surgeries and had to learn to walk again. After three weeks in the hospital she was discharged on crutches, and at last was able to go see her daughter in the other hospital. Which was the worst part of all.

"I saw her and started to shake. She was this little thing full of tubes and machines, and she was there because of me. I did this to her. It was all my fault."

"Does your daughter remember the accident?" I asked, trying to shake the image of an eight-year-old lying in the hospital, unable to see her mother for three weeks.

"Yes, very well. I think that's why she doesn't drive either."

Carmen told me more, about her marriage to and eventual divorce from Mark, about how she liked her job, commute aside, and how lately she'd been thinking it might be time to learn to drive, and how scared she still was to take the leap. I continued to listen and take notes, but all the while my mind was stumbling around, trying to recover something she had said earlier. What was it? It was something that struck me, when she said it, as wrong. Then it came to me. I stopped typing.

"Carmen," I said. "You said you lost control of the car."

"I did. I lost control of the car."

"No. You did not lose control of the car."

Carmen looked confused.

"Mark took the wheel, then you took it back." I took a breath, heat rising in my chest. *"You controlled the car—you were trying to protect them."*

She opened her mouth to speak, faltered.

The words came out of me in a rush then. Carmen, who described herself as passive and insecure, at the moment of truth had done the most courageous thing possible. And she didn't even realize it.

"You went with your instinct," I said, my voice cracking. The thought of her blaming herself for the accident for another minute was unbearable. "You were selfless!"

"I—I never thought of it that way before," Carmen said. A couple of men in suits walked by, laughing about something, coffees in hand. I had forgotten where we were. I lowered my voice so only she could hear.

"Please, Carmen," I said. "Never think of it any other way. You saved your daughter's life. That's the story she needs to hear." My eyes filled with tears that started to spill over. I wiped them quickly. Would I have acted as decisively, as selflessly, in that situation? God, I hope so.

"I never thought of it that way," Carmen repeated softly. For a moment, all her nervous energy fell away, and something like wonder lighted upon her face. From the first time I'd seen her, I'd been taken with her face. There was a subtle and intriguing asymmetry to it. Now I knew why.

"Did Mark blame you for the accident?" I asked.

"No, not outright. He would say things, sometimes, like how since the accident he couldn't run as well as he used to, things like that, which made me feel bad. He never said it was my fault. But I was raised Catholic. I feel guilty about everything."

"Listen to me," I said, hopping off the stool to stand closer to her. It felt good to stretch my legs; our conversation had tied my whole body in knots. "Do not feel guilty about this. Do not tell the story like you're a dangerous driver who caused this terrible accident. You didn't know what to do. You did the best you could given what you knew. Now, if you took proper driving lessons, you'd learn what you need to know, to make the safest decisions."

Carmen nodded, standing up as well. She didn't have to hop, it was more of an unfolding of limbs. She looked taller than before.

"I think I'm ready," she said. "I want to stop being embarrassed. Every time someone asks me why I don't drive, I say because of the accident, which was okay maybe five, even eight years later, but it's been fifteen. I'm forty-seven and I'm tired of being stuck. I want to change."

Her voice, her face, conveyed a sureness, a solidity, that was beautiful to behold.

~

ENTERING NEW ROCHELLE, traffic slowed to a crawl. If I were in Carmen's shoes, I would be a nervous wreck. Every additional minute of waiting was more time to reconsider. "I'm almost there!" I told her over the speaker phone. *Don't run away!* is what I meant. I considered making her stay on the line until I got there, but she sounded remarkably calm, considering.

Fifteen minutes later, I pulled up in front of her building and she emerged in a white sweater, jeans, and strappy high-heeled sandals, hips swaying, and smiling like she was on her way to have drinks with girlfriends instead of facing a trauma-induced fear.

"You look gorgeous!" I said, as she climbed into Storm. "How do you feel?"

"I feel good!" she said, putting her purse and a plastic bag with sneakers in it at her feet. "I just got a pedicure. I figured if I'm taking a day off from work to do this, I may as well live it up." She appeared excited to be on our way.

Carmen's energy spoke volumes about her basic temperament—relaxed and grounded, fun loving and confident—which had been so evident from that first Toastmasters speech, when she'd demonstrated her ability to laugh at herself and invited the rest of us to laugh with her. She reminded me of the girls I grew up a little in awe of, who you could tell from a block away spoke Spanish culturally and linguistically (as opposed to, say, Chinese).

Carmen was dedicated to her workouts, believing that looking and feeling good are things within our control, and we should do the things we have the ability to do. And she already had a track record taking on challenges. She'd learned to swim in her forties. "I got tired of being the one sitting out," she said simply.

So her not driving was not the product of free-floating anxiety or a lack of self-efficacy. It was the result of one really bad experience. Would I be driving right now, if I had plunged that rental car into the river in Montana?

"Hey," Carmen said, interrupting my thoughts, "how did you meet Lynn, anyway?"

I turned off the music to tell her.

☰

MY FRIEND EILEEN, also a native New Yorker, told me that she had learned to drive when she was thirty, because her fiancé wouldn't marry her until she did. "I had a nice driving instructor at the Women's Driving School in Manhattan," she said. "I'm sure they've changed their name by now—it's such an outdated idea!"

A women's driving school? What the heck did that mean? That women need to be taught differently? I thought, hackles raised. A Google search turned up "women's driving schools" in Saudi Arabia, Mumbai, the San Francisco Bay Area, and Texas. There were none so named in New York City anymore, but there was A Woman's Way Driving School in Long Island, created and run by Lynn Fuchs.

If I thought a "woman's" school might mean a softer touch, Lynn's credentials showed she's no lightweight. Her methods have been incorporated into the New York State Department of Motor Vehicles driver's manual. She's been a driver rehabilitation specialist at the Rusk Institute at NYU Medical Center and the recipient of awards and other distinctions. What caught my eye right away was her specialty in working with driving phobias and her personal story.

"Lynn was driving to a friend's house in her neighborhood," I

183

relayed to Carmen, hoping it wasn't bad luck to talk about car accidents while driving across Long Island with someone who'd had an accident on the LIE. It was 1974 or 1975 (interestingly, neither she nor Carmen remembered the year of her accident anymore). Her daughter was a toddler, and was bundled in a snowsuit in the backseat on the driver's side. This was before car seats, before seat belt regulations.

"Lynn had a green light and went through the intersection as another car ran its red light and crashed right into Lynn's car on the passenger side." Her daughter flew up between the front seats and ended up on the floor beneath the dashboard in the front. Luckily, she was not hurt. Lynn, though, had nerve damage and a bruised spleen and would be bedridden and need rehab for a long time afterward.

"I'm not a dramatic person," Lynn had told me. "When you're a parent, you minimize." After being taken to the hospital in an ambulance, Lynn refused to be admitted, saying, "I'll mend at home with a nurse!" so she could stay with her daughter. While recuperating (which she called "layin' there like a latke"), Lynn fixated on what had gone wrong that day. Although others pointed out it was not her fault and concluded with that, Lynn believed there must have been something she could have done to avoid the collision.

We were approaching Valley Stream, and the GPS was recalculating at the worst possible juncture. The roads were full of vehicles to avoid and signage to read. "I need to pay attention to these turnoffs," I said to Carmen. "I'll let Lynn tell you more."

Just before we reached the turn for Lynn's street, I realized I needed to be one lane over and moved left quickly, stopping short as the light turned red. Cars honked angrily. "I'm so sorry," I apologized to Carmen, cheeks burning. It was the last thing she needed right before her lesson. "C'mon, turn green," I whispered to the light. I could see Lynn's office; I'd almost gotten us there without incident. I couldn't wait to pull over across from the brick building with the baby-blue sign and get the hell out of my car.

Just as I put Storm in park, Lynn pulled up behind us in her black Volvo. She rolled down her window and waved us in. "Come in, come in!" she said. "I'm going to take us to a quieter street."

Carmen got in next to Lynn, and I was all too happy to climb in the backseat. With its big Student Driver signage and multiple mirrors and controls up front, the interior had the feel of a construction zone, of important work under way. I could see many reflections of Carmen and Lynn in the mirrors, hesitant and expectant by turns. Lynn drove us onto a side street, where she pulled over, parked, and said nonchalantly, "Let's switch seats and do some paperwork."

I had an image, as Carmen got out of the car, of her running away, hair flying, sandals flapping. *Wait, your sneakers!* I would yell, throwing them after her. *Go! Be free!* To her credit, she came directly around to the driver's side and got back in the car.

"Let's see your learner's permit," Lynn said, opening a Filofax of documents. Together, they filled out forms and chitchatted. After a while, Lynn looked over at Carmen in the driver's seat and asked, "How are you doing there?"

"I'm okay," Carmen said, looking around tentatively, her voice a little husky. "It's a little scary." She shifted her weight in the seat.

"A little scary is better than a lot scary!" Lynn laughed. Then, eyes and face full of warmth, she said, "Look, it's natural for it to feel scary—for you, your fear was not from hearing about accidents in the newspaper—it was a real situation." I had briefed Lynn on Carmen's history. "Right now, if you think about driving, you don't know where to look or what to do. Then you add the fear of what happened before, and of course there's this feeling of *I don't even know where to start!*"

Carmen nodded vigorously. *Yes, yes.*

"But once I educate you and you learn how to do it right, you'll realize you're in control of your own decisions," Lynn promised. "You'll see, you'll be the master, sitting there."

Carmen smiled, a little dubiously, but smiled nonetheless. "That's what I'm hoping for." She shifted again, adjusting the seat belt with her hand.

"Are you comfortable?" Lynn asked. "You don't need to be belted right now. We'll start by getting more of your history."

Carmen held the belt across her chest with both hands. "This thing saved me, that time," she said, quietly. "This keeps me safe."

"Tell me about what happened," Lynn said.

Carmen recounted how Mark had taught her to drive, how the accident had happened. Lynn shook her head while fanning herself like she couldn't believe it. "You were nowhere near ready for that! Local driving for a few hours and then, 'Let's do the LIE'? OMG is my response."

"Well, the first time I did it, I made it, so he felt like I should be able to do it again," Carmen said.

"Yes, but just because you survived, a body in the seat with him pushing you through, doing what he told you to do, doesn't mean you were a driver!" Lynn cried.

"Exactly!"

"Yes, you made it, but you were feeling, 'I could not do this again by myself and be comfortable. I am not owning this.' This wasn't you, looking, judging, making decisions. You were looking for guidance the whole time. This was a scenario you were not supposed to be in."

Carmen kept nodding.

"You thought, 'He's got a license, he's smarter than me about this, I'm going to give it all up to him.' Even though you knew you weren't up for it. Have you thought of the control you could have had if you spoke up? You could have changed that whole story. It was his fault for suggesting it but yours for agreeing. Can you own that?"

Tough love, I thought, cringing a little. I didn't want Carmen to feel more burdened by guilt. But she was nodding, still. "Yes, yes, I can," she said.

"So ever since, you've been punishing your own self: I'm not safe at it, I made bad decisions, I can't be trusted. And you've built up a phobia. That's your story, your old story. Even though the truth is that your skill level at the time did not show you were ready to multitask that way. Even though the truth is, taught correctly, you will be able to drive safely. But you've been addicted to your story and using that story to keep you out of the driver's seat. You've been holding on to it, even though it's not *true.* Because the old story saves you, in a way, from facing the truth."

Carmen stopped nodding and just sat quietly. "That's really profound," she said. I saw the words in her reflection more than hearing them with my ears. "Wow."

Wow is right. "I'm not good at it" is a story line I'm familiar with. Along with "I might hurt someone" and "I don't want that responsibility," it forms a beginning, a middle, and an end to a conversation. As plots go, it sucks.

"So let's see if we can make a new story." Lynn put her hands up, like reading a marquee. *"I want to live in the truth OF WHAT IS.* If you take away that old story, what's left? Who are you, really?"

"Um . . . I . . . a . . . woman afraid to drive?"

"No, that's the old story," Lynn said impatiently, waving it away with her hands. "Look at who you are." She turned to face Carmen, their brown eyes meeting. *"You are responsible, intelligent, safe.* That is the truth. That is the person you have always been. Do you think you would drive, or do anything, in a way that wasn't safe or responsible?" The way she said it, it made so much sense. Carmen's very job, in human resources, was about ensuring that the bases were covered in every situation.

"I wouldn't say that about everyone. Not everyone should be driving," Lynn added. I hoped she wasn't tipping her head toward me. "But you should. Because you're responsible, you're going to be an *asset* on the road. And because you want it so badly, you're going to do your absolute best to learn everything there is to learn."

"I do want this," Carmen affirmed.

"When I'm finished with you, you won't want anyone but you to do the driving!" Lynn exclaimed. "You'll see how much better you are than many of these people who've been driving a long time with bad habits. You'll be telling Patty, 'Give me the keys!'"

"Hey!" I protested, all of us laughing.

Lynn's positive energy beamed out of her, reflecting off every mirror in the car. Carmen was almost bouncing in her seat.

"This is going to change my life. It's going to give me freedom!" she said joyfully.

"It's a new day!" Lynn cried. "A new story—headline it! Responsible Human Being: Better Than Most Behind the Wheel! Say it with me! *I am a safe person. I am going to be a safe driver!*"

The inside of the car became the happiest place on earth. Laughter! Clapping! A seated Macarena! I didn't want to break up the party but . . .

"But, Lynn," I piped up from the backseat, "what about all the bad drivers . . . out there?"

Honestly. The roads are full of them—drivers busy texting; yelling at kids; putting on makeup; taking pictures to post on Facebook; or in the case of the guy who passed me on the right yesterday, eating pizza *while reading the newspaper.* The other night I'd been at a party full of moms who by the sound of it had arrived by the grace of God alone.

"My wipers are so old, I couldn't see a thing in the rain!"

"I'm so tired I can't even see where the road ends and the shoulder begins!"

"I think I may need glasses!"

And we would all be driving home, after a glass of wine, at the same time? I considered staying the night.

With some things, education is power. Take my fear of public toilets, for example. When I had to toilet train Gigi, the thought of lifting her onto the toilet at a city playground gave me nightmares. I wanted a decontamination shower for both of us after every highway pit stop. "Look, missy," I wanted to say, "you can leave the house but you have to stay in diapers. That's the deal."

But then I read in a magazine that girls develop urinary tract infections not from using public toilets but from trying to hold it in. "I have never seen a case of a disease transmitted by sitting on a public toilet," a doctor quipped in the article. The trick was to use public toilets properly: Dry the seat. Hold a piece of toilet paper when you touch anything. Step away from the toilet when flushing to avoid spray. (*Ew.*) Wash your hands with soap. And you'll be fine!

This news changed my life. Airports and gas stations? No problem. It also boosted my productivity at the office and allowed Gigi to go to preschool.

But in driving, isn't too much information TMI? The facts are bad: More than 32,000 people died in motor vehicle crashes in the United States in 2011 alone. Unless you willfully ignore reality, why would you ever put yourself at risk?

"First of all, there are crazy people everywhere," Lynn said matter-of-factly. "You can't control anyone but yourself."

This was not comforting.

"Second of all, knowledge *is* power. The knowledge of what to do to avoid the bad drivers on the road. People, especially people who are afraid to drive, don't realize how many things you can do to avoid a collision on the road. With every accident, if you could pull it apart and ask, 'What went on?' we would see that it didn't have to be."

That, Lynn explained, is exactly what she'd done after her own accident so many years ago.

"How could I have known that woman was going to run the red light?" she asked herself over and over. "My light is green, I can't control her." Then, it came to her like a thunderbolt. There were *clues* that the woman wasn't going to stop at the red light. *Her tires were still rotating when they should have been slowing to a stop.* "If I was looking for them earlier, if I had seen those wheels rolling, I could have applied my brakes and avoided the whole accident."

As long as Lynn was "layin' there like a latke," the theory could only be a theory, but it excited her beyond belief. She couldn't wait to get better and get on the road to test it out.

When she did, it changed everything about how she approached an intersection. She called it the Fuchs Formula of Wheel Position and Wheel Rotation. She copyrighted the method and it was incorporated into the New York State driver's manual in 1991 and was taught to countless students for many years afterward. You can read more about it on her website, but the gist of it is this: If a car is approaching from a side street, do not assume that it will obey its stop sign or red light or that it will turn the direction of its turn signal. Look at its front wheels instead. The *speed* of rotation will tell you if the car is preparing to stop, and the *angle* the wheels are turned will indicate the direction it's heading. If the wheels are not slowing down, pad your brake and prepare to stop or get out of the way, and tap your horn.

World-class athletes, performers, and chess players are said to comb over all their event footage afterward for errors, looking for ways to improve their skills and avoid future pitfalls. Practice doesn't make perfect if you're making the same mistakes over again. Why should driving, where there are lives at stake, garner any less introspection? Accidents are so often chalked up to bad luck, the other guy's fault, or one's own poor instincts—and the reaction is often no more than a prayer that it won't happen again—when what is called for is a clear-eyed examination of what we're doing that is dangerous and what we could do differently in the future.

"Driving is not something people are just good at," Lynn said to Carmen. "You have to be taught how to make safe decisions, how to move your hands, what to do with your feet, where to look." And to bother to look. "I can't see because of the tree," I had said at one point during my lesson with Lynn. "Look through the branches, look between slats of fences, move your car up a little if it helps. Really try to see. It's your responsibility to look for clearance," Lynn replied. "Especially at intersections, you want to look early and deep to give yourself time and space to react to anything that's going to cross your path." It was remarkable, when I paid closer attention, how much visibility I had after all.

"Let's talk about how to judge your position on the road," Lynn said, turning to Carmen. "Do you think we're parked close to the curb or far from the curb?"

Carmen looked through the windshield at the front end of the car. "Um, close to the curb?"

"How do you know?"

"Because the end of the car looks close to the curb?"

"Yes, it does look close; in fact, the front end looks like it's on the curb, doesn't it? But we know it's not, the car is flat on the road. So how do you know what you see is true?"

"Hm. I don't know."

"When we look down, with what's called 'low aim,' what we see is misleading. It gives us the incorrect width and perspective. To get a clear picture of where the car is lined up, you need to use 'high aim.' Focus your eyes up and out into the distance ahead of you and behind you, to judge where you are compared to other objects you see. Are you lined up with the car behind you? How far is that car from the curb?

That will tell you the real story." We craned our heads, looking for landmarks around us.

"People tend to look at things they're afraid to hit, and if you look with low aim, it looks so close! Then they end up veering away from a bumper they're nowhere near and causing an accident on the other side."

How many fender benders could I avoid by applying this advice immediately? I was so excited. The folks at GEICO might never see me again.

"Think of carrying a basket of laundry through a doorway," Lynn explained. "Would you fixate on the doorjamb to figure out how to walk through it? No, that would be weird. You would look straight through the doorway to judge how much space you have and walk through the center."

"Don't fixate on the thing you fear—keep your eye on where you want to go!" I exclaimed, thinking of bicycling, parenting, and life.

The next exercise was similarly revelatory. Lynn got out of the car and walked the length of each side, while Carmen tried to spot her in the mirrors and out the windows. This exercise pointed out exactly where the blind spots were and how easy it is to miss moving objects. Then they practiced looking with high aim out the back *early*, so as not to be surprised by a car suddenly appearing next to you in a lane you want to enter. Carmen was getting acclimated to being in the driver's seat, taking in the world around her, understanding the kinds of decisions she would need to make.

Then Lynn asked Carmen how she would turn the wheel. Carmen balked. She tried to mime it, but second-guessed herself, stopped. She looked flustered. "It's okay," Lynn said, patting her arm. "That hand-over-hand action can take months to get smooth and automatic. We're about at the end of our time."

I looked up in surprise—had we been talking for two hours already?

"I think this was a fruitful consultation," Lynn continued. "Do you feel more comfortable in the car?"

Carmen looked flushed with relief.

"We'll start the driving lessons next week. If you come back, you'll see how we do it, how we'll be breathing, we'll make some jokes in between, and how you'll learn. I think we've made some breakthroughs today!"

"I totally agree," Carmen said, as she sank back in her seat.

"Look at you, you look different, sitting there!" Lynn said with a smile.

"I feel comfortable now." Carmen rested her head back, looking tired but satisfied. Then she popped up. "You two have given me such epiphanies!" She turned to Lynn. "You're right—the accident was my excuse, and it worked! I let myself believe I was a bad driver. People would understand why I didn't drive. So I never had to do anything about it. And you—" She turned to look at me in the backseat. "I didn't lose control of the car. It was taken from me, and then I took it back."

"You are changing something you've held on to for so long. You are very brave," Lynn said with true respect. "You should go home and celebrate with a birthday cake. The birth of a new story!"

"Oh, my grandson just had his fifth birthday," Carmen said. "He calls me Nina. I told him, 'Nina's going to learn how to drive today.' He said, 'I wish I was big so I could go with you!'"

"You will be his good example! He will say, 'I want to be safe, like Grandma.' You are going to break that cycle of fear."

Growing up, Lynn had the ideal role models for driving—her parents and grandparents were all safe and calm at the wheel. "I associated the car with vacations, going to see friends, wonderful times," she said. Her accident never made her reconsider that. "I love driving," Lynn said happily. "It connects me to so many places I want to go, people I love, things I want to do. It takes me to my destination."

Carmen didn't have the benefit of that early experience, but she was proving now that it was not too late to start a new cycle.

Before leaving, I had a question for Lynn. "I've been wondering," I said, "what makes your way a 'Woman's Way'?"

"Oh goodness," she replied, rolling her eyes. "Do you know how many times men have asked me, 'What, you teach women how to put on makeup and have car accidents?'" We all groaned.

"You know what I tell them? 'You're right, women do have a bad rap for driving and I realized why. Who taught them to drive years ago? *Men!* Maybe now that there are more women teachers, there will be better drivers everywhere!'"

We all had a good laugh at that one.

"'A Woman's Way' is my way of teaching," Lynn explained. "I teach men and women with the same approach—I educate and connect personally and emotionally. I use my counseling background when it's helpful. The point is not just to pass a test but to know how to think and react and to enjoy driving for life."

On the way home, traffic stopped entirely leading up to the Throgs Neck Bridge. Following the example of a few hundred cars stopped in front of us, I switched the ignition off and tried to find out what the holdup was, but the traffic report had no information. Luckily, I had packed according to Lynn's philosophy: Always have snacks, a book, and toilet paper in the car, because breakdowns happen and you might as well make the best of them. We ate and listened to music. I handed Carmen my notebook and invited her to write some thoughts about the day while they were fresh. Eventually, the news came across the radio that a ten-wheeled tanker had crashed, causing an oil spill. The cleanup was going to take a while. We didn't say it aloud, but I'm sure we both wondered if anyone was hurt.

"This is why so many people don't drive," I said to Carmen. "Even if you've never had an accident, you see stuff like this." The scene in front of us on the bridge was Exhibit A, B, and C put together of Things That Could Go Wrong If I Drive. The list of things my nondriving or nervously driving friends are afraid of includes (but is not limited to) crashes, flat tires, getting lost, bad weather, darkness, deer, other people honking at them, traffic jams, running out of gas, bridges, tunnels, trucks, detours, falling asleep at the wheel, panic attacks, highways, city streets, and the entire state of New Jersey. Add squeegee men and carjackers for Bronx residents of a certain age. It's hard to let that go.

Then there are fatalistic drivers, who drive everywhere but with a sense of dread in their stomachs every time they pull onto the road that this could be the day when they come up against something they are not equipped to handle.

Sometimes, an early experience with feeling out of one's element can scare a driver off the road. When my mother, learning to drive at age thirty-seven, went on her first big street, a four-lane boulevard in Toronto, the experience was so nerve-racking that she avoided highways from then on. "The teacher said, 'Drive here! Change lanes! Do this!' And I did follow his orders, I did it," Ma recalls. "But when I came home I told Ba, 'You know how people like Liu Chengsi from the Communist air force flew to Taiwan to defect? Oh, and so dangerous for them to do that! Well, I just defected from that road to here, I'm safe now. Liu Chengsi flying over the Taiwan Strait *ye mei you wo ne me jing jiang* [couldn't have been as stressed out as I was]!"

Sometimes, it's a personality trait, a hesitancy to be assertive in the way a driver often needs to be, that keeps people off the road. My friend Eva, who drove during college in New Hampshire but stopped once she moved to New York City, said, "I was never comfortable pulling out into traffic, or knowing when to make a left turn. It was like timing getting into a jump rope or a revolving door. The longer I waited, the more flustered I'd get, thinking of the people behind me getting impatient, and then I'd get more nervous, which makes everything worse."

Eva's also a wary pedestrian, slow and careful when she crosses streets. She wears a hat with reflective fabric when walking through her Queens neighborhood at night. Her fear there is understandable— every year a few pedestrians are hit by cars on Queens Boulevard. Those crazy drivers! Which is actually what made her, after ten years of not driving, consider taking back the wheel.

"My parents are really not very good drivers," Eva once told me in my kitchen. She and her husband, Jeff, were over for dinner. Neither of them drive, and she had just proposed that it made sense, evolutionarily speaking, for some people to be out there, braving the wild animals to bring home dinner, while others tended the home fires and read good books. Eva is a children's book illustrator, her husband a lawyer. They're smart, funny New Yorkers who could make not driving sound like anthropological destiny. For the good of the world!

"I remember them once going the wrong way down a one-way street; another time our car caught on fire." Her parents didn't take care of the car, so they were always having breakdowns. "Once, we barely made it off the highway in a snowstorm. Every time we got out of a situation okay, they would say, 'God is watching over us!' They never once said, 'We were stupid people for bringing our kids out in a storm.'"

"So you associated being in the car with being stressed," I said, pouring us some wine. Even hearing the stories jangled my nerves. We clinked and sipped. To God watching over us.

"Yes. And living in New York City it's easy to avoid being in a car generally. But I realized two years ago, when I was with my parents in their car and *the brakes weren't working,* that I'm not safe with them driving."

"Jeff, what about you?" I asked, calling to him over the sizzling of the vegetables in the pan. He was in the living room, talking to Kent. He had gotten a license long ago but had not driven in decades.

"I prefer to let the professionals drive," he called back.

"He means taxi drivers," Eva said.

I looked at her. She looked at me.

We cracked up.

"You realize that's hysterically funny, right? He trusts NYC cabbies more than himself?"

"Yes, and it gets worse!" Eva said, lowering her voice, giggling. "When we visit his brother in Alabama, his brother drives. His brother, with glaucoma and a bad leg. We are constantly putting ourselves in the hands of people who are not reliable drivers!"

Choosing between feeling endangered in the passenger seat or not seeing their relatives felt like a poor choice. "Maybe I'd be better off just learning how to drive again myself," Eva said, as I turned the food onto a platter.

"You know what I think," I said. "Dinner is served."

≈

WHAT I THINK is that I want Eva and Carmen and everyone I know to get comfortable driving for a lot of reasons. In case of emergencies. To broaden options for travel. To be less dependent on others, especially bad drivers. These are all obvious reasons that every prospective driver weighs against the fear, risk, time, energy, and cost it would mean to take on the challenge of learning to drive safely themselves. But apart from the practical reasons for becoming a competent and confident

SOME NERVE

driver are the emotional ones, which I myself didn't discover until I had to, the summer I was twenty-five.

I had gotten my license when I turned twenty-one in order to get into bars; I resolved the whole drinking and driving dilemma by focusing on the first and foisting the second on Kent. He was the copresident of the car club at his college. He loved cars. He loved me. Why wouldn't he want to drive me around for the rest of his life? I was a nervous driver, flustered by the tension in his voice when I missed a turn and his involuntarily hitting a nonexistent brake pedal at every stop sign. I felt like a bad driver, and bad drivers could hurt people. He was a good driver, so for the sake of society, he should drive and I should talk about feelings on all our car rides, each of us playing to our strengths. The plan had worked for years. Until now.

We were living near Boston at the time. Kent was in law school and had accepted a summer job at a firm overseas. I was telecommuting from our apartment, and because I had no coworkers around and the campus emptied for the summer, it was very quiet for me, home alone. I'd lost my husband and my chauffeur.

At first it was fine. I puttered. I put little leashes on our cats and took them out for walks. I ate breakfast, lunch, and dinner by myself, every day. When I wanted company I walked to Pizzeria Uno and ate at a table for one. Slowly, I went crazy. Crazy enough, after a few weeks, to think about driving the car to go somewhere, anywhere.

I did drive a bit, three blocks to the Star Market and back, when the cats needed litter. But what if I could actually drive myself somewhere interesting? I could visit friends in a neighboring suburb. All I had to do was invite myself to dinner and hop in the car. I could drive to Walden, for . . . more solitude. Scratch Walden. I could drive to the airport and fly somewhere. No money to go anywhere. Okay, I could drive to the airport and . . . surprise Kent when he came home!

It was a random thought, on par with wondering whether I would

198

be happier working in a nail salon. But the thought of the look on Kent's face made me laugh like a crazy cat lady, sitting by myself at Pizzeria Uno. He would be stunned. I had to try.

I had four weeks to get ready before he came back. I plotted out routes on maps, I asked everyone I saw, which was pretty much limited to store clerks, which way they would drive to Logan. I listened to traffic reports, which almost made me reconsider. The Big Dig was on, a massive construction project that turned all Boston's winding roads into a hellmouth of detours and traffic-choked streets. But then I would think of Kent, slack-jawed at the sight of me behind the wheel. And I'd turn back to "Traffic on the 3s" on WBZ radio.

I made friends with the car. It was a hand-me-down Jeep Cherokee stick shift, cranky and always on the verge of collapse. Kent kept it as a badge of honor. Car club presidents don't own nice Hondas with service contracts that never need service. They own cars that present challenges—like windows that, once rolled down, didn't roll back up, and gear shifts that came off in your hand if you clutched them too tightly, which I invariably did. I practiced on local streets, toughening myself up so that when I stalled I could wave cars around me with authority.

A business trip to New York gave me the opportunity to grill two cabbies on the ins and outs of getting to and from the airport. "Talk me through everything you're doing," I said, taking notes on which lane, which exit, which turn, coming and going. They asked when Kent's flight was getting in, probably so they could avoid the roads at that time.

And then the day came.

It was clear weather. It was not rush hour. This was before GPS, when navigating meant memorizing the instructions. I visualized the route. I talked myself through it, like Tom Hanks in *Cast Away*. In fact, I had been my own company for so long that I saw nothing peculiar whatsoever about narrating the entire ride like a tour guide: "And coming up on the right, we'll be merging onto I-93 South, where we'll let this gentleman go first because he clearly has important places to go. We're signaling, we're breathing, all is good." It all went smoothly. I think I got honked at once. When I parked the car at the airport, I got out, locked it like I owned it, and walked to the terminal like a new woman.

I greeted Kent with a big hug, wondering if the world could tell something was different about me. We had our *It's so good to see you*s and *I missed you*s until we got his bags and Kent said, "Where do we get a cab?"

Here it was, the moment I'd been waiting for.

"We don't need a cab," I said, oh so lightly. "The car's parked this way."

"The car's parked? How did it get here?" Kent stopped, trying to compute. "Did you . . ."

The "reveal" I have captured on my memory reel forever after: "I drove!" I triumphed. "I drove here!"

"By yourself?" Kent asked, incredulous, but grinning with surprise and delight. "From Somerville?"

"Yes! All by myself! I practiced all summer!"

"Wow! I can't believe it!" He said it several more times as we made our way to the car, both of us marveling to find it parked between the lines in one piece. "Do you want me to drive us home?" he asked.

"No way," I said, walking to the driver's side and unlocking the door. He climbed into the passenger seat.

"Wow," he said, taking in the different view, turning to look at me behind the wheel. "This is weird!"

Get used to it, I thought, smiling as big on the inside as the outside, as I drove us home.

I was never the same after that summer. "Pushing through fear is less frightening than living with the underlying fear that comes from a feeling of helplessness," states Susan Jeffers in *Feel the Fear and Do It Anyway*. It's scary to not be able to drive, or to drive without confidence in one's own judgment, or to be a passenger in someone else's questionable hands. So much of the fear of driving comes from the fear of losing control or the fear of having control and not knowing what to do with it.

Here is what I learned on the way to Logan Airport: The best way to not lose control is to be in control. And being in control is *awesome*.

If it sounds strange that I would have such difficulty facing my fears in so many areas, but find the resolve to push through them in driving, arguably one of the most legitimately dangerous activities there is, it's a testament to how significant the benefits are. "Being in the driver's seat" is a metaphor for being in charge of your life for a reason. Knowing how to drive means you can get yourself and your loved ones where they need to go. I still feel fear when I drive; I think everyone should. It keeps us alert and careful. But then I do it anyway. The mental freedom from having to rely on others is huge.

≫

A CAR BEHIND US HONKED, startling me and Carmen from our chatting. Traffic was starting to move again. I revved the engine, thinking of what Lynn had said about being honked at. "If someone toots at you, look at the situation. Why are they tooting? Is it dangerous? Are they telling you to pay attention? Or are they just in a bad mood?" If it's the latter, she said, treat them the way you would if they cut in front of you at the supermarket. Smile and say, "Go ahead, have a good day!" and think, *God send her some grace today, she needs it*. I chose to view this toot as a hallelujah chorus.

Turning onto my road that afternoon, I felt like a cowboy returning

to the ranch after a long cattle drive, putting Storm up in his corral—
Storm, whom I'd started the day so mad at for being so big, so ornery,
so difficult for me to control. I now understood so much better how to
maneuver us both more safely through the world.

As I collected my things, I saw my notebook on the passenger seat,
opened to Carmen's page. Here, with her permission, is what she
thought that day:

> I was afraid when I sat in the driver's seat today. I felt tons of
> pressure. I thought she'd want me to drive just so that she could
> see what my driving was like . . . what level was I at.
>
> She asked me if I knew what hand over hand meant . . . I
> mimicked the gesture and realized I was doing it wrong. I
> immediately felt pressure that I'm not going to be able to do this.
> She then told me that this was a skill that could take months to
> learn. I felt relieved . . . I can't believe I can say that when
> speaking about driving. I was scared for that moment, of turning
> the key and getting started. But she made me feel that by the
> time we do it, I'll be ready.
>
> I let go of my old story and am beginning a new one. I feel
> empowered. I feel energized, excited, ready. I am looking
> forward to being able to drive on my own.

A FEW MONTHS AFTER our dinner, Eva did go back for driving lessons in
her crazy neighborhood in Queens. "The fear before was much worse
than actually doing it," she said. The skills she'd once possessed came
back quickly, as did the areas that made her nervous. "It was good being with a teacher who was calm," she said. "When enough people tell

you, 'You're too timid! Go, go, go!' it makes you feel more timid, and it doesn't teach you to figure out for yourself when to go."

Driving is not for the faint of heart. You can cover your eyes in a scary movie, but when it's time to pull out into traffic, you need to do it with authority. In *Nerve*, Taylor Clark writes that driving simulations research shows that "cocky drivers perform best in tense situations: Their arrogance muffles the effects of fear. . . ." The only way to have true authority is to earn it through experience, and not just "more of the same" experience. Clark contends that to become an expert in anything, experience has to be "*challenging*, focusing on your weaknesses, and it has to include *feedback* that allows you to fine-tune your approach." Eva's teacher plans to do just that—he will be making her do the left-hand turns on crowded streets she fears, to practice knowing when and how to make them with confidence.

For Carmen, because of her accident, it will likely take even more exposure, more teaching, more coming up against her fears, because our bodies are wired to remember the events that threatened us the most. "The interesting thing about fear memories is that you can learn them instantly and they last a lifetime," says psychologist Michael Davis in *Nerve*. But the brain is also endlessly eager to learn new things. What Carmen can do is put her fear memory in its place, reframe it as a learning experience, and start over.

≫

A FEW WEEKS LATER, I brought Carmen back to Lynn for her second session, and asked if anything had changed since the first.

"Well, people always ask me why I don't drive, and I used to say, 'I was in a bad car accident' and that explained it, no one would question why I didn't anymore. But since Lynn helped me see what a big excuse it was becoming, now when people ask me why I don't drive, I don't mention the accident at all. I say, 'I'm not driving yet, but I'm taking lessons.' The accident is in the past."

"Well—" I took a breath "—that's a big freaking deal!"

"I thought so, too," Carmen said with a smile.

The amazing thing I've learned about putting something in the past is how much it frees you up in the present. Once you let go of the fear, you have energy and mental space to take in information that before seemed overwhelming. Say bye-bye to the boxes of old papers, Mary Carlomagno had instructed me. And in their space, so much new writing flowed out. Same with Carmen. Good-bye to the accident. All of a sudden, turning a wheel, applying a brake, assessing the road become eminently learnable skills.

After fifteen years, one false start, a turning-point meeting with Lynn, and weeks to process and begin thinking of herself in a new, more capable way, Carmen had turned the page. In Toastmasters, the best storytellers are the ones who are not in the conference room but in the scene. The day Carmen told me the story of her accident she was not in the café with me, she was back in that used silver Eagle. How many times had she told that story, until it was part of her DNA? Now she was ready to trade in the wreck for a much better ride. We can't always choose what happens to us, but we can choose which stories to relive and how to etch them into our memories.

This time, when Carmen got back behind the wheel of Lynn's car, there was no question that she would be driving it before the lesson was through.

Right before she turned on the ignition, Lynn put some spa music on. "Oh, isn't it calming," she murmured dreamily, resting her head back on the passenger seat and closing her eyes. I had just gotten out of the car to film the moment, and now I leaned back in the window.

"Lynn! Don't go anywhere! We need you here!"

She laughed, sitting up. "Don't worry, I'm here. This is just to relax everyone a bit. Now," she said to Carmen, speaking in a low, soothing voice, like Glinda the Good, "turn the key, and you'll hear three clicks. The first engages the electronic ignition, the second turns on the power, the third turns on the engine. Go ahead."

I stepped back and pressed Record, trying to keep the camera steady despite my thumping heart.

Carmen turned the key. *Click, click, click.* High aim.

Aim high, baby.

Carmen looked, signaled. And drove.

CHAPTER 7

STOKE AND PLEASURE

Surfing

adies and gentlemen"—the flight attendant's voice crackled over the speakers—"the captain has turned on the fasten-your-seatbelt sign in anticipation of turbulence."

Anticipation? I thought, checking that my belt was securely fastened. *Does that mean this is going to get worse?* I was on my way to Chicago for a writer's conference, in a window seat over the wing, the row I'd always heard was most stable on a plane. But my seat was rising and dipping like a skiff hopping waves, and out my window the wing was shuddering. Ordinarily I would meditate to calm my nerves, but that never works for me on a plane. There's nowhere to ground my energy when I know I'm hurtling through space.

It was February 29, a Leap Day. If the plane went down today, our death anniversaries would come only every four years. I shook my head, wishing I could pull down a window shade on my thoughts.

I needed a distraction, and fast.

Before stowing my bag I'd taken out a book Patrick, the surfer-writer I'd met at Bread Loaf, had sent me, *Pacific Passages: An Anthology of Surf Writing*, edited by Patrick himself. I'd gotten to know him a bit better after our initial meeting and discovered I'd been wrong about him on a couple of fronts.

First of all, despite his white hair, at a fit forty-eight he wasn't too old to be surfing. Second, he was not some flaky surfer dude. He was a married father of two and a university professor of French who was also savvy enough to build a profession around his passion for surfing by teaching and writing about it. "Is it hard to teach college kids how to bum around on a beach?" I'd asked, not quite believing he was serious.

"Well, they may register thinking it's all about fun in the sun," Patrick had said, "but I sneak in some good history and cultural studies along the way." He'd sent me his book as proof.

I'd started reading it at home and found it edifying to discover that Westerners as far back as Captain Cook's seamen in the late 1700s and New England Protestant missionaries in the early 1800s had greeted the sight of people surfing in Polynesia with horror. The seamen thought of the ocean as full of disease and death, and the missionaries thought playing in it a terrible waste of time. All beliefs I, and my Chinese mother, could get behind.

But I wanted to finish the book before seeing Patrick again at this conference, where I hoped to get his take on how I should face my fear of open water. Besides, it seemed like the perfect midwinter, midair armchair adventure reading. I clicked on my light.

It turned out it wasn't until the mid- to late-nineteenth century that writers like Mark Twain began to write about surf-riding as adventure. Then Jack London, with "Riding the South Seas Surf" in 1907, propelled it into the realm of sport and combat, man versus nature. "It is all very well, sitting here in the cool shade of the beach," he wrote from Waikiki, "but you are a man, one of the kingly species. . . . Go to. Strip off your clothes. . . . Get in and wrestle with the sea; wing your heels with the skill and power that reside in you; bit the sea's breakers, master them, and ride upon their backs as a king should."

The testosterone wafted up from the page. Were I a man, I might feel inspired to go big game hunting now. I looked at my polished fingernails. *No wonder I don't get it,* I thought. *I don't have enough Teddy Roosevelt in me.*

I do, however, have a little M. Leola Crawford in me. She wrote in *Seven Weeks in Hawaii,* published in 1917, about touring Waikiki and meeting Olympic swimmer Duke Kahanamoku, "a splendid looking fellow, about six feet tall and dark as an Indian." I sat up. *Now we're talking.* "I am quite fond of 'the Duke'!" she writes, and he entices her out for a surf lesson. When she gets knocked about in the waves, the Duke pulls her out and gives her a lomi-lomi massage. I sighed. Men might risk death to conquer nature and prove their manhood. Ladies like Leola? Might risk death for a massage.

But who was I kidding? When surfing reached its popular culture height in the late 1950s and early 1960s, it became shorthand for a carefree, partying lifestyle, à la *Gidget.* A main character of that film is the Big Kahuna, whom Patrick describes as "a beach bum who lives to surf and follow the sun." If I had ever taken up with the likes of him, I would have been disowned by my entire family. And by that, I mean all seventy-five million Changs around the world, and probably the Lius, the Wongs, and the Lis, too. There would be no justification for indulging in such a nonproductive activity, only shame in putting personal pleasure first. Without work, hard work, I would have no purpose, no reason for being. No identity at all.

≫

ONE SUSPICION I HAD about Patrick from the beginning turned out to be spot-on. I assumed you'd have to be, as we say in the Bronx, a little "loco in the coco" to surf. But the extent of Patrick's loco became apparent when I opened an e-mail from him at the beginning of February.

It was a link to a surf shop about two hours north of Chicago, in St. Joseph, Michigan.

"You want to surf *LAKE MICHIGAN* in *FEBRUARY*??" I replied. "Are you *CRAZY*?"

"Well, it could be *BRISK*," he wrote back, "but it could also be fun!"

He was planning to go to the conference anyway, he reasoned, and Chicago was closer to open water than he and his "waveless ass" were going to get for a long time, since he lived in Missouri. Besides, he'd never surfed on a lake before. He could write a magazine story about it. The fact that it was winter only added to the drama. The way he put it, it almost made sense. Until he tried to rope me into his plan.

"Aren't you supposed to be facing your fears?" he asked. "Haven't you been practicing for the beach?"

Yes, and yes. I had been swimming laps and practicing what Patrick suggested, like relaxing in the water ("Fighting the ocean is pointless, it just burns oxygen that you need"), and holding my breath while swimming ("You will go under. Practice so you know you can hold your breath when you do"). I was surprised to see how doing the first helped with the second; just as with yogic breathing, staying calm makes everything easier. I drew the line, however, at this: "In Hawaii they practice for big surf by picking up rocks on the bottom of the ocean and running as far as they can along the bottom before they run out of air. You could try that in the pool," Patrick had suggested. "I did it at Waimea Bay. Was fun!"

"That sounds like *SO THE OPPOSITE OF FUN*," I replied. Also, I wasn't about to touch anything I might find at the bottom of the pool at New York Sports Club.

I did, however, practice "popping up," pushing up from a prone position to a surfer's stance on my yoga mat, trying to imagine how I would possibly balance if my mat were moving.

But all this was preparation for the distant future, the warm weather months down the road. Not now.

"No riptides, no sharks, no sunburn . . ." he cajoled.

"Hypothermia! Frostbite! The middle of nowhere with a crazy man!" I replied.

"You just need to keep your stoke up," he said. "Think about it."

What I thought was this: Why does the idea of surfing fill me with fear and Patrick with excitement? What is the "stoke" he's always referring to—what world champion surfer Shaun Tomson calls the "fire being stirred up in the pit of one's stomach" that "captures the feeling surfers get when they see good waves"? When I tried to say, "I'm so stoked!" in the loud, clipped voice of a New Yorker, Patrick corrected me. "You have to say it slowly. I'm *sooo stoohhked*," he said, emanating calm and pleasure in a way I found maddening. I was certain I'd never been *that* stoked. What was so thrilling about surfing that made it worth all the trouble to learn and all the risk?

Once, Patrick got caught inside a wave as the leash attaching his ankle to his board wrapped around his legs, dragging him under; luckily he popped to the surface and the waves washed him in before he drowned. Another time the fins of a board raked across his face, breaking his nose; he still has the scar. He's gotten caught in rough currents that tore his board away or broke it in half. Still, he goes back in. He reminds me of my friend Kus, the coffee roaster at Antoinette's and a race cyclist, who is so able-bodied and energetic you would never know that two years ago he spent six months in a head brace after a bad bicycle crash. After a year of rehab and living a tremendously limited life he found himself full of fear and not only about bicycling. "Bad things happen and it changes your view," he relates now. "I was stuck for a while. But eventually you have to get back to your true nature." He slowly started cycling again and making other shifts in his life, expanding his business, getting engaged. "It's hard to explain, but when I'm on the bike I feel the most free, the most like myself," he says.

The thought of going to such lengths for fun was unfathomable to me. But perhaps it was about more than chasing a high. When Patrick was seventeen he left high school and home and spent three years surfing and traveling with one of his brothers. He says it was a formative time of his life. *Perhaps the search for stoke is his way of keeping in touch with that aspect of his identity,* I thought, *instead of letting it go by the wayside like so many childhood dreams. Perhaps hitching a ride on Patrick's surf safari would show me another reason to face my fears.*

So I said, "Yes, let's do it."

I didn't think it would actually happen.

Even the proprietor of the surf shop—the only one open in winter in the area—sounded dubious when Patrick inquired. "It depends on the ice shelves," he said. *Ice shelves? If the words "ice shelves" are involved, we're not going in,* I thought happily. *We'll drive around and look at the lake, talk about the dangers of surfing while drinking hot chocolate.*

But Patrick was determined. "If there is any chance of going in the water, I'm going," Patrick said. "What is your size for the wet suit?"

I started to get nervous. *Ah, it was a Mary Poppins piecrust promise I'd offered,* I told myself—*easily made, easily broken.* Two days before the trip I chickened out. *I'm at my dr, who says surfing would be a bad idea given my body's current state of decrepitude,* I e-mailed Patrick.

Who is this doctor? he zipped back. *I want to speak to him. Or is it just you, getting cold feet?*

I wasn't making it up. I had just gotten whiplash standing in my very own bathroom, when one of the girls, pretending to be a horse, had reared up while I was leaning over her for the tub faucet and accidentally bashed into my face. ("That's some recoil action you had there," the doctor said. Yes, these things only happen to me.) But I also had cold feet. *Who wouldn't?* I thought to myself as I lay in bed, fretting. What if my muscles seized up? What if I broke another bone, with no medics, no lifeguards on hand to help? Patrick wasn't a lifeguard, although he did know CPR. "Do you have any do-not-resuscitate orders I should know about?" he had asked.

"Let me make this clear. *I WANT TO LIVE,*" I had responded. "Unless a lake monster eats my face. In that case, throw me back."

I didn't want to saddle Patrick with the responsibility of hauling my face-eaten, half-frozen body out of the surf and explaining to my husband what had happened. I could just ride shotgun and write about Patrick going to insane lengths to find stoke in a Michigan winter. I'll take pictures, take notes, I told him. Let the risk taker take the risks.

Whatever you say, Patrick said. He was fine going in alone.

Now, as the flight attendant asked us to prepare for landing, I rummaged in my bag for another book, *Surfing the Great Lakes*, and read about what Patrick was about to do.

Twelve thousand years ago, glaciers more than a mile thick dug deep depressions into the earth's surface, I read. Lake Michigan was created by glacial meltwater in those depressions. In the summer, the water is in the seventies, but in winter, "shelf ice, snow and generally inhospitable conditions characterize Great Lakes beaches."

When I looked out the window, I gasped at the sight of Lake Michigan, whitecaps cresting over water so vast it looked like the ocean, and knew I'd made the right decision. The entire sky hung low on our descent, gray storm clouds racing us to land. Without sunshine the water had a matte density to it.

Patrick, I thought, as the plane finally made its way toward a bumpy but safe landing, *is going to be really freaking cold in that lake.*

WHEN I GOT INTO the rented Jeep Cherokee with Patrick the next morning, the temperature outside hadn't yet cracked forty degrees. He was wearing a flannel shirt, slacks, and hiking boots, with his winter coat tossed in the backseat. I had two sweaters on under my long black down coat, tall waterproof boots under jeans, wool gloves in my pocket. This did not look like the start of a surf outing.

Part of me couldn't believe Patrick would go through with it, although he sure was acting like he was serious. He handed me directions to the surf shop in Michigan as he started the car.

"We may need to go to a dive shop for thicker scuba wet suits," he said, as we drove out of the city. "The surf shop only rents the thin kind."

"The surf shop doesn't rent thick wet suits because no one is dumb enough to want them, dummy," I said.

Power lines decked the highway; a pair of geese flew over the flat brown and gray landscape of Illinois. If the idea of searching for stoke seemed incongruous in this setting, Patrick didn't seem to mind. He taught surf culture to Midwesterners who had never surfed before, after all. He was used to stretching their imaginations by letting them into his.

So as we drove, we took turns telling each other stories about things the other knew nothing about.

Patrick had once discovered the origin of the Hawaiian paddle-out ceremonies held when a surfer dies. "I had to do a lot of hunting, but I found out who the first surfer was to have one in his memory and why," he said. His voice held the pleasure and pride of discovery, both as a surf enthusiast and a writer.

It was a surfer named Jose Angel, back in 1976. "He died diving for black coral. He thought it was two hundred feet down, and tied a twenty-pound weight to carry him down there. But it was actually three hundred and forty feet, and the weight pulled him to his death. His friends paddled out where he used to surf, formed a circle, and told stories about him and bid him farewell and aloha."

We rode in silence for a while, as I pondered whether a sport with a traditional death ceremony is one I should even consider doing. After a respectable time elapsed I decided to meet the maudlin with the macabre.

"Imagine this," I said. "A man, an explorer, is crossing a glacier. Suddenly, the ice crumbles under his feet and he slips into a crevasse. Maybe the crack in the ice is narrow, he only slides partway down. But his foot gets stuck, and the more he struggles to pull it out, the warmer he gets, melting the ice around his body. Maybe the sun is up and he's sweating from the effort, the ice is too slippery to get a hold on. At a certain point he's chest deep in ice and doesn't have enough strength in his arms to pull himself out. Down, down he slides, until he's too exhausted to move. And then the sun goes down and the ice around him freezes solid again," I paused. "Leaving only his head sticking up above ground."

"Like quicksand," Patrick murmured.

"Isn't that gruesome??" I asked, shuddering and grinning involuntarily. Historical novelist Andrea Barrett told me this story when she was researching and writing *Servants of the Map*, a collection which features a surveyor mapping the Himalayas in the 1860s. There's no end to the awful ways explorers have died exploring frozen wastelands. The only way to deal with such horror is to delight in it.

"So, if the water is around freezing level, Patrick, be careful. It might freeze around you, leaving only your head sticking out!" I cackled.

"You like ghost stories, don't you?" he said. "You're like a little girl who likes to be scared."

I actually hate ghost stories. But I don't mind freezing-to-death stories when I'm warm and dry.

Surfing has always been about more than surfing, Patrick said, taking us to cheerier ground. The surf life was about good times with friends, the feeling of well-being after a day spent in and around the water, the sharing of stoke. What interested Patrick was whether that bond between surfers might be even stronger here than in California, because the tribes are so much smaller, the waves harder to come by, the setting more pristine, the conditions less tested. The wild Midwest.

That this drive, from Illinois through Indiana into Michigan, could end in surfing seemed unfathomable, until Patrick said, "Hey, here's the lake," and there it was, out his window, stretching as far as the eye could see. "Let's go take a look."

He pulled off the road by a sign that read Lookout Point, and we hopped out. The point was well above the water. I didn't go anywhere near the edge.

"This is what surfers do on a surf safari," Patrick said, walking ahead of me. The frosty wind took the ends of his words away. "They go looking for the best spot: Where are the waves? What is the wind like? Where are the crowds? Although I don't suppose we'll have a problem with crowds today." The trees were bare, the water was slate green by the shore, light blue on the horizon, and the cold air blew right through my sweaters. There was no one to be seen.

Patrick had explained that waves on a lake, generated by wind, are shorter and choppier than the ocean swells caused by storms miles and days away that bring the powerful, high waves surfers like for the longer runs. But you could travel to sunny Mexico to surf for a week and never get any good waves, too. That was called getting skunked. And here in the great cold North, Patrick was cheerful. No ice shelves in sight.

"There's movement out there, looks like enough to work with. This could work!"

∿

WE DROVE INTO ST. JOSEPH, a town that could have been on Cape Cod. An ice cream parlor advertised malteds, the bright awnings of toy stores and souvenir shops a siren song for sticky children and tired parents. I imagined it packed with families on their way to the lake in summertime. But right now the street had none of the *Endless Summer* vibe. It was quiet.

We walked toward a sandwich board advertising a winter sale at the Third Coast Surf Shop.

"How do they stay open in the winter?" I asked. "How much business can they have?"

"They're not surviving on surfboard sales," Patrick replied. "They sell clothes, gifts. Remember, it's not just about the surfing itself. What they're really selling is stoke."

We stepped into a brightly lit, colorful shop, and caught a whiff of what smelled like the candle on my altar at home. "Smell that?" Patrick asked. "Surf wax. Love that." It was summer in here, the front of the store crowded with bikinis, hats, and sunglasses. I gravitated toward the racks of jewelry and books, as Patrick headed toward the surfboards hanging on the back wall. A saleslady dressed in a fluttery turquoise top introduced herself as Erica and asked how she could help.

"I want to rent a surfboard," Patrick said, "and check out the conditions on the lake. We're just visiting for the day, so if you have any advice on where to go, that would be great."

"Okay, cool," she replied. "Let me check the wind for you."

Okay? Cool? Not, "Are you crazy, it's forty degrees outside, you'll freeze to death, I'm calling the cops!" Michigan folks must be made of hardier stuff than New Yorkers.

"We had a lot of wind yesterday, but it's died down," Erica said, eyes on the weather conditions on the computer. "You might be better off waiting a day or two if you can."

"No, we're only here for the day," Patrick said. "We'll take what we can get."

"Are you going in, too?" Erica asked, looking up at me.

"No," I said.

"Well, she should," said Patrick. "She's writing a book about facing her fears."

"And the last time I tried to face my fear of the ocean a wave broke my foot," I reminded him.

"So this is perfect because it's not an ocean," Erica said brightly. "And especially on a day like today, the waves will be small."

"Yeah, but it's also winter! I don't know if it's a good idea for me to have my first surf outing be in the freezing cold. Would you surf out there on a day like today?"

Erica ducked her head sheepishly and said, "No way! Not that I couldn't, but why? Why be so cold? But I'm from here—I can do it in the summer. Do it while you're here! Tourists do come to surf Lake Michigan as a lark, but hardly any can say they surfed it in the winter! How awesome!"

"But what if I get hurt?" I asked. "What if I die?" Michiganders must be less litigious than New Yorkers.

Erica looked me straight in the eye, and said, "If you die out there today, I promise I will personally start a foundation for you." We all laughed, but she was serious, too. It was a girlfriend's promise, a chick-to-hen vow. I have been pressured by men into situations over my head many times. But I have seldom been steered wrong by another woman. If Erica had doubts, as a woman, she would be honor bound to qualify encouragement with: "Of course, you should do what feels right for you."

What she said was, "I've got a board you can both use. Go to the dive shop and get a wet suit. Face your fears!"

≋

THE LIGHT BLUE BOARD, large and stable, perfect for beginners, was strapped to the car. We got lost on the way to the dive shop, giving me time to get good and nervous. Patrick didn't push, just quietly addressed my every whimper with reason.

"What if I freeze?"

"You'll be cold. But then you'll warm up. We won't be out there too long."

"I didn't bring a bathing suit or a towel."

"You don't need it. You'll have a wet suit. I have a towel."

"What if I can't do it?"

"I have every confidence that you can."

"What if it ruins my hair?" I'd taken the rare opportunity of having only myself to care for this morning to blow it dry and put on makeup, too.

He had nothing to say to that. So he cut to the chase. "I think if you want to face your fear of the water, there are lots of ways to do it, and if you don't do it here, you'll have other opportunities down the road. But we're here. The lake is here. The equipment is here. All you have to do is go in."

I watched the ball sail into my court.

"Oh, and one more thing. When we're done, you'll be able to say you went surfing on Lake Michigan in the winter. For the rest of your life."

He grinned. He had me, he knew it. We're both suckers for good stories.

Gulp.

A FEW MINUTES LATER I was fending off a full-blown panic attack.

Wolf's Marine in Benton Harbor is a warehouse of playthings for those who love the water. In other words, a place I would normally never set foot in. The surf shop had had enough colorful tropical touches to lure me in, enough pretty things to make me want to stay and spend money. The dive shop, in contrast, was huge, cold, damp, and smelled like rubber. A guy land of equipment and tools for taming the sea—boats, tubes, inflatable rafts, snorkels, and scuba suits—hung floor to high ceiling.

Scuba suits are thicker and less flexible than surfing wet suits, Patrick had warned.

"We may look like the Michelin Man. But better to be warmer."

Putting on the scuba suit was like squeezing into a unitard woven out of bungee cords and three sizes too small. It took all my strength to pull it on. I pushed the curtain of the tiny dressing stall open and Patrick looked at me critically. "It's supposed to be fitted. It bulges around your shoulders. Too much room." *That's because of all the shoulder muscles I'm missing,* I wanted to say, but I was breathless, the suit was so tight around my ribs.

"Here, put this vest on under it," he said, handing me another impossibly small swath of black rubber. "That'll fill it out, and it has a hood. Oh, and take off your socks."

In the midst of wrestling out of the suit to get out of my socks, I glimpsed my flushed, sweaty reflection in the mirror. Red welts were appearing on my neck and arms. Hives. *Crap.* They come when I'm stressed or my skin gets rubbed the wrong way or, in this case, both. My hives come on with an itchy, agitated feeling rising in my chest along with a prickly heat over my skin. The way a lot of people who have eczema also have asthma, I feel the hives in my lungs as well as on my skin. The only way to weather them is to calm down, take cooling breaths, and wait for them to pass. Right.

As I pulled the vest over my head, the material got caught on my hair and wouldn't move up or down. A really hard yank might pull it down, but it might also rip all my hair out. As I tried to wriggle out of it, the vest trapped both my arms up overhead, wrapping around my face. I felt like Houdini, except I had no idea how to free myself. And my belly button was showing. It became hard to breathe.

Oh no. I'm not going to die out on the lake, with a medevac rescue and on the ten o'clock news. I'm going to be smothered by this vest in this dressing room. No one will hear me scream. I'll flail around, trip, and fall face-first through the curtain, taking it, and the entire tower of clearance sale snorkel fins down while I'm at it. The salesguy will find me, passed out on the dirty floor like a scene from Law & Order. *Erica will start a foundation. Patrick will lead a paddle-out ceremony. Except I'll never even have paddled out. It'll have to be a dressing-in ceremony.*

I couldn't stand it another second. I yanked as hard as I could. The vest pulled down. The hood slurped up my head like a suction cup, exposing only my face. The sound of my breath and the coursing of my blood roared in my ears.

Once I got the suit back on, I found Patrick standing by the display case next to the cash register, looking at gloves with the sales guy. "I can't hear anything," I said. Patrick said something that looked like, "I know, don't you hate that?" He asked me to touch my toes, paddle my arms. I could do it, but the resistance of the material made every movement an effort. *What if I get tired out? What if I can't hear his instructions?* Tears filled my eyes. Oh no. *What if I cry, and the tears freeze to my face?* That had happened to me once, as a kindergartner in Canada, on the snowy day when no one picked me up from the school yard. Poor me! The universe was closing in on me, the compression from the suit, the shallowness of my breath, the prickling of my skin, the pounding of my heart. The light in the room dimmed, like a computer screen going into sleep mode. I felt dizzy.

Don't Panic. I could picture the book on my nightstand back home. That was its title, and every time I saw the cover, it made me want to panic. What did the book say? I couldn't think. *I can't do this*, I thought. *I need to get out of here. I need to get out of this suit.* And then, *Oh crap, what if I have to go to the bathroom?*

"Can I take off the hood for now?" I asked. *Please say yes.* I held on to the counter, which felt solid and smooth. Patrick nodded, and I peeled off the hood, taking great gulps of fresh, cool air through every pore of my sweaty scalp. "Unzip the back for now—you'll be more comfortable," he added, and I did. *Aaah.* I could hear, I could breathe, I could think. The room came back into focus. I felt so much better.

"Hey, what if I have to go to the bathroom?" I asked.

Patrick smiled. "You know what surfers mean when they say, 'I just gave myself a sauna'?"

My mind was blank.

"It means they went in their wet suit."

Standing there in my rented wet suit, I had an out-of-body experience. One of me was there next to Patrick, absorbing what he was telling me *(me! with my fear of public toilets!)*: that I was essentially wearing a public toilet. The other me was running through the store shrieking and tearing the wet suit off my body in shreds. I would have done it, if the suit weren't so damn hard to take off. Instead, I started to laugh. My tension broke in pieces.

"*Eeewww!*" I said, punching Patrick in the arm. "Now I'm going to spend the entire time wondering if you're peeing in your wet suit."

"It is gross," Patrick agreed. "Don't think too much about it, and you'll be fine." He got his receipt and picked up the bag with his gear. "Ready to go?"

I zipped up my booties. I was.

≋

BACK OUT ON THE STREET, Patrick loaded our gear into the car as I stood around in my wet suit attracting attention. We looked like a Jeep ad. A couple, a bit older than us, walked by. The woman was bundled in a big red Christmas sweater and the man's weathered face was flushed beneath a wool cap. "Did you go out already?" the woman asked earnestly.

"No, we're getting ready to," I said. "I'm wondering if my friend is trying to kill me. Would you go out on a day like today?"

"In this weather?" the woman asked. "No! But you go for it! Ya gotta do things. That's what makes life interesting."

"I'm from New York City," I said. "This is not my natural environment."

The man's eyes twinkled. "You'd make a great Michigander," he said. I had the feeling that was high praise indeed.

Feeling much more cheerful in the car on the way to the beach, I noticed that every bump made me bounce in my seat. *Boing! Boing!* Wearing the wet suit felt like being in a bouncy castle.

"The suit is made of neoprene," Patrick said. "It's a synthetic rubber that's full of tiny bubbles that help insulate you and make you buoyant. Water flows in and your body warms up a layer of it to keep you warm."

I did not like that idea one bit. I had thought the wet suit would seal the water out, not let it in. How was that going to feel, when the water came in?

The parking lot at Silver Beach was deserted. Patrick stopped close to the sand, near a play area of yellow and red plastic climbing tubes and slides. In my normal life, I might have pulled into this spot on a winter's day, to release my cabin-fevered, snowsuited children to play. There was nothing normal about arriving here with a man from Missouri in a wet suit.

"It may be hard to hear out there, with the water and wind and our hoods up," Patrick said. "So let me tell you what to expect."

First, he explained, we would put the surfboard on the sand and practice popping up from paddling position to surfer's stance. If your left foot naturally lands in front, you're a regular foot. If it's your right foot, you're a goofy foot. I had practiced at home—I was a goofy foot. When you're popping up, Patrick warned, keep your head up. If you look down at your feet, you'll fall.

Then we'd go in the water. I'd lie on my belly on the board and Patrick would help get me to the waves, and then he would turn me around and push me into a wave, headed toward shore. He'd shout, "Up, up!" But in case I couldn't hear him, I should just pop up as soon as he let me go. The waves here were short, so I wouldn't have much time to get up on the board before the wave lost momentum.

"What if I fall?" I asked.

"When you fall, relax your body, cover your face with your hands, and go with it. We'll be pretty shallow, because I need to be able to stand. The downside to being shallow is there's less water to cushion your fall. But you'll know you can stand. When you get up, look for your board. You don't want it between you and the wave. Got that? Or it'll hit you in the face. All right?" He knew better than to wait for my answer. He opened the door, and cold air rushed in. "Let's go!"

We were the only people about. I wondered if the birds were

surprised to see us. Patrick lay the surfboard on the sand and patted it. "On your belly."

It's a direction I give yoga students all the time. *Lie down in Advasana. Relax the belly into the earth. All the tension you normally carry, let it go. Let gravity take it away.* I had a feeling this was going to be more stressful.

"Hold the rails," Patrick said. The wind was making it hard to hear. I put my hands where he pointed, along the edges of the board.

"Head up. Now push up, feet where we talked about." I pushed, the suit giving my muscles a surprising spring; I thought I might bounce off the board. "Good!" Patrick said. "But *head up*. The board is big; trust it will be under your feet. Do it again."

The board *was* big, nine feet long and two feet wide, much bigger than the yoga mat I had practiced on. But still I couldn't keep myself from peeking at my feet, just to be sure, every time.

I practiced popping up until I was a little breathless and had worked up a light sweat inside the suit. For a moment, I thought I was warm, until I stopped moving and the wind blew through the neoprene, reminding me how porous it was. Soon, it would be ice water flowing through. I started shivering.

"That's enough," Patrick said. "Let's go—I'll take you in first, and when you've had enough, you can go back to the car and warm up. I'll probably stay out a bit longer."

"But I want to watch you first," I said. I'd never seen anyone surf up close before. I had watched Patrick Swayze in the movie *Point Break* quite closely, but not for technique. I wanted to see how it should be done. No part of me was thinking of it as a delay tactic. None.

Patrick nodded. He squinted at the water, bent down to secure the leash to his ankle. Then he hoisted the surfboard under his arm, flashing its Gnaraloo brand tagline, "Life is better when you surf," and walked into the water. I reflexively tensed, pulling my foot away from the surf. But Patrick walked straight in, climbed onto the board, and paddled out. There was no whimpering, no crying, no running back to land, no carrying on.

Patrick moved quickly, paddling at times on his belly, at times on his knees, looking like a Navy SEAL. His board rode over the incoming waves nimbly, and he covered distance at a clip. Pretty soon he was far enough out that I started to fret. *There's no one else here*, I thought. *I hope he knows what he's doing.*

Patrick's the sixth out of eight kids in his family. He grew up tromping around the woods. "Mom was pretty laissez-faire," he'd told me back at Bread Loaf. "If something was broken, she'd take you to the hospital (maybe), but otherwise we had a home field kit to repair you with and send you back out again." Perhaps that's why he seems so unflappable.

I'd asked him if he was ever afraid to surf, and he had answered, sure, there were times when the waves were just too big and he'd gotten out of the water. But for the most part, "Being nervous is part of the thrill," he'd said. "Falling is part of the fun." He could not resist adding, "By the way, you won't truly know what stoke is like until you're standing on a surfboard, riding a wave, wind in your face, watching the slide fly by. You'll know you're stoked because you'll hear yourself scream. Just FYI."

Now he turned around, caught his first wave, popped up and promptly fell over, then got back to his board and set up again. The next few tries also landed him straight in the water, and although at first I was relieved that he was human—and if he fell, then it would be okay for me to as well—after a while I started to worry that if it was hard for him to stand up, then it would be impossible for me.

Patrick looked tiny out there by himself. I thought of him, out in the world at seventeen, with no one's expectations following him. He was young, strong, daring, and free back then, he remembers.

"Spontaneous enthusiasm is so much a part of surfing as an act and a culture," he once told me. "Perhaps part of searching for stoke or keeping stoke in my life is to try and maintain that even as we get older, more adult, more responsible."

I've never been alone and I don't know what I would do without responsibilities and expectations. Would I feel exhilarated, or simply terrified?

My body was cold. I sat down on the sand, curling myself around my knees. I wasn't sure actually how much was cold and how much was fear—they felt one and the same, the shivering, the contracting, the desire to rock in a fetal position, to close my eyes and disappear. *I don't have to do this*, I thought. *I know where Patrick hid the car key. I could just drive away. Two sweaters. Down coat. Hot chocolate. Hot chocolate. Hot chocolate.*

When I opened my eyes, Patrick was up on the board. "Hooray!" I cheered, jumping up and clapping. He was riding sideways to the shore, on what he called the wall of the wave before it breaks. I would be doing the beginner's version, riding straight into shore on the whitewater that forms after a wave breaks. Yeah, right. He took a couple more runs and then splashed out of the water toward me.

"Hey, you did it!" I said. "How is it out there? Is it really cold?"

He was breathing hard, his face bright red. "My heart's working," he said. "I think it's the cold and the wet suit." *Please don't have a heart attack*, I thought. My last CPR course was ten years ago and it was for infants and toddlers. Patrick was a head taller than me and a lot bigger than the rubber doll I practiced on back then.

"It's so . . . different!" he said, shaking water out of his eyes. "The freshwater, when it first splashed in my mouth, I was shocked. Waves without salt. Just weird! And there's no break between waves, they come one after the other. They're not big, but they're choppy." He looked at me, blinking, trying to focus. "Now it's your turn. Put on the leash. The board isn't waxed, so it's a bit slippery. Don't worry if you fall, okay? You'll be fine."

I closed the Velcro strap around my ankle and realized that at the end of this long journey—after all Patrick's planning, his driving us here, renting the equipment, putting me on the board, and dragging me out into the lake—at the end he would be pushing me away. He would let go, and it would be just me, leashed to this board. God help me.

I waded into the lake, the water slithering into the suit around my ankles like icy snakes. And in my mind I saw myself, and so many other moms I know, self-consciously hiding our bodies in our swim shorts and cover-ups, standing at the edge of the pool, dipping a toe in, shivering, begging the children not to splash us, to let us go at our own pace, with the sun beating down and the water seventy degrees. And here I was, entering liquid four degrees away from being solid, three steps away from cryogenically freezing all the eggs in my ovaries. *One, two, three. Holy mama.*

I was in, waist-deep. Patrick tapped the board, I climbed on. Right away, the board slid around under my belly, like a live animal. I wanted to wrap myself around it and hold on, but Patrick said, "Move your arms, try to paddle." He steered me into the waves, the spray soaking my face. I moved my arms, with Ruby's swim teacher's voice in my head coaching "Stretch!" and as soon as my hands ice cream scooped the water, my gloves filled with it. With every wave my belly clenched on the up, and I gasped on the down. I started giggling. *This is the craziest thing I've ever done*, I thought. *I can't believe this is me.*

"You can turn your face away from the spray," Patrick said. That made it easier. I was grateful he was with me to declare the obvious; it was as if I had no instincts of my own.

Patrick turned me around. The beach, the playground, jostled into view. The water rushed from my feet up over my backside, making me yelp.

"Here we go," Patrick said. The wind carried his voice toward me now. He sounded close. "When I say UP, push up." I could feel his hand steadying the board. And then, with a hard shove, he was gone, I was shooting away from him, his voice calling from another dimension, "UP! UP! UP!" and I tried but my hands and arms would do nothing but clench—for heaven's sake, would a man shot out of a cannon try to stand up midair? Would a woman riding a wild horse try to push up and let go? No way! I clung on to the board and screamed.

I rode the wave, laughing, the water rushing under my belly as if it would never end, until it did and I was tumbling through the water, alone. *Soft body.* I made myself relax. *Don't fight. You'll be fine.* I felt the sand under me. *This way is down.* I stood up. I was fine! I was alive! I sloshed around, getting to the board, bringing it back to Patrick. We tried it again.

This time, I pushed up to a crouching position, and then fell over, inhaling the spray and gulping water, which was shocking both because it was so cold and so fresh. With no salt or chlorine there was no gagging, sick feeling afterward. I had been afraid of swallowing water. I survived that, too.

The third time I fell, my left hip hit the bottom, hard. The fourth time, I landed square on the back of my pelvis. But these waves had only a fraction as much power as the wave at Jones Beach that broke my bone. Those waves had felt like the weight of the world crashing over me. These were like belly flops, as Jenny Javer, my diving teacher, would say: Painful, yes. Career ending, no. After each fall, I assessed how I felt, whether I could move, whether I could feel my fingers and toes. As long as I could, I would try again, I figured. *I'm here, after all.*

"Keep your head up," Patrick said. "You look down, you fall." I tried. I tried to focus on the empty lifeguard chair, the roofs of houses in the distance. But if I couldn't trust the object permanence of the board on land, there was no trusting it once it was moving. I fell again and again.

Patrick gave one piece of feedback after each attempt: "Pop up faster, the next wave is catching up to you." "Keep your knees bent, think 'up' but not straight legs." And my favorite, "My fault! I pushed you too soon."

This is the part where I usually tire, where I start to lose heart. Where each instruction seems insufficient to unlock the mystery, the "click" of finding that balance point. *What if I don't have what it takes?* I might think, right before throwing in the towel. But here, in Lake Michigan, I was having too much fun to stop. The water, the speed, the cold energized every cell in my body. I could see, I could think, clearly. I was *awake*.

I'll try the Law of Attraction on the next run, I thought. Visualize success. I visualized pushing up, standing up, surfing. I fell. I laughed. I floated on my back for a moment, resting. The clouds looked low enough to cover me, a downy, frosty comforter. I had been glad to have no one watching—I didn't want the pressure of a peanut gallery. But now, bobbing in the lake, I remembered Marisa, full of joy, treading water for the first time in the pool, calling out, "Look at me!"

Look at me! my heart sang, to no one, and everyone, at once.

Something curious happened on the next try. Patrick pushed a little before I was expecting it. I scrambled to push up, mind whirling. When I popped up into a crouch, an internal gear clicked into place. My mind locked in: *That's it. I'm balanced.* Then I fell. Patrick knew, too.

"You had it that time—did you feel it? Just keep your eyes up and stand up next time, you've got it!"

The next time, there it was again, a shift within from chaos to calm, and it was not in my feet or my legs, which I had been working so hard to steady. It was in my belly, a growl of recognition between me and the wild horse. I didn't need to look at my feet. I stood up.

Maybe it was two seconds? I remember sucking air in, and then in again, before I realized what was happening.

I'm FLYING!!

I started shrieking, leaned left, and fell. This time, the fall felt from a height, it lasted forever or at least I thought it would never end, until it did, in a splash that felt earned and glorious. Seagulls scattered to the sky. Patrick waved his arms, calling, "That was it! You did it!" I crashed around in circles, in a cacophony of happy screaming with the birds until Patrick caught me in a one-armed hug, and in the space of two heartbeats, I felt mine pounding out *I'm king of the world!* through the neoprene.

We grinned, and as we set up to try again, Patrick said, "Be watchful of the board. It's getting too close to you."

It was good advice I didn't follow, because I sometimes have a complete lack of imagination. One moment, the board was six feet away from me. That's not too close, is it? The next moment, it was smashing into my left hand. Searing pain in a thumb that was halfway numb. *Not my hand! I need my hand to write.* My brain scanned its memory: *What letters do I type with my left thumb?* I couldn't think of any. It didn't matter. I needed my hand. I waved to Patrick, I was done.

On solid ground, he helped me take off the glove. I almost expected frozen fingers to fall right off. To my relief, my hand was bright red and intact. I could move everything, but the thumb throbbed. "My texting thumb," I moaned. "My life is over."

"Good," Patrick said. "You have a battle scar." There was no "poor baby," no sympathy, no charity lomi-lomi massage. But there was respect. A whole new feeling for me to receive and, honestly, a whole lot better.

We moved the leash from my leg to Patrick's—he wanted to go out again. I sloshed my way up the beach toward the car. It was early afternoon now, and although the sky was still dim, the beachfront felt more awake. A couple of people walked their dogs, a mother released her bundled-up preschooler to the playground. *That could easily be me with my kids*, I thought, *counting the hours till dinner*.

Next to our Jeep, an elderly couple sat in their parked car, taking in the view of the lake. Their faces broke open with delight when I walked past. I mouthed the words "Brrr! It's cold in there!" and they laughed, giving me thumbs-up and waving. I imagined them saying to each other, "Isn't that the craziest thing you've ever seen?" or maybe, "Remember when we used to do things like that?"

I thought of myself, an old lady, looking at a winter waterscape and saying, "I did that once. I went surfing on Lake Michigan when it was thirty-six degrees in the water. I was forty-one years old and I thought I was a chicken but I wasn't. I thought I would die but I didn't. I almost didn't go through with it, but I did."

My face broke into the biggest smile of my life at the thought.

Booyah!

Stoked.

≋

NESTLED IN THE CAR with the heat on, fully dressed, it took me twenty minutes to feel my body again. Even then, I was not my old self. My clothes felt too big, like I had shrunk myself in the wash. They felt like clothes I wore a lifetime ago. Was it possible it had only been half an hour? My face, rinsed clean of makeup, felt exposed, new. Actually, everything felt fresh and new. I rubbed my thumb gently. It hurt, but I didn't mind.

Patrick drove with purpose now. The trip back would be predictable; the road-less-traveled portion of our outing was over. "We didn't get lunch," he said, looking at the clock. We wouldn't have time to stop to eat—we had to get back to the conference. "But we did get to go surfing."

I shuddered to think that up until this morning, I would have chosen lunch.

"I don't need food," I said. *I feed on euphoria!* Erica, at the surf shop, had been jubilant upon my safe return, particularly stoked to have inducted another woman into the fold. There are so few lake surfers to begin with—estimates run between 500 to 750 on all the Great Lakes combined—and women are only a fraction of that number, Erica told me. And women in winter? Who knows? And women over forty in winter? I'd like to think that cohort's close to one.

Kent's stepfather set the New Mexico state record for weight lifting in his weight and age (eighty to eighty-four!) bracket in 2010 and 2011. He went on to win a bronze medal at the national masters weight lifting competition in his class. "At my age, there aren't that many competitors," he said, three in his class at the masters, and just him at the state level, to be exact. "You just have to show up and lift the weighted bar overhead with proper technique to place," he says modestly. But still. You have to show up and lift.

"Are you okay? How do you feel?" Patrick asked.

"I feel proud!" I patted my rosy cheeks for emphasis.

"You were great, you worked so hard! The conditions were harsh," Patrick said. "Even though the waves were small, they were incessant. Normally in an ocean there are swells and then there's time to rest in between. Here you had to go nonstop, up and down. You also had the wet suit."

"I know—my body felt so heavy, with the suit waterlogged, it was an effort to push up." I soaked up his praise and heaped on my own.

"And we should have waxed the board. I thought the booties would be enough to hold us on, but it was slippery."

"I'm thankful for all the excuses you're giving me for not standing up on the board for longer," I said, smiling. "I can blame so many things."

"Oh, nothing is ever the surfer's fault in surfing," Patrick said, the California boy in him showing in his smile. I smiled, too, wishing I could absorb the mind-set myself. "Not my fault" is not in my vocabulary. Everything is my fault. It would feel so good to lay that down for a while.

"You did so much of the work," I said, giving credit where it was due. "I couldn't have paddled out myself, I wouldn't have known how to read the water at all."

Patrick was quiet for a moment, thinking. "You know how when our kids first learned to read, it was such a big revelation for them? You go for a while, pointing out the signs on a road, and then one day they realize they can read them. And all of a sudden, the road makes sense in a whole different way? It's the same with the ocean. You look and see wave, wave, wave. Scary stuff. But if you learn to read the water, you can see where the wave is breaking, where the riptides are. And then it makes sense."

The metaphor made sense. I followed *A* to *B*.

B to *C*, however, surprised me.

"And that's what you're doing facing your fears," he continued. "All this strength, this courage, has always been there. You're just uncovering it in different situations and seeing it for the first time in a new way. You're learning to read yourself."

I stopped and considered this. *Has strength always been in me? Then why do I read myself as weak so much of the time?* And how could someone who just met me read me so differently?

"Patrick, how did you know, right from the beginning, I could do it?"

Patrick shrugged. "Kids surf. Old people surf. In terms of physical ability, almost anyone can stand, if the waves are gentle and the teacher is good."

"You make it sound so self-evident," I said. I thought about the former Marine quaking over reading to his daughter's second-grade class. Just because you can do something, doesn't mean you *can*.

"But you did something even experienced surfers wouldn't do. Going out in the freezing cold? Most people would say, 'Nobody does that!' And you did it anyway. I hope you can look at this and think, 'If I can do this here, I can do it in other areas of my life.'"

I thought for a minute about how different Patrick and I are fundamentally. Studies indicate that risk-taking behavior may be hardwired, perhaps 60 percent determined by genetics (as compared to 30 to 50 percent for most personality traits). Other studies suggest that a dopamine deficiency may make the adventurous seek out the thrilling experiences that give them extra dopamine and adrenaline. Or perhaps being allowed to roam freely growing up encouraged Patrick to find adventures and not worry too much about outcomes. I wondered whether, different as we are, he could even understand my fears or I his adventurous spirit—let alone whether I could ever be as brave as he.

But then I paused. A sense memory, of hurtling through water and air, suddenly surprised by how good the wind felt on my face. I didn't think I could tolerate so much fear and take in so many new sensations and enjoy them. I could certainly make more room in my life for *that*.

"I thought I would be terrified, and then happy when it was over. I didn't expect to feel both terrified and happy at the same time," I said. "I would have missed all that if I had let the fear stop me from trying. And I surprised myself. I was stronger out there than I ever thought I could be. So, yes, I think it will help me approach my anxieties differently. But even more, I think it gave me the key to a happy life."

≋

SOMEWHERE IN INDIANA, in the comfortable familiarity of a passenger seat, I felt every ounce of tension drain away. In Integral Yoga, we end each class with a progressive relaxation series in which we tense and then relax every part of the body. "Tighten your legs, then release. Drop them, roll them, let them be." There is something about engaging the muscles actively first that helps them relax more deeply. Surfing, I had tightened every fiber of my being more intensely than ever before, and now the letting go was . . . was . . . My eyelids were heavy.

"You have that look," Patrick said, glancing at me.

"Mmrrmph?"

"That relaxed, après-surfing look. That feeling after getting knocked around, of settling down. That's stoke, too."

"There are chemicals involved," I said, trying to remember my neurology books. "Endorphins, adrenaline, when you're excited, then serotonin helps make you relaxed." That wasn't what he meant by stoke, though. The stoke was something else that took hold in my belly, my heart, not my brain. I knew it, I just couldn't articulate it.

Stoke wasn't about pure pleasure, I realized. It's about pleasure even in uncertainty, relaxing when you're out of your element, keeping yourself excited and motivated for whatever might be coming next. It's about returning to your best, strongest self from wherever you are.

Later, in the hectic pace of everyday life, I would close my eyes and take a breath, and imagine stoke as the space between a leap and a landing, when all thought, planning, worrying, disappears, allowing the spirit to soar. In the excitement of kids' performances and tournaments, I would think of stoke as the exhilaration of the unknown. In the stress of hospitals and school meetings, stoke was optimism in chaos.

For so long, my life had had dread running through its veins, a sense of that twenty-pound weight dragging me below the surface in the face of each challenge. Stoke is the ability to be Houdini in the sea, to be soft and strong and hopeful, in motion and at rest.

"Pure energy," Patrick had called the ocean, in one of our early conversations. Surfing was "riding pure energy." The description froze me to my seat. How could I ride something so much more powerful than me and not lose myself? I had always thought balance came from rooting down into the energy of the earth, so where would I find it if the earth was moving? Standing on the board, it spoke to me in my gut. *Here. Balance, bliss. It lives in me. At all times, whether facing the wave, riding it, or falling, this peace is here.* "This is a wave, I am the ocean," the mantra goes. Stoke is the excited anticipation of wave after wave after wave.

But all that introspection came later.

"I'm soooo stohhhked," I said softly to Patrick. We had crossed into Illinois, the windshield misty from the almost rain in the almost dark.

I don't let myself get knocked around enough, I said to myself. I let my eyes close.

≋

BACK AT THE CONFERENCE, we were returning heroes. I had posted a picture of me on Facebook, just out of the water and grinning like a happy otter, and the reactions were profuse. *"You are insane!" "You are awesome!"* screamed friends as keyboards around the world clicked "Like." At a reunion of Bread Loafers at a local bar the next night, anyone who had seen the Facebook post approached us, asking, "Why, why, why?"

Patrick and I each pushed the other into the center of the story: "It was *his* idea, tell them."

"It was because *she* broke her foot, you tell them."

At Bread Loaf, when I was on crutches, Abe Streep, an editor for *Outside* magazine, had said, "In ski towns, everyone comes to the bar with something in a cast. It's a badge of honor. It means you have a story to tell." I had thought, at the time, *Back where I'm from, a mom who shows up in a cast from an adventure is considered a selfish mom, who would take risks for the sake of a good time.*

But this time, I was the one with a story. And everyone seemed excited to hear it—no one seemed to be judging me. Would I even care if they did?

The best reactions, though, came later, over the phone. Kent was excited to hear I went for it, but, in perhaps the greatest testament to how far I'd come, he was no longer shocked at my daring. I was becoming the kind of person who might do such things. It had been a while, actually, since anyone had said of me, "Mommy doesn't do that."

"Mom! *I LIKED YOUR PICTURE!*" Gigi yelled. Her phone voice was her outdoor voice, calibrated to reach from New York to Chicago. "Did you like the surfing? Do you think I would like it?"

I thought of myself, flying through the spray, mind blown open. Of Gigi, riding pure energy, fierce and free.

"Yes," I said without hesitation. "And *yes.*"

CHAPTER 8

THE UNKNOWN

Death

M ommy, what if you die?"

Ruby, finally clean and covered in sticky lotion under her pajamas, lay on her back with her feet in the air, scratching her ankles and peering up at me through the half dark. She likes to ask penetrating questions right before bed.

It's so typical, I thought, rubbing the excess lotion from my hands into my forehead. Maybe it would help stall the lines forming there. *I worry about something happening to them, while they worry about something happening to me.*

"Be careful!" I call out, a dozen times a day. "It's a parking lot! A busy street! Those are train tracks! You could choke, you could fall, you could get electrocuted. Look where you're going, what are you doing? Watch out!" I might as well be standing on the corner with a megaphone, proclaiming, "The End Is Near." Nobody listens.

Both Gigi and Ruby crashed and bounded through their toddler years like they had a death wish for themselves or for me. "Are you trying to get yourself killed?" I would ask, catching them just before they fell down the stairs or put a plastic bag over their faces. "Or are you trying to give me a heart attack?"

It wasn't their fault. How could it be—they had no idea what death meant. In the phase of naming things that are—*This is a cat; this is a car*—what would you even call the absence of things, the end of things?

When Gigi was three, I tore the sheath in my left ankle that stabilizes the entire joint. I couldn't take a quick step without the chance of rolling the ankle and falling down. "Don't run away, I can't catch you, I'm serious" is what I said to her, over and over. "Run away, see if I can catch you, it'll be hilarious!" is probably what she heard. Once, Gigi ran away from me in a parking lot as the lights of a car backing out toward her clicked on. I don't remember if the car stopped, if she ran past it to safety, or if I lunged and caught her in time. But I was still shaking as we drove away, with her safe in her car seat, her happy shrug at my upset making me furious and terrified. And then I saw a cat lying dead in the road. I drove past it at first, considered for a moment, and then pulled over.

"Where are you going?" Gigi asked, as I put on the hazards and opened the door.

"I'll be right back," I said, stepping outside and walking carefully toward the cat. It was small, black, and crumpled. It was not gory. I weighed for a moment if Gigi would be scarred if I showed this to her. If she would be worse off if I didn't.

"Come here and look at this," I said. I carried her out of the car, held her as we looked at the cat from the curb. "This cat is dead."

We had two pet cats at home at the time. Indoor cats, so they would stay protected. Gigi knew what cats were like alive: full of pride. She leaned out of my arms curiously. This cat looked like a furry puppet, deflated, no animating force inside. I held on to her tightly, spoke softly and slowly. I wanted her to understand.

"This cat was hit by a car. The driver couldn't see the cat. A car is much bigger than the cat. On the inside, the cat is broken. It will never stand up again. It will never go home. It will never see its mommy again."

Gigi started to cry. I felt terrible and relieved at the same time. From the moment we received her picture from the adoption agency, I was overtaken by fear that something bad would happen to her before we could get there. Once home, we ensconced her in safety gates and nonskid padding, assuring her and ourselves that now that she was with us, she was okay, that we didn't have to worry anymore. And now I was cracking open that world, saying she was vulnerable after all. I didn't know how else to keep her safe.

She was more careful after that.

⏫

"WHAT IF YOU DIE?" is the question I feel most discomfited by, the one that even after years of answering it for Gigi still catches me in the throat. Ruby repeated it now, scratching the red welts coming up on her arms.

"Oh, I have no plans to die anytime soon," I said lightly. "Do you want some more cream for your arms, honey?"

Ruby shook her head, *no* to cream, *no* to changing the subject. "Well?"

There are direct, practical answers to this question that I give later in the conversation if she needs to hear them again. The list of who would take care of her and Gigi, starting with Daddy, and if Daddy were to die who the next person would be, and the next. For children who have already lost birth parents for reasons unknown, Plans B, C, D, and E are things they want to know.

There are emotional answers to this question, about how our love would never end, how I would want her to be happy even if she was very sad at first.

There are metaphysical answers about heaven and what it might be like there (I once asked Gigi what she remembered from before her birth mother's belly and she responded without missing a beat, "I was laughing with God") and physical ones about what would happen to my body. If I would be put in the cemetery near the new shopping mall (over my dead body) or in a little drawer with a brass nameplate at church (perhaps) or my ashes scattered over a place they love the most (preferred, unless it's the shopping mall).

But I honestly want none of the above, for the time being, and my first answer is usually this: "Let's count all the things Mommy is doing to live as long as I can." Counting on fingers: "One—I am taking my vitamins. Two—I am careful when I cross the street. Three—I don't do anything crazy." Except surf lakes in the winter.

"Four—you make your body strong," Ruby said, stopping her scratching to climb into my lap. This reassurance was what she was looking for. "You do your yoga." I nodded, while shifting our position slightly. My back hurt; in truth I hadn't done yoga, or much other exercise, for quite a while.

"Five—I don't eat too many sweeties," I said, fudging a little. My stomach was rumbling at that very moment for pie.

"Six—you get checkups like I do," Ruby said, "but you don't get stickers or lollipops." My doctor at my recent annual physical had said I had the lung capacity of a teenager. Although when he palpated my abdomen he clucked, "There's more here than there should be." It was discouraging to have the existence of my spare tire verified but not surprising. Shortly after returning home from surfing Lake Michigan, I'd had some minor surgery requiring bed rest, and all my momentum toward strengthening my body came to a halt. I gained eleven pounds in two months.

We hadn't told the children exactly why I was in bed and going to the doctor so much, except that I had a problem they were fixing.

Maybe Ruby wanted to know if I really was doing everything I could to live as long as I could.

Biologically speaking, we have evolved to procreate and nurture our offspring to independence. It's a fierce drive to protect our young, whether they carry our genes or not (in fact, many adoptive parents I've met feel a double responsibility to stay alive and kicking, so that their children, who have already lost their birth parents, do not have to lose any more). There are parents I know who don't fly or drive long distances without their kids, who stopped activities like skydiving or motorcycling upon becoming parents because, as one former recreational scuba diver told me, "The implications of a negative outcome are just unacceptable."

However, according to the most frankly titled book on the subject there is, *The Thing About Life Is That One Day You'll Be Dead*, by David Shields, the likelihood of dying of the things most people fear breaks down like this: In developed countries, motor vehicle accidents account for 2 percent of deaths, and *all other accidents* for another 2 percent. The vast, vast majority of deaths come from causes within our own bodies: Cardiovascular disease kills 40 to 50 percent of people. Cancer kills another 30 to 40 percent.

Once our biological destiny has been fulfilled, our bodies become essentially obsolete. Up until now, I'd put that process of decline in the "far in the future" file. Like, once my job as a mother was done. After our kids graduate college, boomerang back, move out in their thirties, and I retire from my second career and pay off the house. That file.

The truth is, many of us who feel like we're still on the building-up side of life (finishing degrees, getting married, having children) are in reality already on the breaking-down side of life. The average life span for an American woman today is eighty-one, for a man, seventy-six, putting both me and Kent just over the hill. When you consider that around two hundred years ago, the average life span was thirty-five, it's no wonder our bodies head into this evolutionary overtime dazed and confused. *What am I still doing here?* is the question every body in my age bracket seems to be asking its owner.

"I just cracked my tooth *eating Veggie Booty!*" my thirty-six-year-old sister said, incredulous.

"I pulled my back getting out of bed," a forty-two-year-old man complained. "Even sleeping is too much for me."

"I got a stress fracture from walking," a girlfriend in her late forties told me. "Are you kidding me? I'm *wearing out my bones*? Getting older sucks."

And an old high school classmate posted on Facebook: "I sneezed, and pulled a butt muscle."

As for me, I wake up aching. And it's not like I work in a salt mine. It's like my body is too much for my body to handle.

My friend Michelle Collins, a personal trainer, says that as we age, our ligaments and muscles become less flexible, giving us less range of motion in our joints. We compensate for less flexibility in one area by pulling harder on another, causing dysfunctional movement. All of a sudden, routine motions like taking groceries out of the car or picking toys up off the floor can cause injury.

And aches and pains and broken bones are nothing compared to major illness. Michelle's mother has debilitating diabetes and hypertension, illnesses she could have ameliorated with diet and exercise earlier in her life. Part of the reason Michelle became a personal trainer was to model a healthier lifestyle for her daughters. "Once you're sick, you often don't have the energy to do the things you need to, to get better," she told me, at the coffee shop. I made a note to stop eating so many muffins. "When you're healthy is the time to start exercising. You don't want to wait until it's too late."

Michelle's next point, that weight training and cardio are absolutely essential for bone health, heart health, and keeping our figures recognizable, made me exceedingly unhappy.

Newton's first law of motion states that a body at rest will remain at rest unless an outside force acts on it. Even before the weeks of enforced rest, I always preferred it. I practice yoga. I sit. I lie down. I don't run unless someone is chasing me or there's free food involved. The effects of hard exercise—palpitations, shortness of breath, a feeling that I might vomit and die—mirror those of an anxiety attack. Why would anyone seek them out the recommended five times a week?

But as outside forces go, the look in Ruby's eyes, as she searched mine for answers in the half dark, was enough.

≋

"COME ON, YOU CAN DO IT," Beth Blank said. Petite and wiry, in her black Master Trainer New York Sports Clubs T-shirt, her blond hair pulled neatly through the back of a baseball cap, she moved and spoke authoritatively, the boss.

I, on the other hand, in my sloppy sweatshirt and yoga pants, draped precariously over a large pink stability ball, moaned like a sissy. With each lift of my leg, my pelvis burned.

"Ugh! Arrgh! Is it supposed to hurt right here?" I asked, pointing to where my hip and thigh meet. I was hoping the answer would be "Heavens, no! Stop immediately!"

"Look at it this way," Beth replied. "At least I didn't put weights on your leg."

"Errrgh! As if the weight of my own thigh isn't enough!"

I gritted my teeth. I've avoided gyms ever since I went up two dress sizes in my late twenties. I had been a dancer in high school and college, and becoming heavier than I was used to made me self-conscious about working out in front of people, myself included. My weight has fluctuated since, but the desire to not be looked at while sweating remained.

"I feel like I need to get in shape before I can start working out here!" I'd said despairingly, during my initial tour of the gym the week before. I squinted at a muscular man on the far end of the floor lifting a Prius. Maybe it wasn't a Prius. I need glasses. But it was something big.

"No, what you need is to get strong enough to be able to work out without injuring yourself again," Beth had said. Favoring one leg as I recuperated from my broken foot had done a number on my back, and my insurance coverage for physical therapy had run out months ago. I was worried about going back into the ocean to face my fears lopsided and lame, and here was Beth saying that lopsided and lame did not have to be my default setting. She looked at me the way I look at my yoga students when I know they're going to feel better when we're done. I couldn't believe I was putting down hard-earned money to treat myself to large doses of pain, but I did it, buying a package that would see me through the summer.

The next day I was sore. My friend Michelle, the personal trainer, said it was to be expected. "Sharp nerve pain or joint pain—you back off. But muscle soreness? You have to break down the muscle in order to build it back up. That's gonna hurt a bit," she said. I nodded glumly. My "no pain, no pain" approach to exercise had run out of road.

If I had started the slide toward quitting by cancelling the next session for one reason or another, I wouldn't be the first. The American Council on Exercise polled more than fifteen hundred people with the question "What keeps you from going to the gym?" and a full 19 percent said because they think they are the only ones not already in shape.

But then I heard Isabelle Edwards's story.

≋

ISABELLE WOKE UP FEELING LIKE CRAP, that January morning three years ago. Whatever energy people go on about at the start of a new year was not happening for her. *Why am I so tired?* she thought. It felt like she had been out partying all night. Ha! Those were the old days. These days, with her 7 a.m. start at her midlevel marketing job at a major insurance company, she was early to bed, early to rise. It was Monday, and as usual, she was running late. She hauled herself out of bed.

She decided to dress the way she did whenever she felt down, which meant dressing up. Surveying herself in the mirror, she saw a woman who had it all goin' on. Tina Turner didn't make forty look this good. High-heeled black boots, sheer stockings, a short black skirt and turtleneck, statement jewelry. She was enjoying the way her clothes showed off her figure, now that she had lost eighty pounds.

She looked a lot more confident than she felt, it was true. The nightmare ending to her unhappy marriage, the ugly custody fight she'd lost for her teenage son, the hurricane that destroyed the house she was renting—all that stress had aged her, for sure. But wasn't she still standing? Didn't Shmar, her good friend and colleague, do a double take one day and see her as more than a friend? Weren't they happy now, living together, working together? Yes, there would be a future for them, and for her eleven-year-old daughter. They were all hitting their stride. She just had to focus on taking better care of herself. It would suck to get the flu.

Driving to work, her hands lost contact with the wheel for a moment and the car ran along the skid strip in the shoulder. Immediately she regained control, but the blip in her coordination was odd. *That was weird*, she thought.

Ever since she was eighteen years old, Isabelle had lived and worked on her own. As a biracial kid growing up in Staten Island, New York, her Caucasian mother and stepfather did not approve of her faint relationship with her West Indian father and her chosen identity made things uncomfortable at home. She rebelled against her parents, never saw eye to eye with her sisters. Her first husband had intimidated her, and she'd numbed herself with food through their marriage. She couldn't remember anyone ever asking what was wrong or how she was feeling, so she never really thought about it. Even after being diagnosed with type 2 diabetes, listening to her body's signals never occurred to her. As a working mom, there was always too much to do.

But on this day, once she got to work and didn't pep up like she thought she would, she decided to see the employee health nurse for a blood pressure check.

Her numbers while seated were normal. But when she stood up, they dropped. "You've been running around—the holidays are a crazy time," the nurse said. "Maybe you're a little dehydrated." This made sense. Isabelle never stopped to drink water.

"Can you give me my clearance to use the company gym? I have to get my ass in gear. I want to be healthier," Isabelle said. They made an appointment for a physical the next day.

The next day, Isabelle still felt sluggish. Which no one else would have guessed, because Isabelle at 80 percent or even 40 percent of her usual energy still walks and talks awfully fast.

She chatted her way through the nurse taking her blood pressure, and when the nurse called the doctor in, Isabelle prattled right through his telling her to shut up. He was feeling her pulse, trying to count. "Shut up," he repeated. This time, she did. He let go of her wrist, walked over to the wall, and took the large clock down to look at, so he could count again.

Is he being funny? Isabelle thought. But his eyes were serious as they met hers. "Isabelle," he said, "you're having a heart attack."

"No, I'm not," she said. That was ridiculous. Heart attacks were for old people. She didn't yet know that many women having heart attacks don't have the same symptoms as men. Instead of crushing chest pain, some women get only tightness in the chest or back, sluggishness, dizziness, or nausea, symptoms they can mistake for flu or acid reflux.

"Yes, you are. Lie down. I'm running an EKG." The results confirmed a heart attack. "I'm calling you an ambulance to go to the hospital."

"No way!" Isabelle protested. "I'm not taking an ambulance to go across the street." *Especially since I'm not having a heart attack.* "Call Shmar, he'll drive me."

The hospital campus was directly opposite her office building, so the trip down one driveway and up the next gave hardly any leeway to gather speed or a sense of urgency. Shmar drove carefully; sleet was coming down.

Isabelle and Shmar walked through the sliding glass doors, Isabelle's heels clicking brightly against the polished floor. Her employee doctor had alerted the ER, so a team was waiting. "Where is the patient?" they asked.

"Hello, it's me!" Isabelle said, the bracelets on her wrist sparkling as she waved. She scanned their faces for their reaction. *Do I look like I'm having a heart attack? Obviously not,* she thought, registering their surprise with a satisfied smile.

Paperwork was done, a gown was given. Shmar was worried. A handsome African-American man eight years younger than Isabelle, he sometimes felt more mature than her. She wasn't good at taking care of herself. It was only recently that she'd started to lose weight and dress more fashionably and feel like she was worthy of being adored. And he did adore her. They were going to make a great family. But this . . . this was very concerning.

A woman came in—a doctor or nurse? The weight of her words are what they both remember. "Isabelle," she said, "we can't keep you here."

"You mean I can go home?" Isabelle asked.

"No. We looked at your test results. Your heart attack is so severe, we don't have the equipment to handle you here."

Stop. Rewind. Replay.

"Get out of here," Isabelle said. But the swagger in her voice was gone. It was all suddenly falling out from under her.

"We have to send you to Westchester Medical Center in White Plains. The ambulance will take you. Your fiancé can meet you there."

Strapped to the gurney, in the back of the ambulance, Isabelle could see Shmar's car sliding side to side on the icy road behind them as they pulled away. The oxygen mask pressed into her cheeks. As they turned on to the main road, her eyes filled with tears. She was, she felt in her bones, leaving all safety behind.

Her thoughts skidded from one lane to the next, faster than she could get hold of them. *What did I do to myself? Where is my daughter? Who's going to take care of her tonight? Insurance. Is this covered? Am I going to get cut? Please God, don't let them cut me open. Please God, let me live. I'm going to be a different person, a better person, get me out of this and I will be better. What is going to happen? What have I done?*

In a procedure that proved it is possible to live every minute of every day with one's own heart and not know it is broken, the surgeons at Westchester Medical discovered that Isabelle had no less than four compromised arteries—one that was completely blocked, one operating at 80 percent, and two at 40 percent. In went a stent. Her heart beat on.

In recovery, the cardiologist told Isabelle she was lucky to be alive, that if she had not lost as much weight as she had before the heart attack, she would have been a goner. He told her she was too young and pretty to be in his care. She wasn't too sick to take the compliment in with a smile.

When it came time to release her, the doctor's orders were to "eat healthy and reduce stress." Isabelle had no idea what that meant. All she knew was she had been on a soft food diet in the cardiac unit for long enough. She wanted to go home and eat.

And that's when things got really bad.

Isabelle vomited up her first meal back at home, and food simply would not stay down after that. She rushed back to the ER for antinausea meds, a path she would take five or six times over the next three months. She was dropping weight; she barely recognized herself. What the hell was going on?

What was going on was that her digestive system was breaking down. Eventually she was diagnosed with gastroparesis, a chronic condition where the muscles of the stomach and intestines move food along too slowly, and it ferments or causes blockages in the stomach, interfering with the absorption of nutrients and causing countless complications. Gastroparesis is associated with diabetes and conditions like Parkinson's disease and multiple sclerosis, but in many cases the cause is unknown.

"Every morning for ten months, I woke up and cried," Isabelle said. "The longer I was sick, the more people on the outside didn't want to get too close to me. I felt like a piece of bruised fruit." She was able to go to work, but the energy that took drained her for all else. "Every evening, after work, I'd sit in my terry cloth robe at home. No TV, no music. Just sit there, thinking."

Now that her body had shown fault lines she never suspected, the idea that the Big One could come at any time became all too real. "I would think about dying, about the outfit I would be buried in. I have the dress, I have the earrings. If there's life after death, I want to look the way I want to look!" She laughed. I was sitting across a cafeteria table from Isabelle, trying to imagine her as she described herself back then: racked with nausea, afraid to eat, afraid of exerting herself and causing another heart attack. It was hard to do. "I was afraid, sometimes, of which place I would end up in after." Isabelle swallowed. "Many times," she said softly, "I would miss my mother and my son."

Isabelle was angry at everyone who didn't understand her situation, but mostly she was angry at herself. "I did this to myself, I let myself get fat. I got diabetes, I didn't take care of it, and now see what happened!" There was a big part of her that felt she deserved this. But she knew Shmar and her daughter deserved better.

"Shmar went from being my boyfriend to being my nurse. He helped me pay my bills. He took care of my daughter. He made sure I took my meds. He got angry at me if I didn't hold up my end. And then one day he told me, 'I've devoted my life to taking care of you, *but it's time for you to stand up for yourself.*' He told me he wanted to go back to school. And that's when I realized: *I need to get out of this fucking robe.*"

And that's what she did. Isabelle and Shmar joined Toastmasters, which gave Isabelle an opportunity to find her voice. She made speeches about how life can take a turn on a Monday morning, exhorting people to take care of their bodies. It gave her a reason to stand up and speak.

Isabelle's health situation remained dire. Just because she found the will to get better didn't mean her life got any easier. In the next couple of years she would have extensive hospital stays. Once she almost died from malnutrition, and more recently 30 percent of her leg was removed after blood clots caused tissue there to die ("It looks like a shark bit my calf"). With each challenge, she fell back into the darkness ("I remember sitting in my car, looking at the river and thinking for the first time in my life I understand the mother you've heard about on the news who drives in with her kids"), and each time she clawed her way back out with therapy and support from Shmar and her friends.

Losing part of her leg—and the resulting brace she has to wear—was really hard. "I'm vain, I like my shoes," she'd said to a group of coworkers and friends who had gathered for a birthday party in her honor. There was not a dry eye in the room. To me, she said in seriousness, "I am so humbled by this. All my vanity means nothing."

What does mean something to Isabelle now is helping as many other people as possible to escape her fate. "I don't know how much time I've got left, but I'm going to make the most of it," she said. She became a volunteer keynote speaker for the American Diabetes Association, and now hosts a live Internet radio show called *The Diabetes Diva*. She wears wild curly hair extensions she calls her "battery" because they charge her up. She transfixes her audiences with her powerful testimony.

When Isabelle was unhappy and overweight, she retreated from life. When she got sick, part of her didn't believe she was worthy of getting better. She went toward death, waiting for it in the dark of her room.

"I think people are afraid of living as much as they are of dying," the Reverend Dr. Amy Lamborn says. An Episcopal priest who teaches pastoral theology at the General Theological Seminary in New York City, she is also a psychoanalyst who sees the two basic drives Freud described as the life instincts and death instincts constantly at work within patients and congregants.

"I work with people having a hard time making steps forward in life. They have great spirit, but the death instincts keep thwarting any steps they might take toward their goals. We all do this—we know we should exercise and we don't; we know we shouldn't have the third glass of wine and then we do; or in the extreme, when people don't know how to cope anymore and consider suicide, there is something about the pull to death. When we have the pull, though, I think something else is trying to be born. A part of them is still looking for a chance for something different somewhere."

That part of Isabelle saved her. Isabelle has gone up against death enough times to know how close it is at all times, and her will to live now—fueled by her greater mission to help others, her desire to come through for her daughter, son, Shmar, and the girlfriends awaiting her fashion and dating advice—was also urging her to reach out to people like me.

You can reduce your risk of heart attack, diabetes, and stroke by exercising and eating a healthy diet, her story said to me. Somewhere in my sedentary body, my life instinct ignited again.

≋

"YOU'RE DOING GREAT, PATTY," Beth said as I puffed and crunched next to her at the gym. I'd been working out faithfully for weeks. "Your muffin top is just in the front now, instead of all the way around." It was classic Beth, encouraging but backhanded enough to push me through an extra set. Another incentive was Kent, who after a decade of having a bad back thwart him from all forms of exercise, had also started training with Beth. So far he'd lost ten pounds, and he was looking good. We each wanted to stay in the other's league.

Beth cancelled the next session with a text: "EMERGENCY." She had adopted a newborn baby, her first child, just weeks before. I said a little prayer. When I saw her next, she was wearing her usual uniform but the brash Beth was gone.

"I've never been so scared in my life," she said. There's something about crossing over into motherhood that washes away the carefree innocence forever. Her face, usually bright, was overcast. "My husband was at home with the baby and thought he saw blood in his spit-up," she said. "I freaked out. I ran out of here, got him, and raced to the doctor." The doctor ran tests, and they all came back normal.

I hugged her with relief. Thank God. She patted the table, I hopped up as she put two-pound weights in each of my hands.

"I'm still shaking," Beth said. She held out her hand, and it was trembling. "Every time my phone buzzes . . ." She flinched. Her phone was buzzing. "I do that! I jump." Beth checked her messages. "Everything's fine. But part of me feels like it'll never be fine again, now that I know things can go wrong. I've gotten the call once. What if I get it again?"

The day Gigi started twitching uncontrollably when she was four years old, the subsequent tests and doctor's appointments and diagnosis of "tics of unspecified origin" had changed me as well. It was like a door to the world of what could possibly go wrong had blown open, and I could not get it shut. It took countless sleepless nights before I realized I couldn't think clearly if I didn't get sleep. I couldn't make decisions to help her if I was a nervous wreck. And children need to feel hopeful, not fearful, about their futures. It was emotional strength training, willing myself to not go to the worst-case scenario so that I could focus on doing what we could to get her to the best-case scenario.

Beth was at the beginning of her journey; she would learn this, too, I was sure of it. I made sympathetic, reassuring noises from the table, while lifting my baby weights toward her hands spotting mine.

⇗

I HAD A NIGHTMARE that night. I was on a raft in the middle of the sea. The water was bright blue and so was the sky, the raft a stark white, colors I imagine when I think of Greece. My nightmares are transparent in their meanings. River dreams chased me for years after I was in the Esopus. Kent and I once visited a relative in France on the island of Noirmoutier. To get to it, you can drive, walk, or bicycle across the

Passage du Gois, a two-and-a-half-mile strip of land during low tide. But because it's so flat, once the water starts washing over it at high tide it swiftly and inexorably becomes part of the sea. You don't want to be caught midway. I dream of that sometimes.

In this nightmare I lay on the raft on my belly, terrified of tipping in. I was sure there were creatures in the water. I could feel them, although I could see nothing but blue. Then the water under the raft rose precipitously. I held on, looking down, screaming before nose-diving over a waterfall. I woke up panting.

"If you dream of crashing waves or rocky seas, it may show that your emotions are out of control," according to the British psychic medium Craig Hamilton-Parker in *The Hidden Meaning of Dreams*. Perhaps. But emotional issues aside, this was also a literal fear-of-what's-in-the-ocean dream. I've had them off and on ever since finding out my junior high school classmate Josh Bazell had been lost at sea.

"I have to find Josh," I said out loud, as I lay in my bed, my heart thudding through the sheets.

≋

THE FIRST WEEK OF seventh grade, a girl brought a copy of the *New York Post* into homeroom. The front page headline was "NIGHTMARE IN DEVIL'S TRIANGLE: TV family tell of their ordeal 3 days adrift." It was a crazy story, of a family on vacation in Grand Cayman who'd gone out on a fourteen-foot aluminum fishing boat for an afternoon excursion and then ran out of gas two miles from shore with no food or water aboard. The dad, Robert Bazell, an NBC News science correspondent, swam three miles through barracuda-infested waters to get help that first evening. In the boat remained twelve-year-old Josh, his thirteen-year-old sister, and their forty-year-old stepmother.

The Coast Guard, Navy, and Air Force mounted a "massive" search but turned up nothing. The boat, caught in "unusual currents" in Bermuda Triangle water, drifted for three days and three nights before being spotted by a passing oil tanker. Miraculously, everyone survived.

We squinted at the pictures. The cover shot showed Josh smiling radiantly with his sister after the rescue; inside there was one of Josh leaning on his father's shoulder and another of the family.

"Do you think that's the Josh Bazell in our class?" she asked.

We had just started middle school, and our class was from all over New York City; none of us knew anyone well. But when the Josh we knew walked in, extremely tan and so very thin, he saw us looking down at the paper and then up at him, and he averted his eyes. It was him.

Josh intimidated me. He was a kid who seemed to have been born with gravitas. At age twelve he was already taller than most of us, and his voice had changed. Everything he said in his deep growl sounded authoritative and searingly smart. In our nascent circle of geeks, his science reporter father added to his mystique. Plus, he had survived barracuda-infested waters. I respected him from a distance, and then in ninth grade his family moved away and we lost touch. I never asked him about what it was like for him, out in that boat, but I couldn't get it out of my mind either.

"I know someone who" and "I read in the Chinese newspaper" may be the greatest fear-inducing conversation starters known to Chinese girls. Growing up, my mother used them often. There was always someone whose daughter went rock climbing and ended up paralyzed, or who went for a walk in the woods and got mauled by a bear. I absorbed these stories whole, visualizing and personalizing them. This is why I should never work at the ten o'clock news.

I read every news story there was about the Bazells. I imagined Josh and his sister, as the articles described, scrawling notes on 20-dollar bills and setting them adrift as tiny paper boats. With no radio, no life preservers, flares, or noise-making devices aboard how helpless they must have felt. I thought about how they licked condensation off the inside of the boat for moisture. It paralleled the stories my parents told of how my grandfather, when he was held in a Japanese prison camp, would pick up and eat every grain of salt that fell on the floor. He survived and lived to the age of ninety-three. My parents were implying that these were the genes I had been given, that I, too, was expected to be a survivor (and to eat everything in my bowl and stop making faces already). I always wondered, though, if I took after my other grandparents, whom I'd never met because they died before I was born.

"I know someone who got lost at sea" became part of my own story, and "The ocean is a vast and scary place" a part of my own worldview. *But*, I thought that morning lying safely in my bed, *this didn't even happen to me. So why does it still affect me so?* I had no idea how it affected Josh himself.

I found Josh through an old classmate on Facebook and made contact. *I'm trying to face my fear of the ocean,* I wrote in an e-mail. *Would you tell me your story?* I waited for a response, wondering at my own audacity in asking him to go back and recount a traumatic experience for my sake. Perhaps he was over it, perhaps his mind never went back there anymore.

The reply came: a picture of whale sharks lurking just below a fishing boat.

≶

LIKE KENT, Josh looks better now than he did as a teenager, I thought as he walked into the café to meet me for breakfast. Junior high school boys are by definition unfinished, and in the twenty-five years since I saw him last Josh had filled in the blanks. He's tall, dark, and hand-some; a bestselling author of two thrillers; has an MD and is now in his residency in psychiatry. He still intimidates me. Within five minutes of ordering our food, he made reference to Freud, F. Scott Fitzgerald, and two movies I hadn't seen, and dismissed two scientific theories as bullshit.

In return, I told him I'd never seen *Jaws*. Why? "Because I'm afraid of the ocean, and once I see something scary, I can't unsee it," I said, trying to warm my hands around my coffee cup. Now that the time had come, I almost didn't want to hear more details from Josh. Once I heard them, I wouldn't be able to unhear them, either. It was too late, though. He started in.

Out on the boat, that first night after his dad swam toward shore, there were five-foot swells, Josh said. "We were queasy, hungry, thirsty, but not insanely so, not yet. It was cold. When we woke up, we realized we had missed a ship—we could see its lights as it faded from view."

Josh was still upbeat. "My stepmother had said you could live forty days without food. I had assumed that also meant without water. So I was thinking we were likely to live." In actuality, humans in ideal con-ditions, resting in the shade, could live perhaps a week or more without water. But an athlete sweating in the sun could overheat, dehydrate, and die in a matter of hours. Josh's family, exposed to the Caribbean sun, would push the limit.

"We took turns putting on scuba fins and getting into the water to try to pull the boat by the rope in the front toward shore. There were schools of mahimahi fish that would surround the boat and ram the sharks; they saved us from the sharks. We had these masks—they say you can see a thousand feet down—but it was black down there. You would see a fish but not know how far down it was. Was it a very large fish way down deep? Or a kind of large fish very close up? But we started getting too weak to pull ourselves back into the boat."

They stopped hearing motors. If Dad had made it, wouldn't there be motors from a search party? They began to think he hadn't made it.

"Eventually we lost sight of the island. Then we really were lost at sea."

One of the most beautiful aspects of the ocean, my surfer friend Patrick had told me, is its phosphorescence. A number of marine bacteria, plants, and animals emit light. "The water glows blue-green," Patrick had said, remembering a night spent surfing with his brother in the lit-up sea as one of the coolest experiences of his life.

To Josh, who spent the night in fear of some large creature tipping their boat and eating them alive, the phosphorescence meant something very different. "You could see weird shit all the way down," he said. His recurring nightmare of being trapped in a shark tank in the dark gave rise to a pivotal scene in his book *Beat the Reaper*, and he raises the prospect of lake monsters in *Wild Thing*. We write what we know.

The next day they wrote SOS notes on dollar bills and when Josh reached out to put one in the water, his stepmother yelled, "Move your arm!" A shark came up, biting, and just missed him.

"But at that point I wasn't even scared," Josh remembers. "Once you get dehydrated enough, your teeth get loose because your gums recede from lack of water. Your kidneys start to fail, and then the hallucinations begin. The fish get faces, they talk to you. I saw floating 7-Elevens on pontoons with Big Gulp dispensers.

"I did not feel a fear of death," he said. "I felt at peace. I felt I had lived a good life, for the time I had. My biggest emotion was that I hoped my surviving family would know my peace."

Back at home, in a game of telephone too awful to contemplate, their mother had gotten word through other relatives that Josh and Rebecca were dead. "My mother thought we were dead. My five-year-old brother thought we were dead," Josh said. I gagged involuntarily.

"Yeah, that was tough," he said, with a nod and then a slight shake of his head. "Mothers don't do well with that shit."

Josh and Rebecca weren't dead; they were hovering on this side of life, using keys to scrape notes into the side of their aluminum boat: "We are happy. We are not suffering. Don't feel sad about us." It was Rebecca's fourteenth birthday.

In the evening of their fourth day in the boat, their third day missing, they saw a ship. "We thought it was a hallucination, but we were all seeing it," Josh said. "I had tried to build a flare gun out of a snorkel."

"You *what?*" My jaw dropped. This is why he intimidates me. Josh shrugged.

"It was far from successful."

"I'm amazed you even tried!"

"It was supposed to shoot a lit, gas-soaked piece of T-shirt into the air. But when I tried to fire it, the whole thing burned up, there was rubber everywhere."

Thinking back on it, Josh says, getting lost was not random. Running out of gas was not random. That could have been prevented. But the rescue? Totally random.

Despite the Coast Guard's largest seaborne search at the time, covering a twelve-thousand-square-mile area, salvation finally came from the *Arabian Addax*, a Japanese tanker with a Dutch captain and a South American crew, and one of the few vessels in the area not looking for the Bazells. But once the crew spotted the drifting motorboat they sent a lifeboat three times its size. When they raised the fishing boat that had been Josh's home for three days out of the water, its motor fell off.

"The first thing we said on board was, 'Water, water, water,'" Josh said, reaching his arms out, a man staggering out of the wilderness.

"'We only have grapefruit juice,'" was the reply.

"*Of course!* I thought. *Because I'm hallucinating and I hate grapefruit juice!*" Josh shook his head ruefully. "I have a violent dislike of grapefruit." We both looked down at his plate at the same moment and laughed—uneaten grapefruit sections lay where the fruit salad garnish used to be. "You can't drink water now—it'll kill you," the crew said, taking them to the sick bay. Too much water after dehydration causes electrolyte imbalances. Once they radioed in, they discovered there had been a massive search; that Josh and Rebecca's father was still alive; and that their mother and stepfather were now on the island and, having learned that the children were alive, were waiting to see them.

When they came off the ship, "the whole island was there to meet us," Josh said, choking up for the first time in telling his story. The three of them had drifted without knowing if anyone even knew they were missing. *Unseen.* And the whole time, "All these people had been praying for us, people who didn't even know us." He cleared his throat. "It was very touching."

In the movie *Cast Away,* the character Tom Hanks plays is rescued after being stranded for four years on a deserted island and has a rough reentry into the civilized world. Everything around him looks familiar, but he is different. Josh felt disoriented after four days at sea. He recovered physically much sooner than emotionally.

"I felt like death was everywhere, that I had brought it back with me," Josh said. "I felt like a traveler who comes back with a roach egg in my luggage. I'd look at people walking down the street and think, 'Someone is going to die today.'"

It was a heck of a way to start seventh grade.

"I feel like I had a midlife crisis at twelve. *Life is finite, and it can leave you at any time.* Of course, we're all getting so old now, everyone is having these thoughts. But back then I realized not everyone I hung out with felt that way."

Josh hadn't wanted to talk about what happened. "I saw you looking at that *New York Post* story and I thought, 'Uh-oh, here it comes. Now everyone will know.' But you didn't bring it up, and I was grateful.

"I thought about it every single day for years and tried not to. I had a second-by-second photographic memory of it," Josh said. "I know a Jehovah's Witness who was told his whole life the world would end, and he felt, *Why commit to anything?* I felt the same way, for a long time."

But then a funny thing happened while waiting to die. He didn't.

"You wait to die, and it doesn't happen, and then it dawns on you that life is going to go on long enough for you to have to do something with it," he said. And in writing books, going into medicine, connecting with people (especially his sister—they weren't close before the fishing expedition but have been "like twins" since), he found a way through.

"I was depressed for a time, but I realized no matter how shitty you find your own life, you can help someone else find the bathroom in the hospital." His novel *Beat the Reaper* is full of dead bodies, but the footnotes are like little sonnets to the human body's design, full of anatomical detail and an appreciation for life.

"What do you think happens when you die?" I asked.

Most of us who haven't come so close to death don't think so deeply about what happens next. But Josh had been on the threshold, he'd earned his answer, and I held my breath for it. What he said is something I will never forget:

"I think if there's a heaven, it's the weird time dilation when you die when you come to peace. What people don't realize is that moment, when there's nothing left required of you, is a great feeling."

The writer John McPhee describes the process of writing as going through a "membrane" into a world that is not where you live. Talking with people about their fears is like that, too. Stepping back in time with them, into a moment when they were very vulnerable, is like being led by the hand into another dimension. It feels sacred to me. Josh and I paused there, inside the membrane, where the real world recedes to background noise.

And then I realized I had to go. Traffic outside was heavy. Ruby had an early dismissal from school. I shifted to find the time, and Josh tipped out of the membrane, too.

"I haven't talked about this very much," he said, sitting up straighter.

"Is it okay?" I asked, praying that it was.

"I don't know what I was expecting, but it's kind of emotional." His eyes, which had been so present, retreated from me. Our moment was over.

"But, hey, it's okay!" he said brightly, holding up a shopping bag. "I've got some things to return at Century Twenty-one! Life moves on!"

We laugh at the ridiculousness of it all.

≋

"WHAT DO YOU THINK happens when you die?" This time, I was asking my mom and dad. They're in their seventies, and I'm in my forties. It's not a topic we've discussed in a while. I've wondered, as we've gotten older and phone calls are as likely to bring bad news as good, whether my parents' views have changed. Ba's definitely have not.

"I believe when you're done, you're done," he said flatly, from the front passenger seat. It was so early in the morning the light from a full moon hurt my eyes. Ba's brother, my uncle Henry, was driving us to the San Francisco airport. We were headed home from a trip we'd originally planned to celebrate Nai-nai's (my grandmother's) hundredth birthday. Nai-nai was actually turning ninety-eight, or ninety-nine by the way Chinese people count, which is that you're one at birth. "It's close enough!" she had declared. "I want a party!" But only weeks before we were scheduled to go, she died. We made the trip anyway, to see relatives, to pay respects.

"The body goes back into the dirt. It becomes ashes," Ba elaborated. That didn't sound any more encouraging.

"You don't believe in an everlasting spirit?" Uncle Henry asked. He is younger than Ba by many years and shares half his DNA; Nai-nai was his mother by birth and my dad's stepmother. It's hard to say if genes or birth order or upbringing account for the differences between them, but there are many.

"He's scientific," Ma said, gesturing her head toward Ba. It occurred to me that I should introduce Ba to the Skeptics Society, an organization whose mission is to promote science and debunk paranormal claims, except he would be skeptical of any organization that asked for donations. I, on the other hand, once read ten pages of the Skeptics Society's Executive Director Michael Shermer's book *The Believing Brain* before I got too depressed to continue. I'm all for science, but a life devoid of anything that can't be proven is not something I'm ready to offer my five-year-old at bedtime.

"What about you?" Uncle Henry and I both asked, turning to my mother.

"I believe there is a spirit," Ma said, "but not forever. It stays with the body a little while after the body dies. Especially if the person dies unexpectedly or when they're too young." Both of Ma's parents died when she was in her twenties, her dad of a heart attack when she was in college and her mom of cancer three years later. Ma had left Taiwan to go to graduate school in the United States and never saw her mother again. She would talk about spirits not at rest when I was young, not intending to scare me silly but scaring me silly nonetheless. "It may linger around for a while. But then eventually it goes away."

These, then, had been my options when I was like Gigi and Ruby, worrying, "What if Mom and Dad die?" My parents would either become ashes or ghosts. I did not like these options! There had to be a better choice. This is what drove me, as a college student, to search for a religion. I visited churches and temples, tagged along with friends to their seders and Masses. I lit the menorah with my roommate in our dorm room at Penn. At a Roman Catholic Easter service I sat in a pew next to a friend whose entire family held hands and in perfect unison said prayers I didn't know. *They believe they will always be one,* I thought at the time, aching inside.

Many years later, Radhanath Swami, a renowned monk and teacher in the Krishna-bhakti lineage, would tell me that in Ayurveda, the system of traditional medicine in India, there is a belief that hunger is necessary for proper digestion. When we're hungry, the salivary glands kick in and digestive juices begin to flow, allowing us to break down food and absorb nutrients better than when we're not hungry. "In the same way, in our spiritual practices, if we're hungry or if we're eager or feel a sense of urgency to connect, then when we . . . meditate or pray we'll get the maximum benefit," Radhanath Swami extrapolates. "We'll actually be able to assimilate and *realize* the essence of what we're doing."

I was hungry.

The Episcopal church Kent grew up in comforted me the most. A loving God, welcoming all, a respect for my free will and the use of my brain, music that filled the space in my heart with hope, and a place for me and those I love for eternity. I wanted in.

"Baptize me! I'm ready!" I declared after returning from our honeymoon. I was twenty-two years old, I had just graduated from college and gotten married. I'm not one for uncertainty. These decisions needed to be decided already.

Chaplain Chapin back then was a balding man in his seventies whom I always remember with a runny nose because he would choke up with emotion so often. It always touched me that, having seen so much suffering as a hospital chaplain, he still allowed himself to feel so deeply. He sat, holding on to his cane, looking at me through his glasses, and shook his head. "You're not ready," he said kindly but firmly.

It was just like when we asked him to marry us and he took out a handkerchief and blew his nose, saying, "Please, no. Don't involve me." *Are you even a priest?* I thought. *Do you understand that you're supposed to want to increase the flock?*

But Chaplain Chapin had seen too many failed marriages, too many Christians fall away from the Lord. "I don't want my heart broken anymore," he said. "You can get anyone from the Yellow Pages to do your wedding." We were stunned. We didn't want someone we didn't know. We wanted him.

"If you want me, you have to come to church for eight consecutive weeks and study the ceremony line by line," he said. "It's a marriage we're talking about, not a wedding. You need to know what you're getting into."

We agreed, and by the time I walked down the aisle and said my vows and spent a week at a resort in a state of newlywed bliss, I knew I wanted to be baptized. But Chaplain Chapin disagreed.

"You just got married, you're all happy right now," he said. "You're not thinking straight. Come ask me again after you've come to church every Sunday for a year."

What's that line about not wanting to be in a club that would have you for a member? This was the opposite. I'd known the sting of helpless rejection from trying to rush sororities in college. But perfect attendance to gain entry to the church? *Well, that I can do.*

In the car now, Ba told Uncle Henry, "Patty's a Christian." Of course, that could mean many different things. The Reverend Amy Lamborn was raised a Southern Baptist in the Tennessee countryside. "It was a religion based on fear—fear of anything in life that was too pleasurable, fear of hell if you didn't get born again. People were a lot less interested in this life because, you know, *I'm just waiting on heaven.*" She became an Episcopalian in college. "Growing up, I saw people told on their deathbeds, *Pray now or you'll go to hell.* I didn't want to be afraid anymore that if I died tonight I might go to hell or my soul might not be right because I lusted after a boy or got bored during a sermon."

Working as a chaplain in a hospice, she'd cultivated a very different bedside manner. "I believe with all my heart God's love knows no limits, that God has already accepted us. And if I can offer ease to the dying, helping people cross the bridge to whatever comes next by offering some blessed reassurance, then I've done what I can do." This is why Amy is Ruby's godmother. This is the story I want my children to know.

What of the skeptics, who say that religion is a story we tell ourselves to help us feel better?

"We do all kinds of things to bring on comfort and fend off fear," Amy said. "We drink wine, we have pets, we seek relationships. Who's to say that faith is a worse coping mechanism? And who's to say it's not more than that?" Just as relationships help us cope with life, they also bring true connection and joy, Amy pointed out. Faith brings many benefits, of strength and community, and even perhaps health— a number of studies show that people who believe in something bigger than themselves tend to live longer.

Nai-nai had become a Buddhist in her later years, pursuing the belief that we are on a path to enlightenment, and that in each life we're given we strive to get closer to it. "Do you believe in reincarnation?" Uncle Henry asked. Ba harrumphed in his seat.

"Supposedly, how you live this life determines what you get sent back as, although who's to say what's worse, a fat house cat or a poor man?" Ma said.

"Have you heard the joke about the man who told God in his next life he wanted everyone to give him money? He was sent back as a beggar!" Uncle Henry chortled.

"My father used to say that a bad man should get sent back to earth as a woman. Because women have to work so much harder than men," Ma replied.

The comic potential of discussing past and future lives aside, there is something beautiful about the Buddhist belief that Thich Nhat Hanh expresses in *No Death, No Fear*: "There is no birth, there is no death; there is no coming, there is no going. . . ." We are all like a cloud that manifests when conditions are right into different forms, like rain and the sea. We are sad when a loved one dies "because we are attached to one of the forms, one of the many manifestations of that person," but "matter cannot be destroyed—it can become energy. And energy can become matter, but it cannot be destroyed." The person we love is still there, Hanh counsels. "We can see our loved one in everything."

The subtitle to Hanh's book is *Comforting Wisdom for Life*, and the skeptics would probably dismiss it as a story people tell themselves to make themselves feel better. But watching Ba sitting in the half-light, I wished something could comfort him. The thought of both my parents being gone forever is unbearable to me.

"What's it called when everything is decided ahead of time?" Uncle Henry asked.

"Predestination?" I said.

"Yes! Predestination!" Uncle Henry responded so energetically, it made me jump in my seat. None of us had gotten much sleep. But he was wide awake as he described how his life had been written down long ago.

"When I was a teenager back in Taiwan, I was in a bad way, and my mother was so worried about me she took me to a fortune-teller. It was very expensive, like eight hundred Taiwan dollars. Well, your Nai-nai liked to bargain, and she said, 'What! For a child? You can't have that much interesting to say about him.' He came down to four hundred. But then she said, 'How can you charge that for one hour's work?' The fortune-teller said he would do a lot in that hour, writing everything down. 'I'll write it down and pay you half,' she said. And that's what happened. She paid him two hundred and he ran my birth date, where the stars were, that kind of thing. I still have the piece of paper where Nai-nai wrote down what was in my future. It's all pretty accurate! What he said about life change, job change, moving, it came true."

If all the trials of life were predetermined, Uncle Henry mused, then maybe there was little to worry about, little to fear. He has always been one of my favorite uncles, for the bounce in his step and the eagerness of his smile even when his life seemed so hard, with layoffs, relocations, and caring for aging parents. Perhaps this was the secret to his buoyancy through it all.

"The list runs out at age sixty-eight. So maybe that means when I turn sixty-eight my number will be up!" he said.

"No, what that means is if you wanted him to keep going, Nai-nai should have paid him eight hundred," I joked.

"Oh well, there's nothing to be done about it, if it's already decided," he said cheerfully.

The Reverend Amy Lamborn says that many people she counseled as they lay dying in hospice would tell her what they were seeing, and each person's vision was always his or her own. "It's a blank screen—and we project onto it our deepest longings and fears," she said. "And just as Jesus said in John 14:2, 'In my Father's house are many mansions,' one person may see streets of gold and another quiet nothingness, and I believe there's a place for every one of them."

As for me, my parents, and my uncle, with our vastly different visions of the end, we were nonetheless all laughing as the sun came up over the East Bay. *Perhaps the greatest comfort is being together now*, I thought.

≋

CROSSING THE BAY BRIDGE, I remembered a story in the *New Yorker* by Tad Friend, about how people would cross this bridge in order to go jump off the more famous Golden Gate Bridge, because throwing oneself off the Bay Bridge was considered "tacky."

Since the Golden Gate opened on May 27, 1937, there have been an estimated 1,600 suicides off it in which the body was recovered, and many more unconfirmed deaths, according to a *Los Angeles Times* op ed by John Bateson, author of *The Final Leap: Suicide on the Golden Gate Bridge* and the former executive director of a San Francisco Bay Area crisis center. In 2011, he writes, thirty-seven people died and a hundred people were stopped from jumping, "in other words, every two and a half days, someone went to the bridge and either jumped or tried to jump." It is the world's leading suicide location.

The most harrowing revelation of the *New Yorker* article was that those who jump often regret their decision *midair*. In interviews, survivors said things like, "I instantly realized that everything in my life that I'd thought was unfixable was totally fixable—except for having just jumped," and "My first thought was, *What the hell did I just do?* I don't want to die."

Friend also conveyed that many people want to be talked down; he interviewed a motorcycle patrolman named Kevin Briggs, who had coaxed more than two hundred potential jumpers back from the brink by asking, "What's your plan for tomorrow?" If there was no plan, he'd reply, "Well, let's make one. If it doesn't work out, you can always come back here later."

If history holds true, most of them won't go back. University of California, Berkeley, researcher Richard H. Seiden tracked what happened to 515 people who were stopped from jumping off the Golden Gate Bridge between 1937 and 1971. In his 1978 study he reported that after, on average, more than twenty-six years, 94 percent were still alive or had died of natural causes. The findings show that "suicidal behavior is crisis-oriented and acute in nature," Seiden concluded. If you can get through the crisis, life is very likely to feel worth living again.

Writer Charles Baxter has called an action that takes your character to a place of no return a one-way gate. He has an affair, and becomes an adulterer. She kills someone, and becomes a murderer. They can't ever go back to being what they were before. In art, a one-way gate often leads to a snowball effect of actions spiraling out of control, high drama, and suspense. In America, the land of fresh starts and rehabilitation, there are few one-way gates, where truly what's done is done and cannot be undone.

A successful suicide attempt, though, is one of them. Killing oneself just stops the story cold.

"Even in the pull toward death, there is something that wants to be born," the Reverend Amy Lamborn's voice spoke to me as we crossed over San Francisco Bay.

Don't ever jump.

≫

BOARDING THE PLANE, I noted where the emergency exits were. According to Tim Jepson's *Telegraph* article "How to Survive a Plane Crash," having a plan for what to do in case of a crash is "fundamental to survival." He says to "actually count the number of rows from your seat to exits in front of and behind you—the chances are you might be trying to find your way to an exit in pitch dark and/or thick smoke." So I did that. And then I got ready to sleep.

I was so tired I didn't even pray for the pilots, which I usually do, but I did think hazily about Barry Daniels, who always said a Hebrew prayer at takeoff: *Sh'ma Yisrael Adonai Eloheinu Adonai Echad* (Hear,

O Israel, the Lord is our God, the Lord is One). Except the one time he decided not to.

This is superstitious, it's a ridiculous ritual, he thought on June 26, 1995, as American Airlines Flight 58 from Los Angeles to New York prepared for takeoff. Daniels was a Harvard graduate who liked to think things through. Although takeoffs made him anxious, he'd never actually had a problem on a plane. He was twenty-five years old, about to start graduate school, with his whole life ahead of him. He was going home after traveling cross-country to see friends. It wasn't like he was in some war-torn country trying to escape under enemy fire. What was he worrying about?

"Eh, God doesn't give a shit, I'm not going to say it," he decided, as the plane began accelerating down the runway. He picked up his book instead. And wouldn't you know? A few hours later, above Green Bay, Wisconsin, his plane plummeted in the sky.

About two-thirds of the way through the flight, suddenly and with no warning, the DC-10 rose and then plunged almost two hundred feet (the height of the Statue of Liberty) in less than two seconds. Count two seconds. Imagine your plane dropping almost twenty stories.

The 103 passengers aboard weren't even expecting turbulence—a third of them, including Barry, didn't have their seat belts fastened.

"One moment, everything's cool—*The Brady Bunch Movie* was on, I was sitting in the last row reading my book, my tray table was down," he recalled for me. "Then we're in free fall! I flew out of my seat, and so did everyone in front of me who didn't have seat belts on. They were popping up like Mexican jumping beans." All hell broke loose.

"Every person and thing that wasn't battened down flew up to the ceiling, which was splattered all red." The red wasn't blood, it was wine, a horrifying visual I now can't get out of my mind. "Everyone was screaming, praying, or crying." Barry hit his head on the ceiling on the way up and smashed his leg into the tray table on the way down, somehow managing to hold on to his book. His only clear thought was, *God: You're really going to kill everyone on this plane because I didn't say this prayer? REALLY?*

Barry felt like he was Jonah, whose boat gets tossed in the storm until the seamen figure out it's because of him and throw him overboard to be swallowed by the whale.

"'Sorry, everybody' is what I thought." And then he started praying.

"Remember when we did the seventh grade field trip to Great Adventure?" Barry asked me. We were talking on the phone for the first time, perhaps ever. Although we had gone to middle and high school together, we had different circles of friends, and when I heard he had had a near-death experience and reached out to ask him about it, I didn't know what to expect. So far, I was on the edge of my seat. "Remember Freefall?

"Yes." Freefall was my first and last scary amusement park ride. "I remember taking off and lifting up off my seat, screaming this endless scream, and then, *boom!* Impact and getting flipped on my back. When I opened my eyes and all I saw was blue sky, I thought I had died and this was heaven."

"Wow, it's thirty years later and you remember it that well," Barry said. "So this was exactly like that, except there's no rational part in your head that reassures you and says, I'm in an amusement park. Imagine there's no structure that explains what's happening in a way that you're not going to die."

What was actually going on was that the plane had hit a storm with fifty-mile-per-hour vertical winds. But without knowing that, all Barry could think was that something catastrophic had gone wrong with the plane—a wing had fallen off, the plane was broken and nothing could be done about it.

We're going down, we're going down is what Barry thought, pure panic, with an overlay of disbelief: Wow, nothing is going to stop this from happening. We're not going to be protected. We're not going to be saved.

Because Nancy Spielberg, Steven Spielberg's sister, was on the plane and became the lead plaintiff in a lawsuit against the airline afterward, the incident got widespread media coverage. In an article in *People* magazine, Nancy says, "I went straight up on my head and folded up like an accordion. Everything from the back of the plane was lurching forward, including my daughter. I remember thinking, 'We're going to die.'"

Luckily, the plane was way more than two hundred feet in the air when it dropped, and it still functioned properly. It pitched and tossed as the pilot righted it and then prepared for an emergency landing in Chicago. Barry remembers the pilot getting on the intercom and saying something like, "Sorry, folks. We've alerted the planes behind us about the turbulence," and wanting to scream *But what about the plane we're all in right now?*

Barry, shaking, made his way to the airplane bathroom, and checked his eyes. They were dilating and contracting in response to light; he did not have a concussion. When he came back out into the cabin, it was like entering an alternate reality.

"Everybody looked so sexy, so friendly, I felt this weird mind meld with these other people I didn't even know," Barry said. "I once read an article about people who take magic mushrooms and it was a bit like that, a weird neurological state. We were all one, we had all been through the same trauma, the same terror."

What Barry describes is what happens when stress hormones activate the brain's neurochemical systems that promote attachment bonds. As David Shields says in *The Thing About Life Is That One Day You'll Be Dead*: "Fear and terror, not shared pleasant experiences, are more likely to result in mutual attraction."

SOME NERVE

"You felt like you could kiss anyone. Everybody was talking to everybody, two women asked me for my number," Barry said, adding that eighteen years later, neither had called yet. "Usually we have our own private thoughts, our own interior world—you have your history and I have mine—but here, the boundaries between us were gone. I mean, when you're screaming and crying it's not like your thoughts are private anymore." It didn't matter who was young or old, rich or poor, black or white. "We were all in exactly the same place. It was mind-blowing."

A doctor from the Philippines walked around, attending to people. He had an aura, like he was an amazingly powerful figure. "He was a hero," Barry said.

And then, without knowing what shape the plane was in, they had to prepare for landing. Everyone sat down, some sobbing or whimpering, bracing for what was coming next.

They landed safely. Passengers were told that everyone needed to get off the plane, because of cracks in the fuselage. No one needed to be told twice.

Barry was one of the first off. "There was a blond newscaster who shoved a microphone in my face. She was a vision of the purest beauty of my life. She was *there*. I was *there*. I felt like I was really seeing things for the first time. *We're safe! We're on the ground!* I've never been so happy."

Seventeen of the passengers went to the hospital to be treated for injuries. The rest needed to get back to New York.

"Some people did not get on the next plane," Barry said. "I felt scared shitless, but I also felt like, *Fuck this, I want to go home.*" He boarded the next flight he could.

Eventually, a federal jury would award $2.2 million to be divided among the thirteen passengers who sued the airline for emotional distress following the incident (Barry was not part of the lawsuit). But all the passengers survived that harrowing experience and had something else in common, which is to me the most amazing thing about the story: *Every one of them went on to fly again.*

About 6.5 percent of Americans have a fear of flying so intense they refuse to fly, according to the National Institute of Mental Health. For most, it's anxiety, and not a sensitizing event at the root of the fear. The vast majority have never had an experience like the passengers on Flight 58. Yet the 103 people who actually survived that near-death experience went on to decide that getting where they wanted to go was worth the risk of boarding a plane.

"OMG!!!" was John Viterito's e-mail response to my description of this outcome. Viterito is a licensed professional counselor who overcame his fear of flying "for love—my wife's from Hong Kong, and I flew for her."

I asked him what he thought of the passengers' ability to move on after such a frightening ordeal. He saw it as "proof positive that we bring ourselves to our experiences, even our traumatic experiences. While our negative experiences impact us, they do not determine us. We have the power and ability to respond in a multitude of ways to our experiences and our limitations."

Barry's response to his experience was to research everything he could about airplane crashes. He read National Transportation Safety Board reports and Michael Crichton's *Airframe*; watched movies like Peter Weir's *Fearless*; read books about dying, including Ernest Becker's *The Denial of Death*.

"You went into the fear," I said, with awe. "You didn't push it down. You went toward it, to figure out what happened, to get data for its likelihood of happening again."

"My character structure is very intellectualizing," Barry agreed. "That's the way I handled it, getting over my animal fear with my rational frame."

He flies all the time, for work and pleasure. "The risks in air travel are so much less than in a car." Over the past five years, the risk of a fatal crash on a U.S. commercial flight has been one in 45 million. In 2011, more than thirty-two-thousand people died in motor vehicle crashes in the United States while there were no U.S. commercial airline fatalities at all.

A few months after the incident, Barry took a long flight to Israel, and he brought some prescription medicine along in case he got upset. "I was struck by the absurdity of it," he said. "We started feeling a little turbulence, I reached down to get the Valium—and then I realized, this is to help me have less fear, but I'm not afraid of my fear. I'm afraid of dying in a giant ball of fire. Taking these pills does not change whether that happens. But I took the pills and the turbulence got better, so go figure."

Meanwhile, on my flight home from San Francisco, I woke up when the plane was somewhere over the Colorado Rockies. I got up to go to the bathroom but was sent back by the flight attendant, who pointed to the lit-up seat belt sign. I sat, and tried not to think about what would happen to my full bladder if the plane were to suddenly plummet. And sitting there, I remembered what Barry's brush with death had meant to him in the long run.

"I'm glad I had that experience" is what he said to me. "It was the ultimate moment of my life."

It woke him up.

"We think we know who we are, who others are; we think we know what's going to happen. The revelation to me was that we always live side by side with the void. We think it's in the distant future, but it's not necessarily. Something has to breathe life into reality at every moment." We usually think in terms of matter, not antimatter, he said, but, "When you think in two seconds you're going to be vaporized, you can really see nonbeing."

Rabbi Heidi Hoover of Temple Beth Emeth in Brooklyn, New York, says, "In Judaism, the focus is on this life, perfecting this world. We don't know what happens after you die. What matters more is, are you studying the Torah, are you comforting the sick, are you making the world a better place or not?"

A near-death experience often triggers serious thought about what happens after death and what life itself is for. The closest most young, healthy Jews get to a near-death experience is contemplating it at Yom Kippur, when some even wear a kittel, the simple white robe they will be buried in, as part of the Holy Day's acknowledgment of the fact that we're all going to die. But Barry got a chance to fall headlong toward death and at the last moment pull back toward life. What did that mean to him?

"I can't imagine being more afraid," he said. "But it was also very life affirming. I have treasured life more since then. I've been less into bullshit, I mean I'm still plenty into bullshit, but the questions 'Do we have good grades, a good job, good self-esteem?' paled in comparison to '*Do we get annihilated?*'"

Like Josh, Barry returned to his life changed. When fellow grad students complained about their girlfriends or their jobs, he thought, *Look, you're not residue scraped off a cornfield, stop the kvetching, get on with your life!* Instead of feeling trapped by situations, he thought, *I really do have some degree of freedom when I'm not smoky ash.*

"What do you think happens when you die?" I asked.

"I kinda got the feeling there is no other side," he said. "I used to think sure, there's something of me that could survive independent of my body, but in that moment where it was all about to end, where every cell was saying *THIS IS HAPPENING*, I realized how incredibly embodied we are, how incarnate. We are flesh and blood. If you were stripped away of your body, your memory, your feelings, of the sensation of the sun or the feel of the wind against your cheeks, what would be left?"

But instead of making him think, *What's the point if we're all going to end up dead anyway?* the inevitability and finality of death liberated Barry to live fully now.

"I have really spent zero time worrying about the meaning of life since," Barry said. "Being on that plane made me realize there is no meaning of life except the shimmering experience of being alive for yourself and others. Just the raw state of existing as a pulsating human being and appreciating it is all."

Steve Jobs, cofounder of Apple, was diagnosed with cancer in 2003, and said in a commencement address at Stanford University in 2005, "Remembering that I'll be dead soon is the most important tool I've ever encountered to help me make the big choices in life. Because almost everything—all external expectations, all pride, all fear of embarrassment or failure—these things just fall away in the face of death, leaving only what is truly important. Remembering that you are going to die is the best way I know to avoid the trap of thinking you have something to lose. You are already naked. There is no reason not to follow your heart."

Feeling connected to all those strangers opened Barry up that day, and he strives to stay open and empathetic. For days afterward, he saw the beauty in people, heard the beauty in music, in a heightened state, and he tries to remember that. *Am I spending my days well? Am I experiencing enough? Am I connected enough?* are the questions he asks himself.

Radhanath Swami does believe we have an eternal soul. Within our own bodies, we are constantly changing, and "The soul is accepting new physical conditions, new mental conditions," he said in a lecture titled "Life after Death." "The Bhagavad Gita explains that it is a continuation of the same process at the time of death. The soul accepts another body. What type of body? This is a great mystery."

But before he became a Swami in India, he was a Jewish boy from Chicago named Richard Slavin who at age nineteen set out on a pilgrimage across Europe to discover himself. In his book *The Journey Home*, he writes of near-death experiences he had along the way—by drowning, quicksand, wild dogs, and more. But he kept pressing forward. "Weren't you afraid of getting hurt?" I asked him once, and his answer was one Barry or Rabbi Heidi Hoover could just as easily have given.

"Whether we fear pain and suffering or not, pain and suffering come to everyone," he said. He described sitting by the Ganges River and imagining it flowing from the Himalayas over a thousand miles and around every kind of obstacle—mountains, rocks, fallen trees—to make its way to the sea. "Pain and suffering are like those rocks. They will come. What's the use of being afraid of them? They're going to happen anyway." He chuckled. "Why not just keep our mind focused on where we want to go in our life?"

Or, as Rabbi Heidi Hoover says, "If we thought too much about how many people die in car crashes, we would walk everywhere. And if we thought about how many pedestrians get hit by cars, we would hide in our houses, lying in bed all day. And if we did that, we'd get afraid of our house burning down. And where does it end?"

Barry doesn't think too much about his plane crashing when he travels now.

But he also says the *Sh'ma Yisrael* prayer at takeoff, just in case.

≋

"I'M AFRAID OF SHARKS!" Ruby called to me from her room. I usually sit in the hallway outside her door until she falls asleep.

So am I! I wanted to reply. But out loud, I said, "There are no sharks here."

"I'm afraid of the dark!"

"It isn't dark, Ruby. Your night-light is on, your door is open, the hall light is on, I can see you, you can see me. Now stop talking and go to sleep!"

"I'm afraid of monsters!" This could go on awhile.

"You need to stop sitting there," Kent said, walking past me to go downstairs. I know what he means, that my sitting here could make her think there *is* something to be afraid of, or that she needs me to fall asleep. I know that neither is necessarily true.

But maybe because I've spent so many nights of my life awake and anxious, I don't have the heart to walk away just yet.

⌄

ONE DAY, WHEN I WAS in sixth grade and studying for the entrance exam to Hunter, a highly competitive public school in New York City, the phone rang. I was alone in our apartment in the Bronx. My sister was playing at a neighbor's house one floor down. My parents were at work.

I was annoyed at the interruption. I had a lot riding on this test. The tough girls, who went to the local junior high, got ready for school by slicking Vaseline on their faces in case anyone tried to scratch them and braiding their hair close to their heads so no one could grab a handful and yank them down. I, with my penchant for wearing prairie dresses and reading Charlotte Brontë, wouldn't last a week there, and my parents knew it. "You must get into Hunter," Ba had said. It was Tiger parent pressure combined with real concern. "If you don't, I don't know what we'll do. We have no money for private school. We'll have to find a place in Westchester, and your mother doesn't drive a car." I faced every study session with the thought that if I failed, my entire family would be thrown into upheaval. And now the phone was ringing in the middle of a reading comprehension passage. I'd have to start the section over again.

"Hello? *Wei?*" No answer. People often called, asking to speak to my parents. Perhaps they were salesmen, or thieves checking to see who was home. I usually said I was with a babysitter who spoke only Chinese, but there was no one to say anything to this time. I hung up, went back to work. A while later, the doorbell rang.

"Who is it?"

"The electrician. The super sent me to fix something on this hall, but it's connected to your apartment—can I come in? It won't take long." I looked through the peephole. He was thin, dark haired, with a mustache, a tool belt. He didn't look intimidating. I was so impatient with being interrupted again that I said, "Okay, fine," and opened the door.

He walked past me with purpose. "I just need to check the outlets," he said, but as he walked through the apartment he was looking at the windows. We were on the seventh floor. Was he looking at the view? The fire escape? In the moment I didn't think he was casing the joint, although looking back on it he probably was, and he was probably disappointed. What of interest was there in our apartment? Dishes, what was left of my snack, Stella D'oro cookies and milk. (The Stella D'oro factory on Broadway made our entire neighborhood smell like anise, and whenever I opened a package from the supermarket I assumed it had been freshly baked just for us.) The faux wood table on which the cookies and milk sat in the dining area that was really the foyer and spilled into our living room, the spaces overrun by the usual jumble of toys and newspapers. A small TV. A brown corduroy couch, bought new, but nothing expensive.

In my parents' bedroom my work was spread out on the desk. The lamp cast a warm circle of yellow light on my papers. Even though it was afternoon, I liked the extra light, it focused me. The man pointed to the outlet under the desk and said, "Is it okay if I turn that off while I check it?"

I shrugged. I wanted to finish my practice test, and now the timing was going to be all off. But at least he was doing what he said he was going to do, check the outlet. I wanted him to get out.

The lamp clicked off, and I was standing in the pale gray-blue light coming in the window from a partly cloudy day. It was late afternoon, I realized, it would be dark before long. He lay on the floor, his head and arms under the desk, rummaging.

"Can you help me?" he called out. "There's a plug I can't reach and your hands are smaller." I wanted him to finish already. I wiggled in beside him and said, "Where?"

He tugged at a cord, it must have been to the clock radio. Oh great, now I'd have to reset the time. "Can you reach that?"

I did. He had the plug to the lamp in his hand. "Let's plug them in one at a time, like this." He plugged the lamp in, waited a few seconds, took it out, and did it again. I did not understand what he was doing, but I copied. And then it got hard to breathe.

Of all the stupid, clueless, brainless things I have done in my life, of which there are many, the worst was letting this man into my house. In the cramped space under my desk, with his face so close I could see the oily pores on his nose, I realized he was looking at me, not the outlet. I tried to shrink back to get a little space but he was pressing into me, the edges of the tools on his belt cool, everything else too warm and smothering. Then, and only then, did my stupid brain stop thinking about vocabulary words and start thinking this:

This is wrong. He is not supposed to be here. The realization ricocheted through my body. My ears pounded. I was going to explode.

"I forgot something!" I gasped, pushing myself out from under him, banging into the desk on the way out. I scrabbled onto the familiar Oriental rug, touching it like home base, and then stood up breathing in cool air and daylight.

"What?" He crawled out from under the desk and got up, looking confused.

"I forgot that my neighbor is expecting me—I'm late," I said, and I walked, fast, to the front door and opened it wide. The smells of dogs and dinner and the sounds of Spanish flooding in from the hallway grounded me. *GET OUT*, I was screaming in my head, *THIS IS MY HOUSE*. But to him I said, "If I don't show up, she's going to come looking for me. Call the super if you need to get back in." *GET OUT*, I screamed with my eyes, *OR I WILL SCREAM FOR REAL* and the Dobermans in 7J and the old lady in 7A are going to come out here and you're going to have a big scene. I stood there, holding the door open.

And he did it, he walked away. I watched as he waited for the elevator and got in. I grabbed my keys, slammed the door shut, locked it, and ran, ran down the hall, checked to see that the elevator was still going down, and then I ran down the stairs to 6K, where the Kvenviks sat watching TV and smoking cigarettes and their little dog greeted me at the door as usual and where my sister was playing like nothing was wrong. I burst in and said, "Can we call the super? I need to know if he sent a repairman to my apartment."

Of course, he hadn't.

Of course, this led to mass panic. "*How could you let him in?*" Ba yelled at me. I told my parents everything except the part about getting under the desk. Except the part where I couldn't breathe. My parents, I knew, would not sleep that night. If they knew everything, they would never sleep well again. I was so stupid. What if my sister had been home? What if he had hurt her as well as me?

I refused to go to the police. I was too ashamed. I'm okay, he didn't steal anything, please, no police, I said, trying to downplay what had happened. But by not going, I opened us all up to the question *What if he comes back?* Ba changed our phone number, put big shiny brass locks on all the windows. I think they were meant to make us safe, to make us feel safe. But instead, what I saw was a reminder, in every room, of what I had done to the family. Let an intruder in. Made us all vulnerable. The eldest daughter—stupid, irresponsible girl.

On the scale of harm that could have been done to me that day, nothing that terrible happened. But from that day forward, I lived my life as if it had. Which is to say, I walked around looking at every mustached, slight, dark-haired man on the street for years, wondering if he was looking back at me. Every night before bed, in every bed I slept in from that day on, I made plans. *In case of an intruder, how would I get to the phone, how would I hide my sister, how could we get out?* Exit strategies, physical and verbal. What I would say to protect us all.

The eighties in the Bronx were dangerous times. Once, Ba was shaken down by two men claiming to be cops, until another guy claiming to be a cop scared them away. Three other times, Ba witnessed muggings. He would come home from work and tell us the latest. Once, on the subway, he and a few other passengers apprehended a mugger and held him down until the police came. "I had him by the leg!" Ba recalled with pride. "It was a citizen's arrest."

"*Aiya*," Ma said. "Don't ever do that again. You could have been killed."

I weighed ninety pounds. I knew I couldn't take anyone on in a fight. It made me feel very small.

≋

SITTING IN THE HALLWAY, I listened to the sound of Ruby scratching and Gigi's deep breathing, and thought about what people do who have a fear of being physically overpowered. Gigi has taken karate since she was five years old. Her teacher, Renchi (master) Julio Rodriguez, grew up in Washington Heights at the same time I was growing up in the Bronx, in more dangerous conditions than even I could have imagined. His wife, Sempai (assistant instructor) Crystal Madison-Rodriguez, had been trying to get me to take her women's self-defense class for years. *Maybe I should try a class,* I thought.

We want to protect our children, and we want our children to know how to protect themselves if we're not there. Maybe there's something to be done, apart from praying for everyone's safety every night. Maybe it was time for Ruby to start karate. And for me to get out of this hallway.

≋

"IT MUST BE SO much fun being the fear-facing lady," my friends often say. "You get to do so many exciting things!"

"Fun?" I reply. *"I'm constantly terrified.* Do you know what it's like to be constantly worried you're going to wet yourself? I'm either going to get braver or I'm going to have a nervous breakdown."

I'm joking, to a degree. It is fun, seeing myself do things I never thought I'd do. But the day I finally got myself to Crystal's women's self-defense class at the Riverdale Y in the Bronx, I felt nothing but dread. I grew up avoiding the tough girls I didn't want to fight, and now I was going to pay to relive the sensation on my weekend. *I'm about to get my ass kicked. This is not going to be fun.*

The Y was bustling. I'd put this moment off for so long that the class I finally made it to was the last before summer vacation. All around me were signs of hard work coming to fruition. A woman with an armful of shepherd and Egyptian pharaoh costumes bustled past me as teens in a production of *Joseph and the Amazing Technicolor Dreamcoat* pressed by to get into the auditorium. Outside the racquet-ball court that doubles as the USA Goju-Ryu Karate school, little munchkins in black karate uniforms swarmed around, waving certificates and wooden boards freshly broken by their small bare hands. *It must be promotion day for the beginner belts*, I thought, with a pang.

I remembered Gigi's first karate promotion, her white belt wrapped double around her little six-year-old waist, her black pants also rolled double at the ankles but still too long. The other day we discovered she could stand on tiptoe and kiss my cheek. Was she ever this small?

Standing tall among the waist-high karate kids was Crystal. Even in a hallway with lighting that would make Tyra Banks look like she needed beauty rest, you could not take your eyes off Crystal. She was wearing a sleeveless black karate shirt, showing her powerfully toned arms, over black workout pants. Her black hair swung down to her waist, her head wrapped by a black-and-white bandanna that meant business. She looked like a warrior whose image, in another time and place, would be carved into statues and worshipped.

Crystal had started doing karate after a young man on a bicycle rode by her on the sidewalk and grabbed her ass. "What got me was the smug look he gave me, like it was his to do and he knew he was going to get away with it," she'd told me before. "Well, I snapped. I pulled him off the bike and started hitting him with my shoe." The power of her anger—she knocked him out cold with her platform sandal—surprised and scared her. She ran away, unhurt, but worried about the future. "I was a single mom back then, my son was only four or five. I wanted to learn how to protect myself from guys on the street and protect my child, and also to control my own strength."

"You're here!" Crystal exclaimed when she caught sight of me, beaming surprise and delight. Her skin is so dark, it's light—when she's happy it's as if sunshine radiates from her insides and reflects off the outside.

"I told you I'd come," I said, reaching over a couple of kids to kiss her cheek. "It just took me five years, is all."

"Look who's here!" Toy, the mother of a boy in Gigi's karate class and a student of Crystal's, came up behind me. She, too, had been after me to try this class ever since she started it as a white belt, but I'd always had an excuse. *Too busy. Have an injury. I'm a yogi—a lover, not a fighter.*

I looked at the brown belt tied around Toy's waist.

"In five years, you went from white belt to brown," I said admiringly. That meant six levels of promotion; she was now just one step away from black belt. "What have I done in five years?"

I looked down at my purple sundress, realizing I'd dressed for the hot weather but not for the occasion. I'd worn a tank top and shorts under the sundress, forgetting that everyone else would be in karate uniforms. Shorts seemed immodest for the class, though, so I kept the dress on, preferring embarrassment to being disrespectful. I took my place in the dojo.

Renchi Julio ran the warm-ups, which were familiar to me—I'd watched Gigi, face bright red, do set after set of jumping jacks, crunches, and push-ups to start class every week for years, as I sat in the hallway feeling my hips spread.

I hadn't done a jumping jack in years.

"One, two, three, four, five, six, seven, eight, nine, ten," Julio counted.

I-need-to-pee-uh-oh-I-need-to-pee! I thought, trying to jump and kegel-squeeze at the same time, which was hopeless. The whole room felt like it was shaking. The fluorescent lights high above us had racquet balls stuck in their grates. I hoped none dropped on my head.

When the jumping stopped, the jogging began. We ran around the small room in circles until it was spinning, and then Renchi Julio walked into the middle of the room with a long pole, which he held out into our path at knee height as he turned in circles toward us, saying, "Jump over the stick."

Oh hell no. I'd smashed my foot on an easel that morning, a large stationary object in my own house. How was I going to run and jump over a pole that was moving toward me at a rate I could not control? I ran, I prayed, I jumped. It took every ounce of concentration I had to hurdle over the moving stick again and again.

With each breath now, I was making a high-pitched sound like an animal in distress. I saw Gigi's inhaler in my mind and thought, *Exercise-induced asthma?* Maybe this is what wheezing felt like. I'd never done enough exercise to know.

"Yame!" Renchi Julio called out. "Stop. Good. Get some water."

On the way to the water fountain I saw Mae, Toy's sister, push their mother in a wheelchair into the dojo. Their mother was asleep, slumped over and frail. I have an affinity for most children and elderly people, especially if they're Asian. I often feel I could be related to them. This woman made me think of my own mother in a way that made my heart hurt more than it did from running.

Ma has a degenerative lung condition that keeps her home much of the time now because she's afraid of catching a cold and getting an infection. "Are her fears reasonable?" I'd asked my doctor.

"Do you know what it's like not to be able to breathe?" he'd shot back. *You would be afraid, too*, is what he meant.

Back in the dojo Crystal had us run back and forth across the gym with our bodies turned sideways, an exercise I associate with football players. Crystal, Toy, and Mae looked like athletes doing it. I kept running into the wall, my lack of coordination only accentuated by the purple sundress.

We kept running past Toy's mom, and my classmates' strength compared to her weakness was so pronounced it made it harder for me to breathe. How willingly would any of us transfuse our life force into our parents if we could?

Crystal, running sideways like a linebacker, was saying something encouraging, but since I was facing her rear I couldn't hear it clearly.

"Your thighs might be burning now," she said. And how. Her next words echoed around the room: "Find *homina-homina* deep down."

Find what? What did she say?

"Find *homina-homina*, you know it's there," she said. "It will help you."

What? What will help me? I want to know!

It was like watching *The Karate Kid* and having the tape warp at "Wax on, wax off." What if I was missing the secret to the universe?

But then we stopped, and Renchi Julio came back in. It was time to fight.

≫

JULIO WAS TWELVE YEARS OLD when his father was murdered, shot in the chest during a mugging. His mother was addicted to drugs and alcohol back then. She has since become clean, but for much of Julio's childhood there was nothing but chaos. "After my father died, I didn't know what I was doing," he said. "I had this anger."

But when he was thirteen he saw a martial arts class where all the students were moving in unison. "Everyone was listening, there was no chaos," he remembers with pleasure still. "It was order, uniforms, a stable routine. It saved my life."

About the same time a boy named Chiquito beat Julio up for stepping on his bottle cap. "He did it in front of the whole neighborhood," Julio said. "For a long time my goal in karate was to beat him up one day, and to get vengeance on my father's killer one day."

But his karate teacher "ended the chaos." He knew Julio was introverted, so he put him in front of the classroom to force him to be more vocal. He gave Julio goals to strive for and the discipline to see them through. Eventually, Julio would go to Colgate on a track scholarship, get his masters degree in engineering from Columbia, and become a high school science teacher and karate master. Chiquito, meanwhile, became a drug dealer and was shot and killed.

"If it wasn't for martial arts, I wouldn't be alive today," Julio believes, and when he teaches he wants nothing less than to spark the survival instinct that will help every one of his students to be all they can be, despite adversity. Which means heaping on the adversity in class.

In Gigi's class for six- to twelve-year-olds, he takes kids who might be teased or bullied for being short or gawky or four-eyed and picks them up and teaches them how to fall. "Come closer," he says. *Whack! Whack! Whack!* He pelts them everywhere with a padded stick. They giggle and he cracks a smile, too. It's fun, while it also trains the reflexes to react to the unexpected.

"My job is to put kids out of their comfort zone and have them push past it," he told me in an interview. "I simulate a big obstacle in their life. They feel the fear and then have to overcome it."

His exercises are symbolic of life's greater challenges.

"Be slippery" is one that made my skin crawl when I watched Gigi do it. Three other students surrounded her and she had to evade them somehow, without fighting them. "If a child is ganged up on by other kids, or if an adult tries to grab her, she will not be able to fight her way out. All she can do is be like a pigeon, small and fragile but *fast*." Closing her eyes and giving up was never an option; Gigi always managed to weave and dart her way free.

"Protect your family" teaches the opposite lesson. In this exercise, you have one person behind you that you have to protect, and an attacker in front of you that you have to deal with. "You have to defend yourself and defend someone you love at the same time," Julio explains.

"This teaches more than self-preservation. You can't just run away." In the book *Whatever You Do, Don't Run*, safari guide Peter Allison says that the rule of the bush is that food runs, so a lion may fake charge you in order to test your mettle. Any flinching could mean the end for you. So in the face of a lion you have to make yourself big, steady, and strong and see if it stands down. Often with bullies, it works the same way.

"We were always taught that if someone comes and wants your wallet, your jacket, you give it to them," Crystal's son Waymon once put it. He's a black belt himself. "But if what they want is *you*, you have to fight." In "fight it out" the student is cornered by two or more opponents. "If they're on you, then you have no choice," Julio teaches. "You have to fight your way out."

To the kids, these are games, as much fun as red rover or freeze tag. To me, they are survival skills as important as learning to swim. I wish I'd had this class when I was young.

Instead of now, as a middle-aged woman. Toy was my partner, and although she's a bit older than me and thin as a rail, I knew she could break me in two. "Go easy on me, I'm in a dress," I begged, putting pads on my hands. "Oh, and I have tendonitis in this elbow. And I need my hands to write." She sent both of my pads flying with her first two blows.

By the time it was my turn to punch, my hands were sore from deflecting Toy's hits. "*Hajime!*" Crystal ordered. I stood there, arms midair, frozen. *I can't do this*, I thought. *I'm weak. I'm not even going to land on the target.* The target was a white circle on the pads that symbolized the whites of your opponent's eyes. *I can't stare down a lion. I'm going to look like a fool.*

"*Hajime* means start," Toy whispered.

I did. Tentatively at first, my little questioning punches landing on her pads murmuring, I'm sorry! Is it okay that I'm hitting you? Are you sure?

"Harder," Toy said. "Come on, follow through."

"Don't pull any punches," I'd always heard, but I'd never fully understood the expression until now. All the ways I'd held back through my life—in swinging a bat or a tennis racquet or kicking a ball—started coming back to me. "Follow through, see where you want the ball to go!" coaches had yelled at me from the sidelines, but I never had the conviction that I could get it there. I had dreaded this class, thinking it would be one more experience being yelled at and failing. What if they yelled, "DO IT!" and I couldn't? In five years I'd never considered that I COULD.

Toy wasn't having it. "More, Patty. Come on, harder, you can do better," she said, and I hit harder just to see what that would feel like. *Thud.* "Good, solid, more," Toy said. The instructions in karate are like that—minimal, clear. I focused on the targets and listened to the pattern Crystal was calling out. "Jab-jab, punch-punch." I let it fill my head.

"NO HOLDING BACK!" she boomed.

I hit harder and harder. "Throw your shoulder into it," Renchi Julio urged me on. "And your hips." The more of my body I put into it, the better it felt.

"FOL-LOW *THROUGH!* FOL-LOW *THROUGH!*" Toy chanted, on the beat of every hit.

Jab-jab. Punch-punch.

Sweat was pouring down my face. I stopped to swipe my brow with my sweaty arm.

"Don't stop, don't break your rhythm," Toy said. I put up my dukes again, tried to focus.

"MOVE AROUND, TOY! Move the pads, move your body, make her work for it," Renchi Julio called out. The pads started moving. I swallowed the *Oh no* coming up in my throat and replaced it with *Here we go.*

"NO HOLDING BACK!"

"ALL THE WAY! ALL THE WAY!"

I could no longer tell who was yelling what, or if it was me now, telling myself to quit my whining and just do what needed to be done for once.

"Twenty more seconds!"

It was the longest twenty seconds of my life. I jabbed, I punched, I did it all the way, no holding back, and somewhere deep inside my heart something unspooled, something so tightly wound it made a zipping sound as it went. Hot tears rose in my eyes, a jagged cry in my throat. I kept punching, and the pain in my heart grew.

I saw Toy's mother, slumped in her chair. I thought of my parents, everyone's parents, growing old. I saw Gigi and Ruby, and every hurt they have ever sustained and all I want for them in the future I cannot guarantee. I saw myself, the twelve-year-old under the desk who did not know how to defend herself, with parents who couldn't protect her at the time. And the forty-one-year-old I have become, still afraid to be hurt, still wanting so much to protect those I love. Jab-jab, punch-punch.

I thought of Isabelle in an ambulance, worrying about who would care for her daughter; of Josh's mother, devastated at hearing her son and daughter were lost at sea; of Josh himself, at death's door troubled more about his mother's devastation than anything else. We all want to protect those we love, but we can't shelter them from life and death. We can only hope to teach them, and to learn ourselves, how to be strong to the end: Josh trying to build a flare gun, Gigi playing "be slippery," me punching this pad in the eye.

"Your arms might be feeling heavy now!" Crystal boomed. "Three more seconds."

"FOL-LOW THROUGH! FINISH IT, Patty. You're doing good. Don't stop. FOL-LOW THROUGH!" Toy's voice, her energy and intensity, filled me; we were a closed circuit of electricity.

I didn't know who or what I was punching. Muggers and murderers and slight men with mustaches, who would threaten and hurt people, make them afraid of the dark and of being alone? Myself, for everything I hadn't done and had put off doing or done halfway, because I was afraid to follow through? I had no idea, but I punched, as hard as I could. And somewhere in the last second ("One, one, one, *one* . . ." Was Crystal counting the same second over and over again?) I realized I was punching without fear. Strong (boom!), solid (bam!), unfaltering punches, to the very last one.

"And . . . ONE! *Yame!* Stop!" Crystal boomed.

I obeyed, releasing my hands onto my shaking thighs, head down, gulping air. I stopped the tears from falling, finally wiped the sweat from my face with my arm. I smiled and thanked Toy, I thanked God it was over.

The next morning, sore but not sorry, I got dressed slowly, thinking of Crystal and Julio. I thought how easily their strong bodies could have been built around a core of anger and fear, but how they chose instead to nurture in them hope for the future. I thought of the unspooling in my heart. What was underneath, past the pain and fear? "Find ____ deep inside," Crystal had said. My heart quickened at the memory. What filled in the blank? I stretched my arms overhead and felt the blood coursing through my body, allowing what had been buried deep to flood my being. There it was.

The will to live. The life instinct. The piece always waiting to be born.

≋

"MOMMY, PLEASE, ONE MORE HUG," Ruby called.

I got up and went into her room. "This is it," I said gruffly. "Then I have to go to sleep, too."

Each night, the impatience for her to go to sleep wrestles with the knowledge that each hug is a gift I must never take for granted. It makes me speak gruffly and hug deeply, a mixed message I hope Ruby on some level can understand. The days of my carrying her on my hip are done. And if I don't pay attention, before I know it, I will not have the luxury of holding her for as long as I want, breathing in the scent of her hair. All I'll have is her pushing me away, laughing, saying, "Enough, Mommy!" and the sound of her footsteps running away.

I asked so many people what they think happens when we die, and so many visions, philosophies, scriptural beliefs came forth. Many of the clergy I asked had changed beliefs through their lives—the Reverend Amy Lamborn went from Baptist to Episcopalian in college; Rabbi Heidi Hoover was raised Lutheran but converted to Judaism in adulthood; Radhanath Swami was raised Jewish and became Hindu after his pilgrimage.

I interviewed Radhanath Swami in the food court of Grand Central Terminal in New York City, surrounded by holiday wares of all descriptions and people of all stripes bustling by. He sat in his robes and told me a story.

In India, he told me, he'd met two best friends, one Hindu and the other Muslim. When he'd asked how they could be best friends in a place where there is so much conflict between the religions, the Hindu said, "If a dog has a master, that dog will recognize the master in whatever way the master dresses. The master may be dressed in a tuxedo or a T-shirt and jeans, he may be in a business suit or may be completely naked, but the dog will always recognize the master because he loves the master."

So, too, must we recognize the divine, and the humanity, in each other at all times.

Different stories may speak to us at different points in our lives, and different stories may speak to different people. A brush with death can bring one person closer to God and push another farther away. But everyone I asked, "What happens when we die?" held one belief in common: The most important thing is to not be afraid of life. "The experience of eternity right here and now . . . is the function of life," Joseph Campbell once said in an interview with Bill Moyers. "If you don't experience it here and now, you're not going to get it in heaven."

So when Ruby asks, "What would happen if you die?" I say what I believe and what she needs to hear. That she would be taken care of here on earth and that I would love her from heaven, just as I love her now, in a way that grows without end. I tell her that she is never alone because she is surrounded by the energy of all those who care for her, near and far, known and unknown. And that we will make the best of every day that we're given because every day is a gift.

And then I hug her, without holding back, with everything I've got. I let my defenses tumble down and allow the shimmering, pulsating life between us to take over. It is all we have, and all we need, right now.

CHAPTER 9

FALLING

Heights

Adel clung to the cable, five flights up. The balcony he was trying to climb down to, the balcony to his family's new apartment, was no longer within reach. It had seemed like a great idea a few minutes ago, when he was locked out: go up to the roof, shimmy down the electric cable two stories, get his footing on the balcony rail, and hop down to the balcony. The cable, which ran from a pole in the street to the roof of his building, crossed right next to the balcony, close enough to touch. He'd use it to get into the apartment, unlock the door, and let his friends in—all of them sixteen, or was it fifteen, years old, young and crazy enough to think such a plan could work. But now Adel's body was weighing the cable down, putting just enough slack in it that, as hard as he stretched his leg toward the balcony rail, it remained tantalizingly close but definitely, horrifyingly, out of reach. This was bad.

His whole life up to this point, Adel had been physically adept and fearless. If he were growing up in suburban America, he might have taken up extreme snowboarding or lacrosse. In Damascus, however, options for highly energetic boys were limited, and this was not the first time his hijinks had gotten him into trouble. But this was worse than when he jumped from a second-story landing into a pile of dirt to show the other kids he could. It was worse than the day he used the playground slide like a ski jump, fracturing his arm in multiple places.

This time was different. This time, he had time to think. Below him, far below him, his friends were standing on a path, next to some grass. They were yelling something. What was it? "Should we call the police?" As if there was time for that. The whole block was under construction, the building not even finished. No neighbors to call.

Adel's mind raced through his options. Should he drop onto the grass? Better than the paved path, but he would probably still die. The cable draped lower toward the street; perhaps he could shimmy down and drop at its lowest point? And land in traffic? No. Looking up, he saw his cousin leaning over the roof, looking down at him. The sky was blue. It was a beautiful day.

Adel strained to climb up toward his cousin, but it was no use. His arms were growing more tired by the second. He would have to aim for the balcony and jump.

Kus ucht shaghli. Motherfucking shit.

"But you can't jump if your feet aren't on anything," he said to me, thrashing his foot through the air the way he must have, dangling up there twenty-five years ago, as vivid to him as if it were happening right now. "If you have nothing to push away from, you can't leap."

He was standing in front of me, demonstrating how he had clenched his hands and wrapped his legs around the cable. His dark eyes were blazing. I was transfixed. Clearly he'd survived, but how?

"What did you do?"

"I swung my body back and forth," he said, swaying his hips and knees side to side. "Momentum. I needed momentum. All I needed to get was a couple of inches closer to the building." The cable was so heavy, it didn't budge. "Fucking cable! Move, dammit!" Adel had no other choice, so he kept at it. He could see the middle of the cable over the street, where there was the most slack, begin to sway. A while later, he could feel himself rocking on it, just a little.

"It wasn't a lot of movement, but it was time," he said. "I had to let go."

I held my breath, seeing his body suspended in air.

"I pushed the cable away with my feet and my hands, I still remember the feeling of it sliding out from under me. And I threw myself toward the balcony." His eyes closed, his arms outstretched.

"My feet missed the rail. Oh God, that was the worst feeling. But my body made it over, I crashed face-first into the shutters." He put his arms up, miming the moment of impact. "And then I lay on the balcony. Oh, the feeling in my stomach! I have never been so scared. And that is how I gave myself a fear of heights."

Adel shook his head, and his black hair, tight longish curls, shook over his forehead. He was wearing a hiking rain jacket and carrying a backpack over one shoulder, the suburban dad. We were standing in the kitchen of the Purple Crayon, a community workspace he founded with his wife in Westchester County, New York, as far from Damascus as could be. The memory energized the air around us. We let it shimmer there a moment. Fear, relief, and the pleasure of being safe and sound.

"You are *crazy!*" I said.

"Well, I was young. I did a lot of stupid things. What I put my parents through! You want to hear the funny part? The funny part is that after all that, I still couldn't unlock the door. You needed a key to unlock it from the inside! I had to call my sister to bail me out."

I laughed so hard I coughed and sputtered until Adel got me a glass of water. "So, ever since you've been afraid of heights?" I asked, gulping it down.

"I was so scared after that. That feeling in your legs, where they don't want to move, everything you read about how people feel when they're paralyzed, that's how I would feel every time I stepped near a ledge. I don't think I'll ever really get over it. But I can't let it stop me. I'm an engineer, I have to go up high all the time."

"You're an engineer?" I was surprised. Up until today, I only knew Adel as the founder of this community center, as the kind of visionary who with his wife remade an old church into a gathering space for artists and freelancers, and then painted the building purple in homage to the children's book *Harold and the Purple Crayon*. "So you have to inspect buildings under construction?" My mouth was dry on his behalf. After his story, I felt as if I, too, had a fear of heights. "What a nightmare! How do you do it?"

"My very first job out of college, I was a bridge inspector in Kuwait," he said. My mind flashed to my first job out of college, safe behind a desk. There was a window behind me, but I no longer remember the view.

"I hated looking down at the cars speeding by under me," Adel continued. "I couldn't wait to get down." But he started forcing himself to look over the edge. "It was so hard. I'd tell myself, 'Don't be silly, you're not going to fall, you're not going to throw yourself over, nothing bad will happen.' But I still felt scared. I didn't have to do it, but I made myself, again and again."

I nodded. "You exposed yourself to your fear and you survived. It's what cognitive behavioral therapists do for patients. And you talked to yourself like you are now, an adult. You aren't that teenager who did reckless things anymore. Are you?"

His expression was noncommittal. We laughed.

"Every time I go out, I think, Does this feel secure under my feet? Is this pole solid to hold on to? If this thing I'm standing on collapses, what would I do?" Adel's expression turned serious. "Accidents do happen on work sites. Do you remember the incident at the East Tremont subway station?"

I did. It was on the local news a few years back. A construction worker was in a manlift almost fifty feet in the air when the bucket he was standing in collapsed, spilling him out. He hung helplessly by his harness over the street, like a forgotten marionette, until the fire department came.

"That was my guy," Adel said. "I was in charge of the station's renovation. I told him that morning, 'Wear your harness, you never know,' and look what happened!" Adel was still incredulous. "That lift had passed OSHA inspection, too."

You never know. I don't mind heights, but that's because I don't worry that a guardrail will give way, or that I'll lose my balance for no reason. I trust whatever I'm standing on to hold me. But if there were a chance that in the normal course of my workday I'd end up dangling over the street by my overalls? You'd have to be crazy to do that.

"What about your kids, are *they* crazy?" I asked.

"Yes! They are the ones on the playground hanging this way, that way, making other mothers mad because they give their kids ideas. But here, I can put them in gymnastics. I probably grew up in the wrong place and time."

I left Adel, thinking of what he might have been in another place and time—a stuntman? a gladiator? And then of him leaping through the air in Syria, and landing here. "If you have nothing to push away from, you can't leap," he had said. He pushed away his fear and leaped toward the life he wanted—bold enough to build buildings where none existed before; to create community out of an abandoned church; to take good, brave, reasonable risks forever after. And it seemed to me that in that sense he'd grown up in exactly the right place and time.

MOST PEOPLE ARE AFRAID of heights to some degree, and why not? The instinct to stay intact is a healthy one. Even those who enjoy heights, who seek them out, do not want to hurt themselves, unless they have an actual death wish. They want to stay up high and enjoy the view. Or, if they're skydivers or BASE jumpers, they want to fall and cheat death on the way down. As soon as Adel faced the prospect of actually being hurt or killed, being up high became a lot less enjoyable.

Most of us, though, when faced with normal situations (for example, balconies we step out onto from a building, not drop onto from the sky) are either height tolerant or height intolerant. I'm in the height-tolerant camp, among those who understand that it could be dangerous to be up high but who are able to make ourselves comfortable with it, reminding ourselves that we're safe if we stay away from the edge, that we'll get down the way we came up.

Those who are height intolerant experience more distress, feeling dizzy or scared, in the moment. How the fear affects their lives runs along a spectrum from those who would choose to suffer through a chairlift anyway to those who opt to stay in the ski lodge to those who won't go up to the mountain at all. Fear of having a panic attack can keep people grounded to varying degrees, off ladders, escalators, bridges, observatories, or hiking trails. For the 2 to 5 percent of the general population who have acrophobia, just the thought of going up high triggers anxiety, and rerouting daily life to avoid stressful situations becomes a major preoccupation.

Theories abound as to where such fear comes from. One holds that traumatic experiences with falling are the source. Another is that we have an inborn instinct to self-protect when we're exposed to heights, but the more we're exposed safely, the more we become used to being up high. In this scenario, those who experience persistent fear are those who avoided heights and never got habituated properly. This would be an argument for exposure therapy, to face the fear head-on.

Then again, it could be physical. Our ability to orient ourselves in space and maintain balance depends on a number of bodily systems working smoothly. Our eyes provide visual information, like depth perception. Fluid-filled tubes and nerves in the inner ear form the vestibular system that detects the direction of gravity and helps us maintain equilibrium. The muscles and tendons of the torso and the legs send input to the brain about the body's position. The brain uses all this information to stabilize us, and if any part of it is off, the world can start swimming or spinning around us.

Or it could be psychological. All these systems are affected by emotions. If we feel a little disoriented and become anxious as a result, the more upset we get, the more disoriented we become, perpetuating a negative feedback loop that can feed a phobia.

Oh, and one more thing: All these systems weaken with age. The number of nerve cells in the vestibular system as well as blood flow to the inner ear all decrease as we get older. If we don't keep up our core strength and muscle tone, we become more prone to losing our balance and falling. And we all know what happens to the eyes. *That's* why the Ferris wheel you loved as a kid now makes you feel faint, and the Tilt-a-Whirl makes you want to hurl.

For my middle-aged, height-intolerant friends, it all adds up to this: one heck of an excuse for staying put.

≪

"I AM SO AFRAID of heights!"

I've lost count of the number of people who've told me this freely. Other fears ("I'm afraid of rejection," "I'm afraid to fail," "I'm afraid of my kids") get whispered on the down-low. But a fear of heights is announced with verve, usually with an entertaining reenactment of a terrifying ordeal.

"When I was fourteen, I did a camp trip where we hiked a trail called the Knife Edge," my friend Carter told me one morning when we were on line for coffee at Antoinette's. Carter, forty-nine, is a writer and folk/jazz concert producer. Slightly balding, with glasses, he looks bookish and is soft-spoken. But the minute he started telling this story, he became more animated than I've ever seen him.

"There were sheer drops on either side and I remember dropping to my knees, sweat pouring out of me," he said, his eyes a wide-awake blue I'd never noticed before. "The counselor had to come back for me, everyone had to wait for me to cross. It was terrible." He shuddered as he wiped his forehead, which was shiny with excitement at the memory.

"After you made it across, did you feel proud of conquering your fear?" I asked, stepping closer. I needed caffeine and he was giving off enough energy for a contact high.

"No, I felt like I never wanted to do anything like it ever again," he said emphatically. "I know what you're thinking," he said, spying the glint in my eye. "I'm not your guy." And he stepped away from me before I could suggest a trip to the Empire State Building. In fact I had yet to meet anyone ready to face this particular fear. Many were happy to share their stories of knocking knees atop the Space Needle or the Great Wall of China; to a person, they displayed absolutely zero interest in becoming brave in this arena.

Most of the time, it's easy enough to avoid heights, or peering over the edge from a height, especially as fear of these things is highly socially acceptable. Without the strong intrinsic and extrinsic motivators that Adel had, of wanting to recover a former sense of self or to be able to function in a job, there seems to be little purpose in facing this complicated and deeply seated fear. Why bother?

By the time my friend John said to me at a church picnic, "I have a terrible fear of heights," my first thought was, *I bet you have no interest in facing it, either.* I was eyeing the potato salad on the buffet behind him.

"I remember chaperoning a class trip to a ropes course," he

continued, stepping aside so I could fill my plate. "I was so nervous climbing up the tree, I almost asked them to take me down."

I froze, salad tongs in hand, bells ringing in my head. A ropes course! A place where people are sent to walk tightropes in the name of "team building" and "personal development." A place where height intolerance is not only tested but, in an acrophobic's nightmare scenario, tested in front of bosses and colleagues, strangers and friends. And for what purpose? I wanted to know.

If the mountain won't come to Muhammad, I thought, thanking John for sharing his story and digging into my food with relish, *Muhammad will just have to go to the mountain.*

≋

THE ROAD TO CARMEL, New York, winds through some beautiful land. I glanced down to find my sunglasses, then looked up just as the thick forest that had walled in both sides of the parkway for miles opened up to a lake. For a moment, I felt the heady sensation of flying out over water.

I had tried to rope Carter into coming with me on this jaunt to the high ropes course at Green Chimneys Clearpool Campus, an hour north of New York City, to no avail. *"Gah!"* he'd said at the suggestion, clearly regretting having confided anything to me in the first place. "I have no fears! The only fear I have is of you!" My other height-intolerant friends were putting their finely honed avoidance skills to work by running away at the sight of me.

So it was just me heading into the woods, which from my air-conditioned car looked benign enough. Driving past the entrance to the Chuang Yen Monastery, I told myself to relax. *There are peaceful Buddhists in these woods,* I thought. *Nothing bad will happen here.*

Maybe it's because I grew up next to a fire station and find sirens comforting. Or because of the sleepover when I saw *Friday the 13th* and never slept soundly again. Or the time I discovered an Oreo-sized water bug had climbed into my nightgown *after I'd already put it on.* Whatever the reason, when I'm in nature, I worry. Thoughts like, *It's quiet. Too quiet. What's that noise?* and *Is this poisonous? Oh God! Am I swelling up?* chase one another in my head like dogs in a dog run.

This is where Sybil Ludington rode during the American Revolution, a historical marker along the road informed me. When the British invaded Danbury, Connecticut, in 1777, Sybil, then sixteen years old, rode forty miles on horseback (more than twice the distance of Paul Revere) to rouse soldiers in her father's regiment to ready for battle. A girl on a horse, with a musket and a stick, riding through these marauder-filled woods all night. I shivered at the thought.

At Clearpool the air was simmering with sun, buzzing with insects and lord knows what else. Stepping into the office, I passed a door labeled Bat-catching Net Here. *I'm a stranger in these here parts,* I wanted to say to the lady behind the desk. *Take me to your leader.* Instead, I explained I had arranged with Chris Hendershot, the program director, to observe an eighth grade class on the ropes course. "The group's outside," she said. "Chris'll be there shortly."

Seeing nothing but greenery outside, I took a moment to glance at the pamphlets and research papers I'd stuffed into my notebook.

Clearpool was founded in 1901 as a summer camp for inner-city children. Encompassing 350 acres of natural and protected woodlands, it now offers nature-based education and adventure programs for school and company retreats, and a summer day camp. *Maybe if I had been sent to a place like this when I was a kid, I wouldn't have so many fears,* I thought.

Ropes courses (also called challenge courses) grew out of military training. In France, in the early 1900s, a naval officer named George Hébert developed a "return-to-nature" approach to physical education that included obstacle courses. In England, the first Outward Bound schools in the 1940s trained military cadets in climbing ropes on land as preparation for climbing rigging at sea.

Outward Bound came to America in 1961 and challenge courses have multiplied exponentially since. James Borishade, executive director of the Association for Challenge Course Technology, estimates there are more than fifteen thousand challenge courses in the United States today. Nowadays, their raison d'être is to take people out of their classrooms, offices, and comfort zones and see how they fare. Ropes courses were never intended primarily for fun or sport. They were developed to be good for you.

Which, from the expressions on the faces of the kids walking toward me now, is not something most of us look forward to.

I say "kids" but at thirteen, they were germinating teenagers, all arms and legs and awkward attitude. The traditional class field trip was to Six Flags, but this year their teacher and chaperone, Mr. M., had decided to try something different. He has a fear of roller coasters and a paradoxical love of ropes courses, and he arranged to substitute one excursion for the other. The kids had left their city neighborhood the day before and woke up this morning in the woods. Slouchy and sleepy, they looked like they didn't quite understand how the helmets and harnesses they were wearing had gotten on their bodies. *This is so not Six Flags.*

A big bear of a man wearing a Clearpool Program Facilitator name tag reading "Joe" was leading the pack, and I introduced myself as they approached. "I'm here to observe the class for a book I'm writing about how people face their fears," I said.

"That's so awesome!" Joe replied in a deep and pleasantly growly voice, smiling through his thick brown beard. "Shall I get you a helmet?"

I thought fast. Standing in my closet that morning, I had considered wearing a summer skirt and sandals, which would have given me an out no one could argue with. "I'm sorry, I can't go up there," I could have said. "It wouldn't be appropriate to . . ." and then dropping my voice to a whisper, *"show my underwear."* But I'd reconsidered. I don't mind being up high as long as I don't fall, and there's no real risk of falling while walking a tightrope, safely harnessed. After months of rehab, my broken foot was finally strong again. Why not feel competent for a change? I'd put on jeans and sneakers.

But now, with all these thirteen-year-olds bringing on flashbacks to middle school, my only thought was: *What if this ends up on YouTube?*

"Uh, I'm more interested in how the kids do," I said.

We came to a clearing where what looked like a clothesline was strung midway across the field between two trees, and dangling from it, like an unfinished thought, was a tether. It was hard to tell what it might be for. A ladder stood under one of the trees. "We're going to divide you up into teams," Joe announced. "The ladder team is going to bring this ladder under the tether and hold it steady." He demonstrated, placing the ladder under the dangling tether as he spoke. "Then the pull team is going to pull on that rope over there—" he pointed to a rope lying on the ground across the clearing "—to raise your swinging screaming teammate up into the air."

Excuse me? Did he just say *swinging*? Yes, in fact, the unfinished thought ended in this terrible idea: The victim (let's just call him Vic) climbs the ladder. The tether gets clipped into one self-locking carabiner on his harness near the belly button and the pull rope gets looped into another. The ladder team moves the ladder out of the way, leaving Vic hanging in the air holding his end of the pull rope, which now runs from him across the clearing and over a pulley attached to a tree up about twenty-five feet. The pull team pulls the other end, to raise him twenty feet up and across the clearing. That's two stories high.

Go look out a two-story window, and imagine dangling from it like Vic. And then imagine this: Counting to three out loud, and then *letting go* of the rope. And then? And then you free-fall backward, swinging sixty feet across to the other side, spinning around if gravity so chooses, flying back and forth, reliving the nightmare until you pass out, puke, or the laws of motion slow you down to a stop. There's no brake once you let go.

Can you pass out while standing up with your eyes open? That was me, upon seeing this swing.

≈

"WHEN YOU DREAM OF FALLING, it means you're growing," Ma used to say. My nightmares as a child fell into three categories: being chased by monsters, chewing so much gum my mouth got stuck closed so I couldn't talk, and falling. For a kid nicknamed Chatty Patty, losing the ability to talk probably symbolized nothing short of self-annihilation. But the falling dreams were even worse.

I fell off imagined precipices of all sorts—clouds, buildings, boats, my bed. It didn't matter how high up I started, just the sensation of tipping over would send me into blind terror. I'd wake up gasping for breath.

"Is that really true, or is that something you just told me to make me feel better?" I asked Ma when I was old enough to feel that I should have stopped growing by now but the dreams kept coming. With Ma, I was never sure if what she told me was an old wives' tale, a bit of psychology she'd read in the Chinese newspaper, or a story her heart created to comfort mine.

"It's what I've always heard," she said.

In my waking life, I'm fully capable of climbing or riding my way up to observatories, mountain peaks, even the rigging of tall ships, and enjoying the view before carefully coming down. But the thought of falling makes me ill. That's a survival instinct I have no desire to rewire.

≋

OH NO, OH NO, my brain sputtered, coming back to life. This swing was not what I had in mind. Walking on a rope, holding on to a safety line, I'd trust myself to not let go, to not fall. This was all about letting go and falling. Poor kids. Did their parents know what they'd signed them on for when they sent in their permission slips?

Joe was saying, "Don't worry about the tether breaking. This is three-eighths-inch seven-by-nineteen strand galvanized steel aircraft cable. This is what they use on aircraft carriers to stop fighter jets when they land." So no one would go flying off into the forest. As long as the trees it was bolted to stayed up.

Joe started pumping the kids up. Or trying to. "I'm gonna yell, 'ARE YOU READY?' And you yell, 'YEAH!' Okay? 'ARE YOU READY?'"

The kids, most of whom looked to be East or Southeast Asian and ranged from scrawny and tense to thin and wan, did not look remotely ready.

"Yeah . . ." they said faintly.

Joe growled loudly. "Let's try that again. 'ARE YOU READY?'"

"Yeah." They said it halfheartedly this time, a slight improvement. Some giggled; some groaned. Some whispered in Korean, others in Chinese.

"Look, I know this sounds crazy," Joe said.

"It doesn't sound crazy, it sounds awesome," piped up one girl with curly hair and badass jeans.

Joe smiled at her gratefully. "I was terrified of heights before," he confided to the group. "But the first time I did this swing, it was scary for three seconds and I haven't stopped since. You guys are going to love it."

Mr. M. briskly assigned students to ladder team or pull team, and volunteered to go first. The five kids on the pull team hoisted him up to a smattering of applause, and then everyone gasped as he dropped heartstoppingly fast and far. Swing and scream he did, to the delight of his students, one of the girls saying with a giggle, "He's so cute, look at him." I could imagine how fun it must be for the kids to see their teacher loose like that, whooping away in his T-shirt and cargo shorts.

Mr. M. was pumped. "When you first let go, that initial drop into free fall," he told the students waiting in line, "that's the best part."

The first student to go, a boy with glasses and a baggy North Face sweatshirt that he might one day fill out with muscles, was the picture of agony as he allowed himself to be hoisted in the air. "Ugh! Ouch! It hurts!" He moaned, his body limp, his will to live MIA. He dropped and swung back and forth miserably.

If everyone waiting was hoping to hear it wasn't as bad as it looked, they were sorely disappointed. "It *hurt*," he reiterated, gesturing at his private parts and the offending harness, as he limped his way to sit with the other kids.

The next boy was no better off. His mouth formed a perfect O as he reached the top of the arc. "*Aaaaah* Lord! I wanna pray right now!" he yelled, clutching the rope. "One! *AAAAAAAH!*" He interrupted his own counting to scream. Perhaps he was being a little dramatic.

"Let go!" Joe called up. "The pull team can't hold you forever." He gestured at the kids straining on the pull rope.

"Two, three!" The boy let go but instantly reconsidered, grabbing the rope, which zipped out of his hand as he dropped away. Ouch. Rope burn. *Mental note: When you let go, LET GO.*

Chris the program director arrived, a sturdy-looking man in a blue

Clearpool polo shirt, who didn't need the uniform to show he belonged. It always strikes me how easy and comfortable others can be in environments so foreign to me. He said hello to Mr. M. and shook my hand warmly, and the three of us sat down on a rock in the sun, shading our eyes to look up at what Chris called the Giant Swing.

The next kid's eyes rolled to the back of his head while swinging. The one after that cursed like a sailor.

Then a girl in the hot seat counted to three, let go, dropped only two feet, then stopped with a jerk. The pull rope was stuck. She waited to be lowered down.

I was sweating like crazy. *If that happened to me, I would stay down.* Chris looked at me, fanning myself, and explained soothingly, "That happens, very occasionally—the rope gets stuck. Probably because the girl is so light, she didn't weigh enough to draw it completely through the loop." That would not be a problem for me.

Her second try went off smoothly, and the girl disembarked, high-fiving her friends and looking like she was going to remember the flying, not the faltering.

A girl with round pink cheeks, pearl earrings, and glasses touched her hair and face nervously as she watched. Her blue-and-white striped shirt sagged across her shoulders and arms, the stripes forming sad and worried frowns.

Let's call her Pearl. "How was it?" she asked each kid. The Vics were not reassuring. When it was finally her turn, she let out a loud, "OH MY HOLY CRIMINAL SSSSHHHHH—" as she covered her glasses and swung toward the trees. *"I can't look!"*

"Open your eyes!" Joe called up to her. "Your body wants to know where it is. If you look, your body won't freak out as much."

Pearl swung back and forth in silence, eyes closed, freaking out. It was hard to tell if she was wiping away sweat or tears as she got unhooked and stumbled back to her place on the grass. "Are you okay?" other girls asked, concerned. "Was it scary?"

"YES!" she blurted.

The girl with the badass jeans was next, and for a moment at the top lost her bravado. "Ah, crap," she said, just before letting go and screaming at the top of her lungs. But she bounded off afterward, declaring, "That was awesome!"

And just like that, it became cool to enjoy it.

The next boy flew around doing superhero poses, a girl spread-eagled through the air singing, "I believe I can fly." One boy did an aerial breaststroke as his friends below sang, "Just keep swimming, just keep swimming."

Giant Swing survivors began comparing notes.

"It's not as scary as you think," the girl with the badass jeans said.

"It's scary," Pearl countered.

"No, it's *not*."

"That was the coolest thing ever," pronounced Superhero Boy.

"It hurt my testicles," said another.

"It did hurt," Superhero Boy cheerfully agreed. "The harness cut in, like—" He gestured to his groin and then stopped, glancing at me apologetically. "It was still fun."

A good-looking man, athletically built and wearing a harness, stood by the boys, listening. I didn't know if he was on the staff of Clearpool or was with the visiting students. He looked like he might spend his days scaling mountains or climbing trees, but his next comment told all.

"Guys, I got a stomachache now," he said, shifting his weight, looking decidedly uncomfortable. "I gotta go to the bathroom." He made himself scarce.

"Where'd Mr. K. go?" the principal asked as the last of the students lined up to swing. Mr. K. was a special ed teacher and chaperone, the students explained to me. When he came back, the principal urged him to take his turn. Mr. K. crossed himself as he got hooked in. "I'm king of the world!" he joked at the top before exclaiming, "*What the*—!" at the drop.

Meanwhile, Chris and Mr. M. were trying to convince me to do the Giant Swing. Chris was the good cop, pointing out how safe it was. ("The trees the ropes are bored into are oak," he said. "That's a hardwood." *Very reassuring,* I thought. *Not.*) In truth, today's challenge courses are created and maintained to a high degree of safety, largely thanks to the formation of the Association for Challenge Course Technology in 1993, to support the standardization of challenge course practices.

Still, this was me we were talking about. "I got whiplash once standing in my bathroom," I said. "This swing could herniate every disk in my back."

Chris moved to reassure. The injuries that happened at Clearpool were the ones where kids sprained an ankle walking to the dining hall. Could happen anywhere.

"You might as well try this, because God knows what will happen to you walking to your car!" Mr. M. quipped.

The group was finishing up. It was time to decide.

"You don't have to do this today," Chris said. "You can think about it and come back another day if you want."

Mr. M. was not having it. "I'm giving you my harness, right here, right now," he said, unbuckling at an alarming rate. In one fluid motion, he stepped out of the blue straps and threw them down on the rock next to me. *Wait! I'm not convinced! I'm not ready!* But with all the authority of a teacher whose word is law, Mr. M. looked me in the eye as he handed me his helmet.

"Do it," he said. Discussion over.

I knew I should have worn the skirt.

≋

THE CLEARPOOL APPROACH IS Challenge by Choice, Chris had explained. "We don't want to terrify people. We've gotten a lot of kids
and adults to try things by going slow." Of the three hundred to four
hundred guests Clearpool had over the course of the school year, despite an "Oh hell no" initial reaction by most, 99 percent ended up participating to some degree.

"The adults tend to have more fear than the kids," Chris said. "For
some, all they're ready to do is stand on the ladder. For them, that's a
big step. We consider that participating."

So I could have gone two steps up the ladder and said, "Enough." I
could have let myself hang in the air and asked to come down. That last
part, letting go, was up to me. I could have just refused to let go.

But I didn't think of it. I was too scared. I stepped into Mr. M.'s
harness and allowed Chris to buckle me. I climbed the ladder, blowing
out pretend birthday candles to steady myself. "Go up one more rung,
I'm clipping you in," Joe said. I looked into his brown eyes, surprised to
see a baby face behind his beard. He was, what? Twenty-five? Was he
even old enough for this job?

"Now I'm looping the rope through and then I'll hand it to you." He
spoke in a low and steady voice. There were birds singing, kids laughing, me Lamaze breathing. I tried to part the sea of noise. What was
Joe saying?

"Hold the rope with both hands but don't pull. When you get to the
top, count to three and let go."

"You look like a kind person," I said, thinking, *Petting a cat reduces stress* and wishing I could pat his beard. Some people's brains come up with exactly the information they need in a life-and-death situation. Mine? Busy grasping for self-soothing techniques not at my disposal. "You're going to do a good job, right?"

"Yes," he said calmly. I noticed his black T-shirt's heavy-metal logo, Mayhem Festival.

"Let the pilot worry about flying the plane" is standard advice for the nervous passenger. *Trust the equipment* plus *trust others to do their jobs* can seem like leap upon leap of faith. But when you speak to people who have stayed with these jobs, they generally know what they're doing. Chris had told me how nervous he was at being responsible for kids' lives when he first led groups on the ropes course, how seriously the staff takes their role in keeping people safe.

Joe looked completely grounded. Even as I stood steps above him on the ladder, he seemed larger and more solid than me. I wanted to ask him something else, to keep him there. But there wasn't time. He took his hand off the rope. It was in my hands now.

"The ladder is going," he said, as the ladder team took my connection to the earth away. I hung, a thief caught in a net, totally hosed.

"Sit back. Let the harness hold you." *Trust your equipment.* "You're good to go!"

The pull team pulled like sled dogs hauling a large Eskimo woman who'd put on some layers of fat for the winter. Were they actually grunting? By the time I reached the top, I was afraid of giving them hernias. Their mothers would kill me.

"One—two—three!" I didn't recognize my voice. It was so hoarse. The voice in my head was clear and strong: *Let go when you let go.*

I let go.

I fell. Really fast.

Open your eyes, Patty. I was falling away from the sky, away from the sweet, upturned faces of the teenagers watching me, who'd already braved this. I was screaming, the air thick and warm but doing nothing to slow me down. The rope twirled and I flew down toward grass, then out toward trees, and just when I thought it would never stop, I reached the other side of the invisible half pipe and paused at the top for a sickening second before turning and falling face-first again.

It is said that when Buddha told his followers that whatever they believed had to be let go (including the belief that they had to let their beliefs go), the vast empty space that remained was too much for them, that some even had heart attacks at the news. People need certainty. We need to know what's real. When everything you thought you knew falls away, there is no way to cope. The heart stops, the brain checks out. *La, la. Nobody's home.*

"To the extent that we stop struggling against uncertainty and ambiguity, to that extent we dissolve our fear," the Buddhist nun Pema Chödrön writes. "The synonym for total fearlessness is full enlightenment—wholehearted, open-minded interaction with our world." Perhaps this is what the monks at the monastery up the road were meditating on as I swung past terror at falling, into relief at being caught, into terror at falling again.

"Quiet the monkeys chattering in your brain," the swamis say. It's the hardest thing to do under any normal circumstance. But right now my monkeys were stunned to silence. And in their stead? A sudden, unexpected joy. I did not pass out. I was *awake.* I did not die of a heart attack. I was *alive.* I gave in to terror. And on the other side was *relief.* Was this enlightenment? I don't know, but I stretched out one sweaty arm and then another, feeling the breeze, feeling free.

I stopped screaming. My throat was sore, my mouth dry. My lips cracked a little when I pressed them together in a contented Buddha smile.

"Ommmmmmmm," I hummed, hands clasped at my heart, eyes open, swinging through the sky.

≫

THE NEXT TIME I saw Carter at Antoinette's, he put up a hand before I could speak. "I know what you're thinking," he said. "I'm not your guy."

"Ropes course, Carter. You and me."

"I *embrace* my fear of heights," he said. "It doesn't affect my life."

We laughed and chatted for a while, then, about what life is like for him, about to turn fifty, with a daughter in college, an aging mother to look out for, and a comfortable groove for him and his wife in the middle. "I remember a trip we took to Colorado," he said. I knew that was his wife's home state. "We rode a gondola over a deep mountain gorge, and I felt so sick, all I could do was stare at my shoes." It was the first time he'd conceded that the fear of heights had any effect on his life at all.

As usual with friends of a certain age, we kvetched about getting older, about feeling less physically capable than before. But in a sign of how far I'd come since I met him (he had been in the group of friends surrounding Barb here the day she first said hello to me and Ruby), I wanted to turn this conversation to the kinds of experiences that make us feel more alive, that give us hope that the future might still be about growth instead of diminution.

"The most amazing thing happened at the ropes course," I said. He was standing by my table near the door on his way out. "Do you have time for a story?" I patted the seat next to me and cleared a space for his coffee cup next to mine. He sat.

≫

THE STORY WAS ABOUT MR. K., who'd been chaperoning the class trip. He gets positional vertigo and is afraid of heights. He's the father of four, and the Giant Swing was like the carnival rides his kids make him go on—he could "stomach it" if all he had to do was sit and wait for it to be over. But he did not want to walk a tightrope.

On the high ropes courses, the kids took longer than expected, and the group started running out of time. I saw Mr. K. off to the side, blending in with the foliage, and I stepped carefully around the perimeter of the clearing to join him; we weren't supposed to cross the space in the middle without a helmet.

"What do you say to your students who say something is too hard for them to try?" I asked when I reached his side. We had spoken a bit about the rewards of working with special ed kids, the satisfaction of seeing progress that is hard-won somehow twice as sweet.

"Well, I say that's unacceptable," he said. "You have to try."

I really wanted him to try the tightrope. He had told me that he wanted to enjoy things with his kids more, not to dread going places with them. He had said that it was embarrassing to be a man and afraid in certain situations where other people were fine. "One day I'll get a handle on this fear," he'd said.

I wanted to say something inspiring, maybe that famous quote attributed to Karl Wallenda, "Being on the tightrope is living; everything else is waiting." Except that Wallenda had died falling off a wire strung ten stories above the pavement in San Juan, Puerto Rico, at age seventy-three. Bad example. I decided to keep it simple.

"So it would be inspiring for your students to see you try something hard for you."

We were both looking up at a kid on a tightrope who was saying, "Mr. M., I'll do this if you give me an A."

It didn't take much to connect the dots. Mr. K. excused himself to see what some kids were doing. I went to observe some others up on different courses. A while later, I heard Mr. M. say, "If you get on the bus without even trying, you're going to hate yourself." He was trying to convince the last of the students to give it a go.

I looked over at Mr. K. and his harness was off. Had he gone up while I was watching another course? I looked at him inquiringly. He shrugged, pointing at his watch. "Out of time," he mouthed.

Oh hell no.

"Did you hear what Mr. M. just said to the students?" I called over. I wanted everyone to hear it—all the people I care about who'd rather live in a cave because it's what they know than step outside and see the sun. Including myself.

He was so close. He was here. The equipment was here. Who knew when he might get this close again? I strode through the clearing, breaking all the helmet rules, pointing to my notebook with my pen. "Do you want your story to be that you did it or that you didn't?"

We looked at each other. Two heartbeats, then three.

I almost crumbled inside. I want people to like me. And if looks could kill, there would be nothing but a scorch mark in the woodchips where I was standing. *Take it back. Tell him he should only do what he's comfortable doing.*

But then I remembered: He wanted to face this fear "one day." *What about today?* I held my ground, notebook in air.

He blanched. "That I did. Of course."

He broke our gaze and walked away.

≈

"YOU ARE ONE TOUGH COOKIE," Carter said, peering at me through his round glasses. He looked both impressed and terrified. "What happened—did he go up?"

"Yes, he did," I said, with a great big grin. The import of what he was about to do didn't even register on me until he was twenty-five feet in the air on a three-quarter-inch tightrope, and his students, his colleagues had all gathered to watch. I realized that whatever happened would be all over school the next day, and if it was a disaster or a disappointment he would have to live it down. Immediately I started praying for safe passage. "It was like a nightmare, these teenagers were catcalling, saying things like 'Yo! Don't look down at the rocks!' And 'Break a leg!' He was *shaking*."

Carter looked like he might be ill. I hurried to the best part of the story. "And then, he started down the tightrope and do you know what happened?" Carter shook his head. "The kids were *impressed*. They started saying things like 'OMG, he's really doing it!' They started cheering for him! It was like out of a movie."

I picked up my mug and inhaled the scent of warm coffee. I love these stories better than chocolate-chip muffins. "Do you know how long it took him to do the course, Carter?" He shook his head again. "*Two minutes*. The story will last a lifetime. He's going to show the pictures to his kids."

After a pause, I came to my point.

"So, I'm putting together a group to go back to the ropes course," I said. The secret to recruiting people to face a fear is to show them exactly how exhilarating it might be, I'd discovered. After posting a picture of me gasping on the Giant Swing on Facebook, I'd been flooded with inquiries about what the heck I was doing. Once I arranged for an adult group excursion to do high ropes courses at Clearpool, the slots filled themselves. "I've got three women who are afraid of heights who're going to come with me a week from Thursday."

Carter stiffened. "My back hurts—my shoulder hurts—I don't know if I'll have the car—I'm really busy—I get dizzy just looking up," he said. The excuses sat there in their well-trained line, hoping to be patted on the head. I sat quietly on my hands.

I was learning. When it comes to facing fears, the first *no*, the loud, afraid, reflexive *no*, needs to have its say. Then you wait, for the inner *yes* to be heard.

"There's room in the car for you," I said.

"Maybe next year," he replied, getting up and moving toward the line to get a cup for the road. The door was closing.

"Sure," I called after him. "No problem. Because next year, when you turn fifty-one, it will have just as much symbolism as it would right now, turning fifty." He was facing away from me, but I could see him take a breath, hold it a moment, and then let it go. When he got his cup, he had to pass my table to get out the door.

He paused, asking, "Where would we do this, anyway?"

"Carmel. It's beautiful there."

He shook his head. His lips said *no*. But his expression said, *Well . . . maybe . . .*

≫

IT WAS A MERRY BAND that filled Julie Haas Brophy's car the next week. Carter, in charge of the music, had made a mix for the occasion and we all burst out laughing as the sound of the Beatles singing "HELP! I need somebody!" filled the car. Julie, a thirty-eight-year-old artist, mother, and fellow blogger, was driving, and I was next to her. Carter was sitting behind us along with Esther Kinderlerer, a thirty-six-year-old hypnotherapist and mother of two; and way in the back sat Amy Carr, a forty-three-year-old librarian and mom. They all knew me but not each other, not yet. Still, we were starting off with some common bonds.

Julie had lived in Manhattan for ten years and had never been comfortable going near windows up high, but after 9/11 (her father worked at Marsh & McLennan, a company that lost 295 employees when the World Trade Towers fell), she became even more anxious with heights. "In general, before kids, I did more," she said, keeping her eyes on the road. "When my husband did some work for Goodyear Tire, we got a chance to ride in the blimp and I did it! Would I do that now? I don't know." She did not want her anxieties to get in the way of her kids' enjoyment of life. "I've been putting off taking them to the Empire State Building. I know I will do it eventually, but I hope it won't be really scary."

Esther's husband is a rock climber, and in that "lovey-dovey early stage" of their relationship she'd gone with him in France, but got scared on a high ridge, slipped, and injured her shoulder. Apart from that, she'd had two panic attacks in her life, "but having nothing to do with heights," she said in her English accent. "Both times I was pregnant. So I tell myself as long as I'm not pregnant, I should be fine." She was really coming on the trip, she said, to "face my fear of becoming boring in middle age."

Tom Petty's "Free Fallin'" came on and I said, "Goodness, I hope that doesn't happen on this trip!" I was starting to crash from the excitement of getting under way. The night before, my stomach had hurt so much I'd spent much of it in the bathroom "just in case," wondering if I should reschedule the trip. I was in no shape to be jostling the contents of my digestive system while suspended above ground. But when morning came and the sun was out, I thought about how nervous the others probably were, how losing this opportunity might open the floodgates to reasons to back out of a rescheduled outing. "I'm just going to gut it out," I'd said to myself, I hoped not literally.

I turned and looked back at Amy. "How are you doing back there?" I called out. She and I go back the farthest: We met when her daughter and Gigi were toddlers. I had just stopped working full-time and was trying to get a handle on my anxiety via yoga. "You should be a yoga teacher," she'd said after I shared some relaxation techniques with our mother's group. It was the kind of stunning statement you have to hear from an outsider because you would never think it yourself. She became one of my longtime yoga students, always bringing a quiet, receptive presence to the class.

"Amy, what brought you here?" I asked. Amy is tall and thin and has cropped hair that's flecked with gray. I knew from yoga class that she was stronger than she looked. She smiled as she said, "The thought of feeling powerful when I'm done."

⟫

HARNESSED AND HELMETED, we stood around Joe, trying not to look up at the ropes hanging in the trees behind him. We were the only Vics this time—because I'd arranged with Chris to come on a day they were training new staff on the course, there were no other groups scheduled. "This isn't going to be like getting a haircut from a beauty school student, is it?" I'd asked, a little worried.

"No, Joe and several of our experienced staff will be there," Chris had said. "You'll be in excellent hands."

Now Joe was pumping us up. "I want to see you pushing yourself a little beyond what you know you can do," he said. "Every time we push ourselves beyond our comfort zone, our comfort zone becomes a bit bigger. *We* become a bit bigger."

The method behind the madness is this: The *perceived* risk on a ropes course is very high. You feel like you're dropping into oblivion. But the *actual risk* is very low. The ropes will hold. You will not hit the ground. But even though the rational mind understands this, even though you've seen others do it before, the moment you're in the precarious position of not feeling any familiar touchstone, you think you might die.

People don't like this. How many times do we stop ourselves from trying something that feels dangerous but actually isn't?

By *not letting fear stop you*, you strengthen the part of you that can tolerate uncertainty, that can deal with the possibility of pain, that can open you to new experiences. The experience itself becomes the touchstone. You no longer need a literal or figurative floor, wall, or person to hold you up. The next time you feel yourself on the edge of something big and scary, you have the experience of survival to hang on to.

You don't have to skydive or bungee jump or even do the Giant Swing to get this experience. But you do have to step out of your comfort zone. The Clearpool staff encourages full participation. But they won't force or carry anyone over the threshold. Often when people freeze, they can get unfrozen with prompting and direction. "The group leader will always ask for just a step or two more," Chris had said. "Most people end up going much farther than they ever thought they could."

We're going to need all the encouragement we can get, I thought, as Joe introduced us to the Three-Line Bridge. The first line was the aircraft cable we'd be walking on tightrope style. The other two were safety lines strung waist-high to hold on to on either side. The bridge was thirty feet up and thirty feet across. We gaped at it from below, until Carter stepped up. He wanted to get this over with.

"Belay means to fasten or make safe," Joe had explained. Through a pulley system, he would counterbalance Carter's weight. Should Carter slip, Joe would lower him down slowly. Joe clipped him in, and Carter started up the ladder.

Once you're on the ladder, you're on the apparatus. There are no platforms to hang out on. It's just one foot in front of the other, unless you decide to back down. And it's so complicated getting onto the tightrope that, once up, most people decide to just finish the damn thing.

Carter climbed twelve rungs, and then had to navigate several large eight-inch staples bolted to the tree. But at least these are bolted in firmly. Then comes the wobbling rope. For Carter, the setup—the bolts, the tree, the cables from the belay system, the safety wires, and tightrope—was unlike anything he'd ever seen. The instructions being called up to him might as well have been in Swahili. "That cable by your head, you should be able to hold it with your right hand instead of wrapping your arm around the tree. Good! Now put your left foot on that staple. Now go ahead and push up. Perfect. Now this part's a little tricky: You're going to do a foot switch. Move that foot onto the cable. Now here's the next tricky part. You have to get under that cable that's next to your waist to get situated on your foot cable. Try to hold the cable that's closest to you."

If it sounds baffling here, believe me, it's worse when you're three stories up and trying to concentrate over the pounding of your heart. Carter, who had been processing all the information slowly but responding steadily, came to a halt.

"I don't know how I'm going to do this now," he said uncertainly. He was facing sideways, with both feet on the tightrope but his body outside the safety lines, both hands on the far line and the near one pressing into his belly. His entire body was wobbling with the ropes. "Which way am I going?"

"You have to go under the safety rope by your stomach," Joe reiterated.

Carter puffed a breath, bent both knees deeply and took one hand off the safety rope and leaned back, ducking under the near rope and then grabbing the far rope again, then repeated it for the other side. He emerged, standing between the safety lines, on the tightrope, facing forward. Mission accomplished.

"YEAH!" Everyone on the ground cheered.

"Dude," Joe said sincerely. "Well done."

It had taken Carter a full two minutes to get up onto the tightrope.

"Okay, whenever you're ready, start walkin'."

≋

IT HAD BEEN LIKE an alternate reality on the Three Line Bridge with the eighth graders. Pearl, who had covered her eyes on the Giant Swing, walked the tightrope with more confidence than she walked on land. The kid in the North Face sweatshirt sauntered across and when they asked him to stop in the middle and let go of the safety lines to clap three times, he clapped *nine* times like it was no big deal.

But some kids who had been full of wisecracks and bluster on the swing went white-knuckled on the ropes. "I'm freaked out now," one girl said, voice unsteady.

"That's totally legit, that's perfectly normal," Joe said. "I have you—the cable will hold you. Give me three claps."

She refused, so he asked for one. And then two more.

"You're hesitating," he told a girl who looked like she might be starting to panic.

"I know I'm hesitating!" she snapped back. "I can't do this!"

"It's a hundred thousand times worse because you're hesitating. You're never going to find perfect balance. Just clap."

Afterward, he asked her, "Remember that part where you said, 'I can't' and then you did?"

"Remember the part where I hate my life?" she retorted.

Joe, wise beyond his years, didn't miss a beat.

"That part won't last," he said. *If you don't let it.*

≋

"CARTER, you are doin' fantastic," Joe said.

Carter was stepping, breathing, trembling his way across the wire, sweating through his olive green T-shirt that blended in with the trees. A steady stream of encouragement flowed at him from below.

"Good job, man."

"You got this."

"Focus on that tree."

"Eyes on the prize."

I was so focused on filming him that it took me a while to realize how far he'd come. "You are halfway there!" I exclaimed.

Later, Carter would tell me, "I was surprised I had come that far." The rope was shaking (the ropes are actually designed to shake, to make the course more challenging), but he realized that he was the one causing the shaking and that shuffling in a straight line was much easier than maneuvering to get on the tightrope had been. "And all of a sudden I felt like it was going too fast, that it was all going to be over before I knew it." The staff on belay were already discussing his dismount. *I'm almost at the tree*, Carter thought. *And they're not going to ask me to clap.*

He shuffled a few more steps, took a deep breath, and the rope stopped shaking. He was in balance. "Wait," he said. "I want to clap!"

"You want to try?" Joe asked, impressed already.

After all it had taken for Carter to get to this moment, he wanted to take it in.

"I'll try," he said. "I'll try one."

"Do it!"

"Ready?" Carter asked, a last bit of prefacing.

"When *you're* ready!" we bellowed back. I could hardly stand the suspense. There was background noise from belayers directing Esther and Amy on other courses, ambient chatter among the staff. I wanted to shush everyone so we could hear. But when Carter's two hands came together, the sound was unmistakable.

CLAP!

"*Wooo hooo!*"

"Yeah!"

"POWER CLAP!"

The crowd went wild.

The traditional way to end the walk upon arriving at the tree is to hug it, saying, "I love you, tree." Carter's face broke into a wide-open smile as he approached. "Oh, tree," he said. "I'm gonna give you a big kiss when I get there." And he did.

AS STOKED AS I WAS for Carter, waiting my turn to go on the Elvis the Pelvis course, I felt doomed. I'd asked Esther how she felt as she was getting unclipped after finishing it, and she gave me ten seconds of speechless silence before saying, "It's scary."

At twenty-five feet above the ground and twenty-five feet across, this course is a little lower and shorter in length than the Three-Line Bridge. The tricky part is, although you are held on belay, this course does not have safety lines on either side, and you do not walk facing forward. Instead, you walk sideways, reaching for a series of five ropes hanging down for balance. The ropes start off close together and are spaced farther apart the farther out you go. You can imagine the hip gyrations required to stay on the wire. Elvis himself would have trouble walking this line.

My stomach flipped over just looking at it. I was exhausted from lack of sleep and worry over how the group would do. *Now that they're all having a great time, can't I just call it a day?* I thought, wishing we weren't so far from the bathroom. But then I thought of Mr. K., and how I'd pressured him into doing this very course. *Two minutes. I can stand anything for two minutes.* I stepped onto the ladder. *Let's just do this thing,* I thought.

"*What are you doing?*" the staff shouted in unison. Amy grabbed my arm. "*You're not on belay!*"

I looked down at my harness. I was about to mount the tightrope freestyle. "Somebody help me," I said. "I clearly need help."

The new staff member tying the knot in my harness to put me on belay took a full five minutes to figure out how to tie it properly. I'll call her Sally.

"Man, it's getting humid out," Joe said.

"Yeah, it's hot!" said someone else. They were keeping an eye on Sally's work, but wanted her to do this herself.

I wish she'd hurry up already, I thought, as Sally murmured, "It's too tight, I have to do it over again." I mean, I wanted her to do it properly, but *for God's sake let's get this done before I hurl!*

I must have looked awful, because Amy said, brightly, "Patty! Do what you always tell me to do. Stand tall, feel the energy run through your legs, tuck your tummy, shoulders back, head up toward the sky." She demonstrated mountain pose.

"Do I really say that?" I asked. I wanted to sink into the woodchips and take a nap.

"Yes, you do. Gosh, I hear you in my head all the time. You just need to hear yourself."

"All set," Sally said.

From the moment you step on the ladder and it sinks a little under your weight, you know that everything you consider normal is about to be taken from you. By the time I was up the twelve rungs and three staples and teetering on the edge of a narrow wooden block bolted into the tree, I had no bearings at all. "Put your foot on the wire," someone said.

Joe's firm voice came next: "No second guessing!"

I should just follow directions, I thought. *I'm good at that.*

I put one foot on the wire, then the other. With one hand I held a bolt in the tree.

"Awesome! Now reach for that rope."

Unfortunately, I have wee bitty arms. The rope dangled just out of my reach like a cat toy. I swiped at it to no avail. "It doesn't matter how close the rope is if you can't reach it," Chris had explained. "It isn't coming to you, so you have to go get it. It feels like it's ten feet away."

I wiped my face with my hand and then tried again.

"You can do it, Patty!" Amy encouraged from below.

"You might have to shuffle your feet toward it," Sally said. That was, after all, the idea, to *walk* across the tightrope. But my feet did not want to move. I leaned my hips out to see if that put me closer, but it didn't.

I wiggled my feet a few inches.

"That's it! Quick snatch!" Sally directed, and I did it. I had the first rope in my left hand. Whew. Except now I no longer had the bolt in my right.

"If your legs start to shake, take a deep breath," Joe said, just as the world started swaying around me.

"*Holy crap*," I gasped.

"It can get crazy," he continued. "That single cable action can make it very hard to stop the shake."

Look at something that's not moving. Isn't that what you're supposed to do when dizzy? Well, what do you do when *everything* feels like it's moving? My entire body was shaking. Not quivering, not trembling, but *shaking* involuntarily. *This is what "involuntary" means*, I thought. *It means it's not what I want! It means I have no control! It means . . .*

"You're fine," Esther's voice cut through the wailing in my head. She's a hypnotherapist for a reason. "You can do it, Patty."

On the way to Carmel, Esther had explained how she handles fear. "When you're afraid, the body releases adrenaline, which gives us a burst of energy to do what we need to do," she said. "If you allow it to come, it will help you. The problem happens when we put ourselves too much in the future, into thinking what might happen. That's what leads to panic attacks, when we overload on worst-case scenarios instead of staying with what's happening right now." Esther had talked herself through the Three-Line Bridge, even though she felt scared, by staying in the moment and telling herself, *My body can handle this.*

"You look calm!" the person belaying her had observed. "I'm a hypnotherapist," she quipped from above. "If I can't look calm, who can?"

The first time I'd picked up Susan Jeffers's *Feel the Fear and Do It Anyway*, I put it right back down after seeing the all-caps directive: "ALL YOU HAVE TO DO TO DIMINISH YOUR FEAR IS TO DEVELOP MORE TRUST IN YOUR ABILITY TO HANDLE WHATEVER COMES YOUR WAY!" The idea, she says at the end of chapter one, is to be able to say: "WHATEVER HAPPENS TO ME, GIVEN ANY SITUATION, I CAN HANDLE IT!" *That's bogus,* I'd thought. *Mental institutions, prisons, recovery groups are full of people who couldn't handle what life dealt them. Who's to say I can?*

And now here I was, thinking, *I cannot handle this,* every muscle straining to hold on. Then people below started singing, "I'm all shook up!" I amended my thinking. *I cannot handle this. But I'm not staying up here listening to that.* I looked at the rope in my left hand and tried to figure out what to do next.

"How do I . . ."

"Switch your hands," someone said. I passed the rope over to my right hand, freeing up my left to reach for the next one. This time I quickly shuffle-stepped sideways and grabbed the second rope.

"Well done!" The crowd approved. I was shaking more than ever. The horizon appeared to be undulating, as if I were in the crow's nest of a tall ship. *Why is this so hard? I'm not afraid of heights! This is not what I was expecting!* The third rope was spaced farther away.

"Take a breath through your nose and take your time," Esther called up. "There's no hurry."

No hurry, except for the feeling that I was about to pass out.

AN EIGHTH GRADER LOST her footing right here on Elvis the Pelvis last time. She didn't scream or make a fuss. Most of the group didn't even notice. I looked over when I heard the woman belaying her say, "I'm gonna have to let you down. Unless you think you can pull yourself up." The girl, so very thin, in a sweatshirt and long pants that looked too big for her, was wrapped around the tightrope by her arms and legs, sweaty and looking flipped out by the entire situation. I couldn't imagine that her hands were anything but clammy and slippery. It was impossible. Bring her down!

But the girl refused to be lowered. She tilted, this way and that, stretching one leg, then an arm, following directions at times from below, other times from some internal voice we couldn't hear. Slowly, she got herself sitting up on the rope. She pulled herself up to stand, teetered, and slipped back to sitting. "I'm sorry," she whispered.

"I'm going to bring you down now," the belayer said. It had been an excruciating effort; there was no way the girl had anything left in her.

"No," she said, more to herself than anyone else. "Can I just try one more . . ." She looked in the direction she wanted to go.

"Summon all your strength!" the belayer called. Where was this strength coming from? The girl had no muscles! But somehow she powered herself up, somehow she finished the course.

She shook like a leaf afterward, hiding her face in her hands. The other kids left her alone. After a while I approached her, saying, "That was one of the bravest things I've ever seen." In my head I was calling her Wonder Girl. She was overcome, whispering words in response I couldn't hear. I let her be.

"These challenges are only worth it if you succeed," cautioned a friend whose experiences on ropes courses have been nothing but torture. "If you get up there and it's even worse than you expected, then it's a different story entirely."

For this girl, if this was her first scary experience with heights, slipping off the rope in front of her classmates could become what hypnotherapists call an initial sensitizing event. It could become the source of social anxiety or a fear of heights for years to come. If she had a fear of heights already, this could confirm that fear.

Or this could be the best thing that ever happened to her. She could view this experience as a triumph, as the moment she realized, perhaps in a way she could not have known before, her inner strength.

Will her peers praise her or tease her back at school? Years from now, will she tell this story proudly or wish it away?

There's no guarantee when you face a fear that everything will go smoothly. So often making it through without incident is considered a "successful" outing. But success can be in the attempt more than in the outcome. Staying on the wire is succeeding at crossing a tightrope. Getting knocked down and getting back up is a recipe for succeeding in life.

≋

I DID NOT WANT TO SLIP. *I am no Wonder Girl. I have much less collagen in my joints.* If I fell, I was not getting back up. So I had to stay up.

"One more step and you should be able to grab the next rope," Esther said. I did it. Number three. "Superstar!" she called out. "You look like Angelina Jolie."

I had no funny reply, I was too busy puffing like a steam engine. The oxygen was clearing my head and I was busy using the brain power to curse Mr. K. for making this look so easy. Even while shaking, he had cracked jokes ("I'm glad I have insurance! Thank God I packed an extra pair of pants!") his entire way down the wire. "This is crazy," he'd said at one point, and the kids started singing, "'Here's my number, call me maybe!'" and he laughed along.

If he was mortified by being on display in front of teenagers who could have been tweeting his every move, he didn't let on. A recent study shows that teenagers use the part of the brain that is most concerned with what others think of them in determining what they think of themselves. That may be why a middle school humiliation can scar us for life. But adults in the study were able to define themselves without using that part of the brain. It's a good reason to not let a teenage trauma keep us from trying things as an adult. Mr. K. burned up the course, crossing it in two minutes flat, and when he reached the tree, he looked surprised, as if it had appeared out of nowhere. "I LOVE YOU!" he yelled at the tree, hugging it with all his might. "I LOVE YOU!!!"

⌆

I HAD THE FOURTH ROPE in my hand.

One more.

Hello, fifth rope. Hello, tree.

"Woo, Patty! Now you can kiss the tree!" the voices clamored below.

"I love you, tree," I said, my voice barely a squeak. I leaned toward it, then burrowed my body into its solidity with relief. I wanted to wrap myself around it like ivy over oak. It had taken me five minutes to get here. But the hardest part was yet to come.

"Now you need to take three steps back and turn your back to me," Sally said. *No way, José. I don't need to do nothin'. I am not leaving this tree.* "You can turn first or step first, up to you. Don't let go of the white rope. Use it to guide you."

"Oh my God," I whispered. I was completely disoriented. I tried to

337

push myself away from the tree with my left hand and felt the sensation of falling. *"Ack!"* I emitted, before catching myself on the tree again.

There were a lot of people talking—a belayer was coaching Julie on another course, and Amy, Carter, and Esther were watching me. I couldn't tell who was telling me what.

"Put your other foot behind you, Patty. There you go, spin around. You're almost there—take that one step around, come on, one step with your left foot."

I slowly turned around, until I was leaning into the tree with my butt and back.

"Now take three big steps," someone said.

I tried, but I couldn't pull away from the tree. When I realized why, I wanted to cry. "I'm stuck."

"You're *what?*"

"My harness is stuck on this bolt," I said, my lip quivering.

"Your *harness?*" Sally the trainee sounded incredulous. It didn't sound like a solution was forthcoming.

"When you feel like you're going to die, is when you need to *keep going*," my friend Penny, who ran her first marathon at age forty, once told me. I had tried to apply this while swimming laps—instead of stopping when I started to tire and take in water, I tried everything I could to stay afloat. I wouldn't just be able to give up in the middle of an ocean wave, I figured. I'd have to keep going.

So I kept going. I wiggled my hips, and the harness popped loose from the tree. Now I was back on the wire, and the wobbling started all over again, taking my breath away.

"I feel very, very unbalanced," I said.

"You are very, very unbalanced," Joe responded. Good old Joe. "Let go of the white rope. Let go of the tree." He kept it simple. "Put both your hands on the orange rope. It will hold you. Trust your gear."

The question was could I trust myself. My legs started to give way.

"Don't bend your legs! Keep them straight!" they called from be-low. My legs were buckling—there was nothing I could do, it seemed. *Against my will* is the phrase that came to mind. My bottom was drop-ping lower and lower—*it's gravity, people, how can I fight it?*

But that's a lie, I thought, surprising myself with the truth. This is not being done to me by some stronger external force. *Surely my will is strong enough to straighten my legs!* It took five seconds to find the will, but it was there. I pushed the tightrope away with my feet as hard as I could.

⋙

THE REST OF THE DISMOUNT was a blur. I made it down; my friends were proud. I felt chastened. For a fear-facing woman who professed to have no fear of heights, I did not exactly rock Elvis the Pelvis. It had taken me almost eight minutes to complete what Mr. K. had done in two. And I'd been *scared out of my mind.* After seeing all the thirteen-year-olds brave the ropes, after knowing intellectually there was little risk of being hurt, after telling Carter that it would be so worth doing, the course just about brought me to my knees. Literally.

Fortunately, the rest of the gang had a blast.

"I think I succeeded in becoming a little less boring today!" Esther declared, as we all swigged water and ate granola bars in the car. Gone was the morning's *nice to meet you* demeanor. The ride back was full of convivial chatter between friends.

"Committing to doing this was the hardest part," Julie said. That was quite a statement from someone who'd done the Catwalk, a bal-ance beam suspended *fifty* feet in the air. "I didn't leave room in my brain to feel fear once I was there. I charged up those ladders! I was much more nervous last night."

"Committing is usually the hard part," Amy agreed. "It would have been easy to say, 'This would be great, it would push me, I would learn things . . . but I don't have time.'" She had taken a day off work to come, and had spent it leaping from plank to plank on a course three stories above the forest floor. If she ever got tired of the library, she could moonlight as a stuntwoman.

"I'm a big procrastinator of things that are hard for me," Carter said. "Now that I've done this, I feel like it's all up here." He pointed to his head. "Just because I now qualify for my AARP membership, that doesn't mean I've stopped growing in my ability to do new things."

"It's funny, I love to learn new things," Amy said. "But I'm not a huge fan of the learning process. *What if I can't do it? What if I get scared? What if I look stupid?* I like to be good at things. *Look! I'm a master at this already!* I prefer it that way." We laughed. I told her about how at age forty Kent bought an electric guitar to fulfill a lifelong dream to play it, and when he picked it up the first time and didn't sound like Eric Clapton, he was ready to give up. "You need to take lessons first," I'd said.

"The thing is, if I stop doing things where I can't be a master from the start, I can see my life getting smaller and smaller," Amy added. "And what does that show my daughter? That growing up is about giving things up?"

"I can't wait to post pictures of this to Facebook," Julie said. All at once the car buzzed with excitement about what friends and family would think.

"I want to do it again and bring a group of friends," Esther said.

"We should do this again," said Carter. "What fear could we face next?"

A lively conversation ensued.

I watched these animated, sweaty, fully embodied people talk and laugh and felt the way Barry described feeling for his fellow passengers on Flight 58. We had all been through something together. I had wanted the world to know how it felt to be a little braver, to enjoy life a little more. *And this is how it starts.*

⌇

WHEN I FIRST STARTED trying to face my fears I wondered if I would, as books and seminars promised, one day "master" my fear. Rabbi Heidi Hoover says one of her favorite quotes is from Rebbe Nachman of Breslov: "The entire world is a very narrow bridge. The most important thing is not to be afraid." Could I do this? Would I ever get so strong, mentally, physically, and spiritually, that I could view any potential situation with an *I can handle it!* attitude?

What I realized on the high ropes is that I am still terrified of falling, of the unexpected, and of being out of my element, even when strapped into a harness. I thought facing my fears was going to get easier, yet this was *hard.* Perhaps it's because I didn't feel well, because I'm middle-aged, because I'm . . . a hundred other excuses I might dish out to avoid things that are hard, but this tightrope didn't care. It wasn't going to magically turn into terra firma. It wasn't going to let me off the hook.

And that's what life is like.

The ocean is indiscriminate, I had thought, and I was right. The wave that broke my foot didn't care that I had kids to care for or work to do. The night that Sybil Ludington was called to duty, it didn't matter that she was sixteen years old and a girl and it was the middle of the night during a war. Sometimes you don't get to choose what life dishes out. You do, however, get to choose what to do about it.

Two days later, still sore from the ropes course, I ran into Barb at Antoinette's. She was also sore, although she wasn't sure what it was from. She had just come back from camping with her sons. "It could have been the kayaking," she said, rolling her shoulder. "Or the biking. Or the hiking."

I laughed. "Only you, Barb, would have so many activities to choose from." She smiled. As always, she was full of good energy even in difficult times. Her silver earrings looked like labyrinths, a good metaphor for where she is in life, the divorce she's going through, and all the uncertainty that that implies. When I asked her if her adventurous spirit helps her through, the answer was an unreserved *yes*.

"There are moments when I'm afraid of having all this responsibility," she said. "How am I going to navigate this divorce? And find a job? And keep everything going for the boys? But then I think, 'I am handling it. Look at how you helped Jonah last night when he was upset. Look at how the person you met yesterday connected you to a job opening today.'" Barb reminds herself of her strengths; she makes herself laugh. She grounds herself in reality.

I remembered once at the Albert Ellis Institute hearing a woman onstage tell the counselor John Viterito that she was in a deep depression after being laid off. She'd "lost her footing," and without her job, her identity, she had little to look forward to or live for. It was like she was clinging to a nonexistent platform, thirty feet in the air, instead of realizing that the only way to go was forward. Viterito said her fear of free fall was a mirage, that the reality was she had skills, she had resources. "You can be very concerned and even worried without being destroyed," he said.

A friend, who was widowed three years ago, says, "Every morning is still like realizing it again." But every day, from the beginning, she did something to move herself forward. "I learned to program the TV, I learned to pay the bills online," she said. "You have to keep yourself going."

At times, life feels safe, the world comfortable and known. But then something happens and we're reminded that the world is actually a narrow bridge. Nothing is ever guaranteed. It is hard to not be afraid when what we know falls away. But instead of keeping us clinging to where we are, it can propel us, like Wonder Girl, up on our feet, eyes set on where we want to go. When we stop thinking about what we lost (firm ground) and start assessing what we have (a rope), we can start plotting a path to the future.

Fear of the unknown is a given, but the unknown goes both ways, Barb said. "I wonder what's going to happen. Maybe I'll get a great job. Maybe I'll meet someone. I don't know how it's going to turn out. That's exciting, actually." The future may be better than we can possibly imagine, if we keep ourselves open to new things.

I was about to tell her how her adventurous spirit had helped me, from the moment she invited me to go boogie boarding, from the moment I said *yes*, but just then, Carter came in, smiling at the sight of us.

"Did you hear about our adventure?" he asked Barb. To me, he said, "Where are my pictures? People want proof!"

"We'll have a viewing here one morning," I said. "Let's spread the joy."

Carter picked up his coffee from the counter and pulled up a chair right next to me.

"So," he said, leaning in, with a glint in his eye. "What's next?"

Becoming Brave

S omeone once told me that fear and courage are like lightning and thunder," Lawrence Block writes in *Write for Your Life*, an image I now call upon every time I feel the electrical sparks of fear crackle through my body. "They both start out at the same time, but the fear travels faster and arrives sooner. If we just wait a moment, the requisite courage will be along shortly."

So far, I was feeling plenty of lightning, as I bobbed on a big pink surfboard. This was going to be, without question, my last run of the day. In a three-hour group lesson run by Elliot Zuckerman of Surf2Live on Long Island, I had face-planted countless times. Lake Michigan may have been colder, but the Atlantic Ocean was rougher, and I'd spent the morning careening from the thrill of victory to the agony of defeat. I did get up on my board for one sun-drenched, glorious run. ("Did you see?" I asked Elliot. "Yeah, it was hard to miss, with you screaming *ELLIOT!!!* and waving your arms all over the place," he'd replied with a chortle.) I rode all the way in to shore, stepping off the board as if I were stepping off the subway, as if this were something I did every day. But near the end of the lesson, I fell and let the board get between me and the wave. It crashed into my head, and I stumbled to shore, seeing stars.

As if on cue, the sun had gone behind clouds, and kids began coming out of the water, complaining of being tired and cold. Elliot came to check on me, and then waved the whole group in. "Come on in!" he called. "Good job, everyone. That's a wrap."

I held my head. *I don't want to end like this.* "Elliot," I said, "do you think I should go back one more time?" The Greek Chorus tripped over itself trying to catch up to me: *Concussion, Not Thinking Straight, Go Lie Down!*

Shhhh, it's okay, I can handle this, I murmured back. "Or do I need an MRI?" I cracked.

I trusted Elliot. He's not a reckless teen; he's in his late fifties, a grandfather. If he told me to go to the ER, I would pack it in. He'd been surfing for more than forty-five years and had almost drowned more than once. Still, he went back out. "You can decide never to go again, or turn it around and say, 'This is a part of life, relax and you'll be fine.'" I wasn't sure what he meant by "This is a part of life," except that *everything*—risk, pleasure, awareness, fear, uncertainty, pummeling, ecstasy, even death—is a part of life. To live is to experience it all, and I wanted to live.

Send me back out there, I'd said with my eyes, doing an internal double take at my own audacity. The old Patty Chang Anker quits when she's ahead *and* when she's behind! Who was this new person begging to be put back in the game?

"You want to go back out?" Elliot asked, and then he'd answered in one go: "Then go back out. Hey, Sport!" He called to one of his instructors who was wading out of the surf, shivering. Elliot couldn't remember names to save his life, so we all went by nicknames in the water. "Take the Old Lady out for one last run."

Sport's lips were blue. "I'm sorry," I apologized, and explained that I didn't want to end the day with a whimper. In fact, as he'd pushed me out into the water, that's all I'd wanted to do. But I knew by now: The feeling of fear never goes away. It comes as surely as this wave, and the next, and the next.

"Fear is about self-preservation," says yogini Victoria Ramos, "but you can preserve yourself in a way that's glorious and expansive and not limiting. The question to ask yourself is how."

In the space between waves, the moment of uncertainty that Barb calls "the best part," we have choices. To jump, to dive, to ride, to play. To face what's coming without running away. We can learn not only to tolerate the fear but enjoy the suspense, to get knocked around and pop back up for more. "Keep your stoke up," as Patrick would say, in the water and in life. In facing fears, there are so many things to try. Keep trying.

In the story of my life there were many times when I did not dive in, literally or metaphorically. Until I decided I wanted better stories. "Tell us about the time you went surfing in Lake Michigan," my girls have asked at bedtime. "Start at the beginning, and don't leave anything out." What stories would you like to tell, over and over, until they become part your DNA? What stories would you like to pass on to the wider world?

For energy travels in all directions, and whether you start off facing your fears for someone else or hoping to transform yourself, you will end up profoundly changing yourself *and* everyone you come into contact with. We start to shimmer, and the world is never the same.

≋

LATER IN THE SUMMER my family would go to the beach together, Gigi jumping waves with Kent, Ruby splashing next to me in the shallows. All of us part of the fun, part of the human experience. All of us growing by choosing, in a thousand small acts each day, to become braver than we thought we could be.

"What's your plan for tomorrow?" the highway patrolman asks the person ready to jump off the Golden Gate Bridge. "Don't have one? Well, let's make one." What would your tomorrow look like, if you were planning to save your life? What would your future hold, if you wanted to fall passionately in love with the person you were meant to be? How do you want your story to end? How soon are you willing to start?

Jeff, the aquatic therapist, told me about a student who overcame her aquaphobia at the age of ninety-two and remained an avid lap swimmer until she died at ninety-five. It's never too late to begin. But how many years of swimming could she have enjoyed if she'd faced her fear at sixty, fifty, forty, or before? It's never too soon to relish life, either.

So let go of *I can't* and say *I'll try*. If you say *Oh no*, follow up with *Here we go*. Or do as Gigi advised when I balked at the top of a spiral waterslide. "Say '*wheeee!*'" she said with a smile. "*Wheee!* makes everything less scary."

"I get it," Sport said, like it was a simple truth that bonds us all, teen surf instructors and midlife housewives alike. "End on a high." He turned me around to face the beach.

The water rose. I could feel the rumble start within my belly. The pink board stuck out in front of me, Mick Jagger's tongue. *Come on, courage, come on,* I incanted.

He pushed me in. "Up, *UP!*"

I stood up, whooping and laughing and alive.

ACKNOWLEDGMENTS

For a person with enough fears to fill a book, writing that book was its own terrifying process. The Greek Chorus had a field day every day, chanting *Writer's block! Bad reviews! Change your name!* If it weren't for the incredible support of family near and far, friends, my publisher, and fear-tamers and fear-facers alike, I never would have had the nerve.

I am so grateful to those who gave me the courage to start by supporting me and *Facing Forty Upside Down* from the beginning. Thank you to Barb, Bill, Amy, Zulma, Zerlina, Iris, Kirsten, Solveig-Lynn, Alice, Melissa, Laura, Michael S. Kaye and the TOL gang, the Good Counsel of Ken Obel, T. J. Allan, Albert Taylor and the FKSA fan club, Facebook fans (especially Matt and David), my guest bloggers, and the blog communities of *Circle of Moms, BlogHer,* and *babble.*

Eternal gratitude to *Good Housekeeping* magazine for publishing the post that made my friend Laura Rossi ask, "Have you ever thought about becoming a full-time writer?" and to Laura herself for then putting her publicity skills to work to help me get started. *Audrey* magazine, *The Huffington Post,* George Rede, Bob Brody, Robin Gorman Newman, Rene Syler, and many others gave me opportunities to write, and longtime mentors and friends like Louise Brockett, Alane Mason, Paul Golob, and Pamela Duevel helped me at every juncture.

In facing any fear I recommend looking for believing eyes—the people who see past your self-doubts to your potential, and *know you can do it*. I cannot thank my beautiful and brilliant agent, Brettne Bloom, enough for believing in me and representing this book so wholeheartedly, and for leading me to my editor, Rebecca Saletan at Riverhead. Luckily, Becky does not have a fear of betting on a first-time author like me, but does have enough of her own fears to feel passionate about the topic. For her guidance and commitment to this book, I will always be grateful.

Nothing relieves anxiety about the quality of your book like filling it with great content. I am in awe of all the brave people who stepped up to challenges and allowed me to witness their moments of vulnerability and triumph. For the sake of privacy I won't list names here, but to everyone who shared memories and made memories with me, thank you. You inspire me continuously.

I am also thankful for the experts—psychologists, teachers, therapists, coaches, and clergy—who generously shared their knowledge in interviews or sessions/lessons. All hail the fear-tamers: Mary Carlomagno, Wendy Tomkiel, Karen Clay, Jennifer Paolicelli, Jeff Krieger, Jenny Javer, Thomas Lachocki, Rick Frishman, Tony Smith, John Viterito, Joe Rhinewine, Elaine Rogers, Ettie Shapiro, Victoria Ramos, Michael Star, Dan Suraci, Lynn Fuchs, Patrick "Bon Courage!" Moser, the Reverend Amy Lamborn, Rabbi Heidi Hoover, Radhanath Swami, the late Chaplain Oliver Chapin, Beth Blank, Michelle Collins, Crystal Madison-Rodriguez, Julio Rodriguez, Chris Hendershot, Joe Apuzzo, Esther Kinderlerer, Elliot Zuckerman, Elina Furman, Roger Tsao. Only a few of the staff and volunteers at Toastmasters International, Green Chimneys, Albert Ellis Institute, Bike New York, Aquabilities with Jennifer, Surf2Live, Integral Yoga, and BOCES are named in the book, but all of them are helping people to transform their lives every day. And special thanks to Dr. Ted Roth and Dr. Leslie Gibson for professional reads of the manuscript and personal support, and to Vijai Wilansky, my longtime yoga teacher, for teaching me everything about sitting quietly and listening.

ACKNOWLEDGMENTS

In writing the book, I was blessed to have the wise teachings of Jane Brox and Cornelia Maude Spelman at the Bread Loaf Writers' Conference and Heather Sellers at Kripalu Center. Britta Alexander listened to my brainstorms and told me when I was making sense (and when to go get some sleep) and eased me through my fear of criticism by giving sensitive and honest feedback on my first draft. Kimberly Meisner gave me her sharp editorial eye and her expansive best friend heart, showing up with coffee or Kleenex depending on the need, and cheering me on every single day. Barbara Feinberg taught me by word ("Just do the work") and example ("I can't talk now, I'm writing") how to simply keep writing. Jean Kwok's and Beth Kephart's encouragement always lifted my spirits. I channeled my first real-world writing teachers, Bert Shanas and Neill "Cut 200 Words" Rosenfeld constantly. Anne Lamott, Natalie Goldberg, and Betsy Lerner became my BIFs (Best Imaginary Friends) through their writings on craft.

Janet Hansen's book jacket, Gretchen Achilles's interior design, Alison Sheehy's photography, and the enthusiasm of Riverhead publicists Jynne Martin, Katie Freeman, and Glory Anne Plata embody the joyful spirit of the book perfectly. Thanks, too, to Kate Stark, Lydia Hirt, Mary Stone, and the rest of the Riverhead marketing and sales team, as well as to Julie Cottineau, Steve Kane, and Ben Dattner for additional marketing savvy, and Zak Young for website genius. I am also grateful to the Penguin Speakers Bureau, Gildan Audio, Alysia Reiner, and Mothers & More for their support, and to Lily Rudd for answering every question.

As a catastrophizer with a fear of making even minor mistakes, I am profoundly grateful for the meticulous factchecking of Sarah Yager, the legal prowess of Linda Cowan, and the ministrations of a team of copyeditors and proofreaders (who exorcised my comma demon).

I am not alone is perhaps the most profound comfort to the fearful. The leap it takes to create something that wasn't there before kept me up every night, and I could not have survived without a community of seekers by day. Many thanks to Sarah and Adel Hinawi and my fellow Inc. members at the

Purple Crayon Center, the Fabulous Bloggers of the Rivertowns, Women's Media Group, the Listen to Your Mother sisterhood, my yoga students, and Kus and the gang at Antoinette's for keeping me motivated, caffeinated, connected, and sane. And as G. and R. would say, "infinity!" thank yous, Likes, Favorites, to all who make FFUD and our online communities a vibrant and welcoming place to share support and resources for facing fears and trying new things in midlife (www.pattychanganker.com).

And because the best way to face fear as a writer is to draw strength from those who make us feel safest, bravest, unconditionally loved, thank you to my father, who taught me to speak my mind, my mother, who taught me to feel deeply with my heart, and my sister, who is my touchstone.

Thank you to G. and R. for teaching me everything. And to Kent, who read my college application essays as I wrote them and twenty-five years later still reads my first drafts; who never asked to be a supporting player in a blog or book yet allowed me to make him one because he supports me, period; and who, more than anyone, has been with me in the darkness and the dawn.

And finally, thanks be to God, whose divine presence is the only way I can account for how all these precious souls came into my life and sparked such stories to tell.

INDEX OF FEARS

INDEX OF FEARS